H. P. Blavatsky and The Secret Doctrine

Cover art by Jane A. Evans

H. P. Blavatsky and The Secret Doctrine

Edited by Virginia Hanson

This publication made possible with the assistance of the Kern Foundation

The Theosophical Publishing House
Wheaton, Ill. U.S.A.
Madras, India/London, England

Published 1971. Second Edition 1988

The Theosophical Publishing House
306 West Geneva Road
Wheaton, IL 60187

A publication of the Theosophical Publishing House, a department of the Theosophical Society in America.

Library of Congress Cataloging in Publication Data

H. P. Blavatsky and The secret doctrine.
Bibliography: p.
1. Blavatsky, H. P. (Helena Petrovna), 1831-1891.
2. Theosophy. I. Hanson, Virginia.
BP585.B6H23 1988 299'.934 87-40523
ISBN 0-8356-0630-9

Printed in the United States of America

Contents

Preface to the Second Edition

The Secret Doctrine first appeared in a world at the depths of materialism, dominated by the notion of billiard-ball atoms and consciousness as an offshoot of chance evolution. The religion of the day was extremely narrow with no possibility of incorporating science into its purview. Today, a hundred years after that first publication, the predominant world view is changing dramatically. Holism, interdependence, ecology, interconnectedness characterize the view of reality that is emerging from the new physics and also from sociological and anthropological studies. H.P. Blavatsky's grand vision of the universe as a single entity with all its parts interrelated is very much more in harmony with the world of 1988 than it was in 1888. It seems fitting in the centenary year of the publication of her magnum opus, *The Secret Doctrine*, to issue a new edition of this anthology, which is a tribute to her and to the sweeping concepts about which she wrote.

This book first appeared in 1971 as a companion volume to the newly published *An Abridgement of The Secret Doctrine*, edited by E. Preston and Christmas Humphreys. It now commemorates the centenary of the publication of *The Secret Doctrine.*

To update the volume, five new articles have been added (by Adam Warcup, Doss McDavid, Michael Gomes, John

Algeo, and Ralph Hannon). Two articles were not included because they were not closely related to the subject or were too repetitious of ideas discussed in other articles (Elsie Benjamin and Norman Hankin). A few of the articles have been very lightly edited to bring them up to date.

It seems likely that in the century ahead H.P.B.'s insights will be even further corroborated, that the bicentennial of her major work will find that many more of her ideas have become mainstream.

Shirley Nicholson,
Editor of the Second Edition

Preface to the First Edition

In the spring of 1969, *The American Theosophist*, journal of The Theosophical Society in the United States, paid tribute to the memory of H. P. Blavatsky, one of the principal founders of the world-wide Theosophical Society, in a special issue devoted to a discussion of her contributions to the intellectual, moral, and spiritual atmosphere of the world and to her magnum opus, *The Secret Doctrine*. So great was the demand for copies of this issue that it was decided to enlarge its scope by the addition of further material and to publish the whole as a Quest Book. This is intended as a companion to the Quest edition of *An Abridgement of The Secret Doctrine*, which has made available to thousands of readers (without alteration or rearrangement of the original text) an abbreviated version of H.P. Blavatsky's challenging treatise on the nature and origin of the cosmos and of man. It is dedicated to all seekers for deepened understanding and widened horizons of living.

Virginia Hanson

Contributing Authors

John Algeo, Ph.D. is professor of English at the University of Georgia. Formerly editor of the journal *American Speech*, he has been a consultant for the National Endowment for the Humanities as well as several university and commercial presses. He is author or co-author of a number of scholarly books and the Quest book *Exploring Reincarnation*, and a frequent contributor to theosophical journals. He is currently Vice President of the Theosophical Society in America and lectures on theosophical platforms both in this country and abroad.

Sri Madhava Ashish is English by birth and Indian by adoption. He went to India in 1942 and, in 1946, became a pupil of Sri Krishna Prem, well-known author of a number of works on yoga, with whom he collaborated in writing the book *Man: The Measure of All Things*, relating to Cosmogenesis as set forth in *The Secret Doctrine*. Since the death of Sri Krishna Prem, Sri Madhava Ashish has followed the earlier book with *Man, Son of Man*, based on Anthropogenesis in *The Secret Doctrine*. He continues to maintain the ashram founded by his distinguished predecessor.

Seymour Ballard, formerly General Secretary of the Theosophical Society in Puerto Rico, served as assistant editor of *The American Theosophist* and assisted with the publications and editorial work at the international headquarters of the Theosophical Society in India. He has lectured to audiences in a number of countries on Theosophical subjects since 1949. He now resides in Oxford, England.

Geoffrey A. Barborka (1897-1982) was educated in the Theosophical school at Point Loma, California, and matriculated at the Theosophical University there. While attending the university, he set up on the monotype for publication the books *Isis Unveiled, The Secret Doctrine, The Key to Theosophy,* and *The Voice of the Silence,* all works of H.P. Blavatsky. Among his major writings are *The Divine Plan*, a commentary on *The Secret Doctrine*, and *H.P. Blavatsky, Tibet and Tulku.*

Katherine A. Beechey, daughter of an English clergyman, was educated in England. She was in charge of the Theosophical Society Archives for some years and in 1964 became Recording Secretary for the international Society. She assisted in the publication of *H.P.B. Speaks*, edited by C. Jinarajadasa; compiled the book *Meditations from the Letters of the Masters*, first published in 1949 and reprinted many times; and was editor and publisher of the Adyar *News-Letter*, which she inaugurated in 1960.

Boris de Zirkoff (1902-1981) was a native of Russia, where he received his early education. After the revolution, he studied in various European universities, specializing in languages and the classics. Emigrating to the United States, he went directly to the headquarters of the Point Loma Theosophical Society, where he worked for eighteen years in literary, scholastic, and secretarial capacities. In 1925 he began compiling and editing a uniform edition of H.P. Blavatsky's *Collected Writings*, which is now in its fourteenth volume. He was editor of *Theosophia*, an independent quarterly published in Los Angeles, where he maintained a Theosophical Information Center. Mr. de Zirkoff was the last known direct relative of H.P. Blavatsky.

E.L. Gardner (1869-1969) was born and educated in England. He was one of the principal founders and served as the first chairman of the Theosophical Research Centre in London. He was also chairman of the Theosophical World Trust for Education and Research and helped to found the theosophical estate at Tekels Park, Camberley, where he lived from 1953 until his death. From 1924 to 1928, he served as General Secretary (President) of The Theosophical Society in England. His numerous writings have greatly enriched theosophical literature, his most notable contributions perhaps being *The Web of the Universe* and *The Play of Consciousness*.

Michael Gomes's articles on various facets of the Theosophical movement have been published in journals in England, Canada, France, India, and the United States. He is currently a research student at Columbia University, specializing in the nineteenth century interpretation of India and the East. He is under contract to produce a volume titled *Theosophy in the Nineteenth Century: An Annotated Bibliography,* to include about 1200 titles. This is part of the series on social science put out by Garland Publishing. The author is a Canadian citizen, born in Trinidad, educated in Toronto, and residing in New York City.

Ralph Hannon, Ph.D. is Professor of Chemistry at Kishwaukee College in Illinois. He received the B.S. in physics at Eastern Illinois University, the M.S. in physics from Northern Illinois University, and the Ph.D. in chemistry, also from Northern Illinois University. He is co-editor of *The Theosophical Research Journal.*

Christmas Humphreys (1901-1984), native of England and resident in London, was by profession a barrister-at-law, Queen's Counsel. With Mrs. Humphreys, he founded the Buddhist Society in London in 1924. He was Vice-President of the World Fellowship of Buddhists, Vice-President of the Tibet Society, and author of some twelve books on Buddhism, including *Buddhism* (Pelican Series), *Zen Buddhism, Walk On*, and *Karma and Rebirth*. More recently he collaborated with Elizabeth Preston in editing *An Abridgement of The Secret Doctrine.*

F.L. Kunz (1888-1972) was President and founder of the Foundation for Integrative Education and Editor of its journal, *Main Currents in Modern Thought.* He attracted many prominent scholars to the Foundation, the object of which was to find philosophical principles to integrate the various areas of modern knowledge. He drew on Oriental thought and theosophy, as well as Western philosophy.

W. Doss McDavid, Ph.D. is an associate professor at the University of Texas Health Science Center in San Antonio, Texas. His responsibilities include teaching and research in the area of radiological physics. He is on the Editorial Board of *The Theosophical Research Journal.*

Joy Mills is Director of the Krotona School of Theosophy in Ojai, California. She served as President of the American Section from 1965 to 1974, and as International Vice-President of the Theosophical Society from 1974 to 1980. She continues as a member of the Society's General Council. Formerly a teacher of history and English, she has spent most of her career in work for the Theosophical Society, lecturing in over fifty countries of the world organization. Her writings have been published in theosophical journals throughout the world, often translated into other languages, and her books include *An Abridgement of the Key to Theosophy* and *100 Years of Theosophy: A History of the Theosophical Society in America.*

Gerrit Munnik, Litt. D., is a graduate student from the Royal Academy in The Hague, the Netherlands, and received the Litt. D. degree from the University of Amsterdam. For a number of years he taught art and art appreciation in several colleges and is presently a permanent member of the faculty of the Krotona School of Theosophy, Ojai, California.

Hugh Murdoch, M.S., Ph.D., a Senior Lecturer in physics at the University of Sydney, Australia has done research in radio-astronomy.

L. Gordon Plummer was born at the headquarters of the Point Loma Theosophical Society in California and received his education at the school and college there. After his graduation, he taught at Point Loma and continued his studies in "Outdoor Education" in San Diego County. He has devoted his life to theosophical lecturing and writing. His published books include *From Atoms to Kosmos, Star Habits and Orbits,* and *The Mathematics of the Cosmic Mind.* Keenly interested in astronomy, he has lectured for visitors at the Mt. Palomar Observatory.

Jean Raymond, M.D. (1934-1980) was a practicing physician in Sydney, Australia. She was born in Singapore of English-American parents and later went with her parents to the international headquarters of The Theosophical Society at Adyar, Madras, India, where for six years she attended the Besant Theosophical School. She completed her education and earned her medical degree in Sydney.

W. Emmett Small was educated from age two in schools of the Point Loma Theosophical Society. For several years he was Assistant Secretary General of the Society, Assistant Secretary of the Theosophical University, and Secretary of the Cabinet. He considers his main contribution to have been in the literary field. For sixteen years he was one of the editors of, and a regular contributor to, *The Theosophical Path, The Theosophical Forum,* and *Lucifer, the Light-bringer.*

Alfred Taylor, M.A., Ph.D. (1896-1973), before his retirement in 1965 as head of cancer research in the Biochemical Institute of the University of Texas, had published more than one hundred articles in the fields of science and philosophy. He was a Fellow of the American Association for the Advancement of Science and of the New York Academy of Science, and a member of the Society for Experimental Biology and Medicine. He is author of the Quest books *A Human Heritage* and *Understanding through the Ancient Wisdom and Modern Science.*

Corona Trew, Ph.D., D. Sc., a graduate and Doctor of Science of the University of London, before her retirement was a Senior Lecturer in chemistry at that university as well as a lecturer and writer on theosophical subjects relating to science. She was a member of the Theosophical Research Centre, London, an organization composed of scientists in a number of disciplines.

Adam Warcup, B.S.C., received his degree in human and physical science from the University of Surrey, England. His career is in the computer industry, where he serves as consultant and instructor. He lectures widely and gives workshops in England and other parts of Europe on a variety of theosophical topics. He authored *Cyclic Evolution: A Theosophical View* and was invited to give the Blavatsky lecture in London in 1981, which he titled "An Enquiry into the Nature of Mind."

Helen V. Zahara (1917-1973) was the first editor of Quest books and co-ordinator of special programs sponsored by the Kern Foundation. She was a New Zealander by birth but came to the United States from Australia, where she served for eight years as General Secretary (President) of the Australian Section of the Theosophical Society, edited the theosophical journal published there, and conducted a weekly radio program. Miss Zahara was a certified public accountant by profession.

I

H. P. Blavatsky and the Inner Side of The Secret Doctrine

1

H. P. Blavatsky: The Mystery

L. GORDON PLUMMER

For countless generations hath the Adept builded a fane of imperishable rocks, a giant's *Tower of Infinite Thought*, wherein the Titan dwelt, and will yet, if need be, dwell alone, emerging from it but at the end of every cycle, to invite the elect of mankind to cooperate with him and help in his turn enlighten superstitious man. And we will go on in that periodic work of ours; we will not allow ourselves to be baffled in our philanthropic attempts until that day when the foundations of a new continent of thought are so firmly built that no amount of opposition and ignorant malice guided by the Brethren of the Shadow will be found to prevail.

But until that day of final triumph someone has to be sacrificed—though we accept but voluntary victims. The ungrateful task did lay her low and desolate in the ruins of misery, misapprehension, and isolation; but she will have her reward in the hereafter for we never were ungrateful. As regards the Adept—not *one of my kind*, good friend, but far higher—you might have closed your book with those lines of Tennyson's "Wakeful Dreamer"—you knew him not—

> How could ye know him? Ye were yet within
> The narrower circle; he had well nigh reached
> The last, which, with a region of white flame,
> Pure without heat, into a larger air
> Up-burning, and an ether of black blue
> Invests and ingirds all other lives. . .

The Mahatma Letters to A.P. Sinnett (p. 51)

Someone said not long ago: "I wish I could have lived in H.P.B.'s time. I should like to have known her." It would certainly have been a great experience, but I could not help but wonder how many of us would have understood her. While we were not present to participate in the work as it was carried out in her time, and we missed the benefit of her "word of mouth" teaching, nevertheless, I am inclined to think that we have a certain advantage brought about by the span of years. As a recent writer pointed out, it is difficult to see the picture when you are inside the frame. Because we are now looking at the picture from a distance, we can select the facet of H.P.B.'s life that we wish to examine. A book might be written, giving an entire section to each of such aspects as her childhood, her travels, her training, her books—not to mention the numberless articles that she wrote—and, finally, her true nature. Had we lived in her day, we would have received the full impact of this amazing person, and it might well have been a bewildering experience, as it undoubtedly was to many of her contemporaries.

In the brief space allowed in a magazine, it seems better to pass by the incidents of her life, as would be required in a biographical sketch. Instead, I will focus attention upon some of the factors in her own nature that made her what she was. This is of particular interest to her students, and might give much food for thought to all.

We must divide H.P.B.'s life into three periods. First, her childhood and early womanhood, during which she traveled widely, for she had an insatiable appetite for adventure. Her natural leanings toward the mystical and the occult led her into many by-paths that would be overlooked by the average traveler. She delved deeply into Eastern philosophy and wrote vividly of her experiences. Her first major book, *Isis Unveiled*, was to a large extent the fruit of her travels, as was *From the Caves and Jungles of Hindustan*. Both of these books make absorbing reading. It is a matter of historical record that the first edition of *Isis Unveiled*, comprising 1,000 copies, was completely sold out in ten days! I do not know how many editions have appeared since it was first published in 1877.

The second portion of her life that must be understood, to a degree at least, comprises those years of her intensive training for the work that she was destined to do. The nature of this training is not easily understood for the reason that nothing resembling it exists in Western countries. Modern psychology is not equipped to analyze a nature such as hers, and that is why she is so misunderstood. No one can be blamed for not understanding her, although the crude attacks which have been made upon her cannot be condoned. In order to understand her at all, we must realize first of all, that she lived in a "frame of reference" quite different from that of the ordinary person, and it is my purpose to give a picture, if possible, of this peculiar frame of reference. In one respect, understanding her is something like accepting some of the more recent scientific explanations of time and space; they are difficult for us to understand because they do not fall within our experience, or frame of reference. In like manner, there is much about H.P. Blavatsky that does not fall within the experience of any of us. Nevertheless an effort to understand her has its beneficial effect, as I hope to show.

Her training was the natural outgrowth of her childhood. She was a most unusual child. Although unmanageable in her rejection of authority and her wild tempers, she nevertheless had certain characteristics that fitted her for precisely the kind of work she was to do. She was more than just a protester. Like so many of the present day, she saw through the shams and hypocrisies of life, but unlike the run-of-the-mill protester, she had something unique. She had certain qualities essential to a program being initiated by certain members of a Brotherhood of Adepts long in existence in the East but totally unknown in the West. These Brothers are known by various names in the East, such as the Mahatmas, the Masters of Wisdom, the Elder Brothers of humanity, and so on. They have worked for countless generations, as indicated in the extract from *The Mahatma Letters to A.P. Sinnett* quoted at the beginning of this article. Their home is in the trans-Himalayan fastnesses in Tibet. H.P. Blavatsky was trained by these Mahatmas for the work that was required. She was instructed by them to inform the West about them and their work. One very important aspect of their endeavor took the form of a correspondence carried on by them with A.P. Sinnett from 1880 to 1884. The originals of these letters are now in the British Museum where arrangements may be made to examine them. They were compiled and published in 1923 by A. Trevor Barker.

During the early years of H.P. Blavatsky's life she was mediumistically inclined and was constantly surrounded by psychic phenomena. Naturally, she became a center of interest, as well as of controversy. While The Theosophical Society of today does not encourage psychic practices and is ever ready to point out the dangers to health—physical as well as mental—incurred by anyone seeking to develop such faculties, nevertheless, the very fact that she was endowed with a strong psychical nature made her peculiarly adaptable to the type of training that was in store for her. Since it was necessary that she should give undeniable proof of the existence of nature's finer forces, she had first of all to become a complete master of the strange powers which she possessed. The first stages of her training then were in the nature of a cleansing of all of her lower psychic tendencies and substituting for them *genuine occult powers*. There is a vast difference between the two. The task was accomplished at great cost to herself. She became dangerously ill on more than one occasion, but through these crises she brought her psychic nature under complete control. Thereafter, with the help of her Teachers, she was able to perform wonders that would today strain the credulity of any but the student already versed in the esoteric philosophy.

It should be stated that H.P.B. met her Teacher face to face for the first time in London on her twentieth birthday. At that time he made known to her in general outline what her destiny would be, if she was willing to accept it, and all the trials and sufferings that would necessarily accompany it. She was given a choice, and as the work involved the most genuine and soul-satisfying service to the human race, there was never any doubt in her mind.

If she had been difficult to control as a child, she was now willing to undergo the most gruelling training at the hands of her Teachers, for having once recognized them, her devotion to them was unswerving to the day of her death. It would have never occurred to her to rebel, no matter how difficult the discipline might be. In short, she gave herself completely to the task of fitting herself to be the transmitter of teachings that her Masters desired should be promulgated to the world.

She was very reticent about the nature of her training, but we may be sure that it had at least two aspects. One of these was in the nature of intensive study of the doctrines of Eastern religion and philosophy, and to a far greater depth than that afforded in exoteric systems of thought. Her Teachers were in possession of the esoteric philosophy, and she was taught far in excess of anything that she was permitted to reveal. This was necessary in order that she might have the necessary background from which to work. The second aspect of her training was in the nature of a transformation of her own being. And here psychology must give way to pneumatology if we are going to understand the difference between H.P. Blavatsky the woman and "H.P.B." the teacher. The Ancient Wisdom holds that within every human being there is a divine essence at one with, because derived from, Deity itself. Between this divine essence and the physical body there are many grades or levels of consciousness manifesting themselves in the various selves in man which have come to be known as the *seven principles*. Although each such self or principle is an entity in its own right, learning and growing, nevertheless the whole stream of consciousness that is man might be compared to the spectrum of light ranging from red to violet. Each of the seven colors is considered to have its own characteristics, yet in the spectrum the gradation is such that it is impossible to tell where one color leaves off and the next begins. The illustration of the spectrum will be used again in order to bring out a very mysterious and important fact of occult training.

However, it should be made clear at this point that the

various "selves" in man have likewise their own characteristics. The one in which his consciousness is focused, and which therefore assumes the greatest importance, is the personality. This includes the mind, the emotions, the desires, as well as the senses which function through the appropriate organs of the physical body. Now, this personality does not stand very high in the spectrum of man's nature. Some of his higher selves have long since evolved out of the mediocre state that the personality finds itself in. One of these higher selves is the inner Guide or Teacher. It may well be that this concept has little meaning for some, but one who has learned about the existence of his inner Teacher and who strives to find it does ultimately learn how to recognize it. He discovers that the real secret of meditation is the ability to place oneself in the attitude of a learner before his mentor, and he eventually develops the ability to take knowledge, as we might express it. He finds that his own inner Teacher is a source of wisdom as well as knowledge, and he develops a relationship to it that changes his whole life.

It is only when a student has developed this faculty of recognizing his own inner Teacher that he is then able to recognize a Teacher such as those who taught H.P.B. Such Teachers can do nothing for anyone until he has discovered his own Teacher within, for until that occurs, the pupil has not awakened the faculty of understanding. This is nobody's fault—certainly not the Teacher's. It is just a matter of the growth of the student, and this must proceed in its own good time. Thus it is that it is difficult for the Teachers to find just the right person to undertake the particular training for the exceedingly difficult work which must be carried on toward the eventual enlightenment of the human race. That is why, in the following passage from *The Mahatma Letters to A.P. Sinnett* it is stated that the "Chiefs" searched fruitlessly for over a century for just the right person. Here is the quotation from Letter XXVI, p. 203:

> After nearly a century of fruitless search, our chiefs had to avail themselves of the only opportunity to send out a

> European body upon European soil to serve as a connecting link between that country and our own. You do not understand? Of course not. Please then, remember, what she tried to explain, and what you gathered tolerably well from her, namely the fact of the *seven* principles in the *complete* human being. Now, no man or woman, unless he is an initiate of the "fifth circle" can leave the precincts of *Bod-Las* and return back into the world in his integral whole—if I may use the expression. One, at least of his seven satellites has to remain behind for two reasons: the first to form the necessary connecting link, the wire of transmission—the second as the safest warranter that certain things will never be divulged.

A few of the terms require explanation. Bod-Las is one of the names for the spiritual home of the Adepts or Masters of Wisdom. The "fifth circle" referred to is the fifth degree of Initiation, that one by which the learner moves from the state of discipleship to Adeptship. Only an Adept can leave this spiritual home and go into the world to work, retaining the full spectrum of his consciousness, for he can be relied upon to know with certainty how to work without the special type of help from his own Chiefs that the disciple needs. The latter has not yet developed to the degree that he is able to work entirely upon his own. So, the term "one of his satellites" refers to one of his selves or principles. Which one is not indicated, and it would probably be fruitless for us to speculate upon this, for it might be that circumstances will vary with the individual so sent out to do the spiritual work of the Brotherhood.[1]

Here we shall return to the illustration of the spectrum. Pure white light when directed through a prism will produce a continuous spectrum. However, if the light is made to shine through some chemical vapor (for the moment, let us suppose it to be sodium vapor) a dark line will appear in the yellow portion of the spectrum. The chemist learns to identify the chemical element by the presence of well-recognized lines in the spectrum. That is the way in which the chemical elements in a distant star may be detected. What happens is that as the light passes through the vapor (sodium for the purposes of our explanation) the atoms absorb just those frequencies of light to which they are resonant. Since these frequencies have been absorbed, they are no longer present. Hence, the dark lines are really gaps in the continuous spectrum.

In this case of a Messenger of the type that H.P.B. was, there were gaps in the continuous spectrum of her consciousness, because in the process of leaving the spiritual home in which she was trained, certain portions of herself were withheld. This is a very strange doctrine to be sure, but it is a fact that explains much about every Messenger who appears. It makes the life of the Messenger a martyrdom indeed, but it is an absolute necessity. At the conclusion of the tour of duty, all is restored to normal, and the Messenger has gained enormously in experience and knowledge. But during the lifetime of service under these peculiar circumstances he works under a serious psychological handicap. In certain respects, he might be said to be a cripple. This explains in part H.P.B.'s unorthodox behavior and the difficult temperament that was hers. These of course are the things that are seized upon by her critics, who completely overlook her intellectual and spiritual qualities which far outweighed the disadvantages under which she worked.

It may seem to the reader that the path of occultism is unnecessarily harsh. It is indeed harsh, but not unnecessarily so. There is a reason for everything connected with it. There is nothing arbitrary in the laws governing the life of the student. All are rooted in the very fabric of nature itself. It cannot be otherwise.

Why then, should such a one as H.P. Blavatsky undertake the training at all? For the same reason that it has been undertaken by thousands before her: coupled with the stern discipline and the suffering, there is also the intense joy of service, a joy that has no equal. It is a state of consciousness beside which all our notions of happiness and contentment pale into insignificance. This joy comes from a knowledge that one is privileged to bring light to a darkened world. It is the strange paradox in the nature of the Messenger which makes this joy a possibility, and for the following reason: the gaps in the spectrum of the consciousness of the Messenger are arranged for with a certain lofty end in view. When the Messenger undertakes the training, he is made fully aware of this purpose, and readily assents to it, even though adequately warned of the dangers and the suffering that this will entail for the duration of his life-time.

The service the Messenger renders takes this form: the intellectual vitality of the Teacher works through the psychological nature of the Messenger, and the entrance is made through the "gaps" that have just been described. This is the only way in which it can be done. Now, the Teacher is not working at all times through the Messenger. When he is, then the Messenger (in this case, H.P.B.) speaks and writes "*ex cathedra*" as the saying goes. It is not the Messenger speaking; it is the Teacher speaking through him.

A great portion, if not the majority, of H.P.B.'s writings were accomplished by this form of occult dictation. Many of the Mahatma Letters were written to A.P. Sinnett in this manner, relatively few of them having been in the Mahatmas' own handwriting. They were letters from the Mahatmas, none the less.

So here we have an important difference between a medium and a *mediator*. There are gaps in the spectrum of the consciousness of a medium, but these did not come about through training; rather they betoken an unhealthy state of the psychological apparatus of the individual. He is often a prey to his own psychic powers, over which he has no control. Such a person is unfortunate indeed, for the reason that entities which are not welcomed by the trained student gain entrance unhindered into the nature of the medium while in the trance state, and during such times he is unaware of what he is saying or doing; thus, upon awakening, he does not remember. It is said that these destructive tendencies are almost certain to be carried over into a future life. This is one of the most important reasons why the development of psychic power is strongly discouraged by the Teachers. Only they know when the time is right. Such development, if it takes place at all, is for the purpose of making these powers the *servants* of vastly higher powers—the genuine spiritual powers—which are first to be awakened.

The case of the mediator is entirely different from that of the medium. During the time when he is working as the mouthpiece of his Teacher, all of his faculties are awake and alert. This activity is not accompanied by a trance condition. The mediator knows exactly what he is doing and gladly gives of himself so that he can transmit the message that the Teacher wishes to promulgate. Thus we see that the word "mediator" is synonymous with messenger.

The ability to perform this work is what makes all of the suffering and misunderstanding worth while. No better words could convey the spirit of H.P.B.'s work than those which appeared in her magazine *Lucifer* for September, 1891:

> There is no danger that dauntless courage cannot conquer.
> There is no trial that spotless purity cannot pass through.
> There is no difficulty that strong intellect cannot surmount.
> For those who win onwards, there is reward past all telling, the power to bless and save humanity.
> For those who fail, there are other lives in which success may come.

Notes

1. In *The Letters of H.P. Blavatsky to A.P. Sinnett*, beginning on page 305, there is a letter to H.P.B. from A.O. Hume in which he expresses his skepticism about this whole matter. He makes the statement: "Now I know all about the Brothers' supposed explanation that you are a psychological cripple. . . ." The Master M. appends the comment: "He is mistaken—he does *not*." And immediately after further words of Hume's, to wit: "Therefore to me this explanation is not only not satisfactory—but its having been offered—throws suspicion on the whole thing," the Master has inserted: "Very clever—but suppose it is neither *one of the seven* particularly, but all? Every one of them a 'cripple' and forbidden the exercise of its full powers? And suppose such is the wise law of a far foreseeing power?"

2
The Sources of The Secret Doctrine

BORIS DE ZIRKOFF

It is a well-known fact that *The Secret Doctrine*, H.P. Blavatsky's *magnum opus*, is partially based upon a number of stanzas translated by her from the *Book of Dzyan*. As a term, *Dzyan* is simply the Tibetan and Mongolian way of pronouncing the Sanskrit term *Dhyana*, which means meditation or contemplation. As a book or manuscript, it is an integral part of a well-known, more or less common, Tibetan series of works called by the general title of *Kiu-ti*. According to H.P.B.'s own statement, there are some thirty-five volumes of *Kiu-ti* of an exoteric character for the use of the layman, and these may be found in the library of almost any Tibetan monastery. There are also fourteen books of commentaries and annotations on the same by initiated Teachers.

The exoteric portion of the *Kiu-ti* series is full of myths, blinds, and legendary material as is the case with popular beliefs all over the world. The fourteen volumes of commentaries, however, with an ample glossary of occult terms, contain a digest of all the occult sciences and are derived from "one small archaic folio, the *Book of the Secret Wisdom of the World*." The exoteric volumes of *Kiu-ti* are comparatively modern, having been edited within the last millennium, while the earliest volumes of the commentaries are of untold antiquity. Their relation to the exoteric books is somewhat similar to the relation between the Jewish *Qabbalah* and the so-called Mosaic Books.

The *Book of Dzyan*, which is the first volume of the commentaries upon the seven secret folios of *Kiu-ti*, while recent in its physical form, is extremely ancient in regard to its substance, as the teachings contained therein go back into Atlantean times and beyond. It deals mainly with the cosmogonic building of the worlds of our own planetary chain of globes especially, and with the appearance and development of man through the various Root-Races and Rounds. It is definitely stated by H.P.B. that she is using only excerpts from certain stanzas and that her translation of these is made from Chinese, Tibetan, and Sanskrit translations of the original Senzar commentaries and glosses on the *Book of Dzyan*.

To limit oneself, however, to the *Book of Dzyan* as the chief source of *The Secret Doctrine* would be somewhat one-sided and therefore incomplete. H.P.B.'s monumental work is not a mere translation of ancient passages, with her own commentaries and explanations thereof. A considerable part of her two volumes[1] was produced in quite a different manner and originated from another yet co-related source. In order to understand the situation, it is necessary to consider some of H.P.B.'s characteristics as an occultist, and to bear in mind the ancient esoteric doctrine of *Tulku*. This technical Tibetan term (Sanskrit equivalent being *Avesha*) describes the condition when a living Initiate sends a part of his consciousness to take embodiment, for a longer or shorter period of time, in a disciple or chela whom that Initiate sends into the outer world to perform a duty or to teach. The chela then acts as a transmitter of the spiritual powers of the Initiate. H.P. Blavatsky acted frequently throughout her public career as the temporary *tulku* of one or another Adept or Initiate of the Trans-Himalayan Brotherhood. *Tulku* is performed without loss of consciousness and with definite and complete knowledge of what is taking place, the occultist maintaining his self-conscious awareness at all times, and merely lending his astro-physical organism to the temporary usage of a higher consciousness by mutual consent. *Tulku* stands at the opposite pole from mediumship, and is one of the powers acquired as a result of occult training. Other powers, developed by means of extremely arduous, severe and strenuous occult discipline, are spiritual clairvoyance and clairaudience, powers which stand in relation to their psychic equivalents as the brightness of the noonday sun stands to the pale and deceptive moonlight.

When these facts are taken into serious consideration, it becomes easier to understand how H.P.B. produced some of the most outstanding passages of *The Secret Doctrine.* Considerable portions thereof were dictated to her by one or another Adept, not as an employer would dictate to his secretary, but by direct transference of ideas from one mind to another in the condition of *tulku.* Other portions are descriptions by H.P.B. of what her trained spiritual consciousness actually *saw* in the akashic records marshalled before it. These indelible records were either evoked by her own powerful will, or unfolded under the superior will of the Adepts, in those cases when she was unable to do it herself. Still other portions of the manuscript were precipitated by one or another of the Initiates she was working under, and worked over by her, edited, re-arranged and incorporated into her work.

It was not for the first time that these circumstances were taking place. They were, to some extent, and most likely to a greater extent, the repetition of what occurred in connection with the writing of *Isis Unveiled* some ten years previously.

Writing from Würzburg to A.P. Sinnett in November, 1885, H.P.B. says:

> I am very busy on *Secret D.* The thing at N.Y. is repeated —only far clearer and better. I begin to think it *shall vindicate* us. Such pictures, panoramas, scenes, *antediluvian* dramas and all that! Never saw or heard better. . . .[2]

Writing from the same city to Dr. Franz Hartmann in December, 1885, she says:

> Now, as you know, I also am occupied with my book. It took possession of me (the epidemic of writing) and

crept on "with the silent influence of the itch," as Olcott elegantly expresses it—until it reached the fingers of my right hand, got possession of my brain—carried me completely into the region of the occult. I have written in a fortnight more than 200 pages (of the *Isis* shape and size). I write day and night, and now feel sure that my *Secret Doctrine* shall be finished this—no, no, not this—year, but the next. . . .[3]

Writing again to A.P. Sinnett on March 3, 1886, she explains:

> There's a new development and scenery, every morning. I live two lives again. Master finds that it is too difficult for me to be looking consciously into the astral light for my S.D. and so, it is now about a fortnight, I see large and long rolls of paper on which things are written and I recollect them. Thus all the Patriarchs from Adam to Noah were given me to see—parallel with the Rishis; and in the middle between them, the meaning of their symbols—or personifications. . . .[4]

Writing from Würzburg to W.Q. Judge on March 24, 1886, she tells him:

> . . . I want you badly for the arrangement of *Secret Doctrine*. Such facts, *such facts*, Judge, as Masters are giving out will rejoice your old heart. . . .[5]

In a letter received by Countess Constance Wachtmeister from Dr. William Hübbe-Schleiden, who visited H.P.B. at Würzburg in the early part of 1886, he says:

> In many respects her work was then carried on in a very similar way to that which Col. Olcott describes in Chapter XIII of his *Old Diary Leaves* . . . I also saw her write down sentences as if she were copying them from something before her, where, however, I saw nothing. . . . I saw a good deal of the well-known blue K.H. handwriting as corrections and annotations on her manuscripts as well as in books that lay occasionally on her desk. And I noticed this principally in the morning before she had commenced to work. I slept on the couch in her study after she had

> withdrawn for the night, and the couch stood only a few feet from her desk. I remember well my astonishment one morning when I got up to find a great many pages of foolscap covered with that blue pencil handwriting lying on her own manuscript, at her place on her desk. How these pages got there I do not know, but I did not see them before I went to sleep and no person had been bodily in the room during the night, for I am a light sleeper.[6]

Early in January, 1886, Dr. Hübbe-Schleiden, after leaving H.P.B. on his last visit to her in Würzburg, found in his copy of Richard Hodgson's *Report* a precipitated letter signed by Master K.H. The last sentence of it said that "the undersigned is happy to assure him that *The Secret Doctrine* when ready, will be the triple production of M., Upasika and the Doctor's most humble servant." *Upasika* stands for H.P.B. and means female disciple or chela.

Together with this letter there was another one signed by Master M. which stated: "If this can be of any use or help to Dr. Hübbe-Schleiden—though I doubt it—I, the humble undersigned Fakir certify that the 'Secret Doctrine' is dictated to Upasika partly by myself and partly by my Brother K.H."

In the well-known letter from Master K.H. which Col. Henry S. Olcott phenomenally received on board the P. & O. Mail Steamer *Shannon*, August 22, 1888, the day before he arrived at Brindisi, occurs the following passage:

> I have also noted your thoughts about the 'Secret Doctrine.' Be assured that what she has not *annotated* from scientific and other works, we have given or *suggested* to her. Every mistake or erroneous notion, corrected and explained by her from the works of other theosophists *was corrected by me or under my instruction*. It is a more valuable work than its predecessor, an epitome of occult truths that will make it a source of information and instruction for the earnest student for long years to come.[7]

From the various documents quoted above, it is abundantly clear that *The Secret Doctrine* is actually a great deal more than just an explanation of, and a running commentary on, certain stanzas translated from the *Book of Dzyan*. Throughout its pages there are a great many passages which begin with such expressions as: "Occultism teaches," "the Secret Doctrine states," "the Esoteric Philosophy affirms," "Occult Science declares," etc., etc., followed by a succinct exposition of certain occult truths expressed in direct and unequivocal language. When such passages are linked together, it becomes obvious that *The Secret Doctrine*, in its essential framework, is a comprehensive outline of the heretofore secret science or philosophy of occultism, publicly given out by at least two Initiates of the Brotherhood of Adepts through the intermediary of their direct messenger, H.P. Blavatsky.

Its text contains several different yet interrelated levels, from the scientific arguments and philosophical dissertations of H.P. Blavatsky as a student of mystical lore, to the inspired ideas, penetrating thoughts, and prophetic statements of an initiated occultist—H.P.B., and beyond these, to the lofty pronouncements and stirring passages directly derivative from the minds of Higher Occultists and which, at times, resound like the peal of organ music in the vastness of space. Unless this complex scheme of the work is grasped, the real nature of *The Secret Doctrine* will not be understood.

Some students, impressed by the vast amount of collateral information contained in this work, and dealing mainly with supporting evidence drawn from various religions, philosophies, and mythologies the world over, have imagined *The Secret Doctrine* to be a syncretistic work wherein a multitude of seemingly unrelated teachings and ideas are cleverly woven together to form a more or less coherent whole. Nothing could be farther from truth than this erroneous conception.

H.P.B.'s *magnum opus* is intended to present a wholly coherent outline of an ageless doctrine, a system of thought based upon occult facts and universal truths inherent in nature and which are as specific and definite as any mathematical proposition. The teachings of that system as a whole cannot be deduced from, or found in, any of the known exoteric religious or philosophical schools of ancient or more recent times, although separate ideas and single tenets can be occasionally found, or at least hinted at, in the works of ancient writers, suggesting the existence of a parent doctrine carefully hidden from view.

The stupendous Cosmogenesis and Anthropogenesis presented for our consideration and study are completely *sui generis*; they are not copied from any of the world-scriptures, nor are they pieced together from a number of them. They challenge investigation as the most extraordinary literary problem of our age. Unless H.P.B.'s own explanation concerning their source is accepted, no other explanation is of the slightest value.

Already as early as 1883, H.P.B., while discussing various conflicting views about Buddhism on the part of Western Orientalists, took occasion to point out that:

> The only way in which they will solve the problems raised, will be by paying attention to the direct teachings of the Secret Doctrine which are now being given out to the world through the columns of this Magazine [*The Theosophist*] for the first time in the history of the subject.[8]

The Secret Doctrine is the first major work in *several thousand years* which is intended to, and actually does, outline in a consecutive and coherent manner the foundation-principles of that universal occult doctrine—the *Brahma-Vidya*, the *Gupta-Vidya*, the *Gnosis Pneumatikos*—which was the original knowledge of the *Manasaputras*, who brought it to nascent mankind in this Round and left it in the care of its then highest exponents as a perennial fountain-head of spiritual truths.

It should of course be distinctly borne in mind that *The Secret Doctrine* outlines but a small portion of that universal occult tradition which in H.P.B.'s own words is "the accumulated Wisdom of the Ages." It is but the lifting of a corner of the mystic veil which hides the higher degrees or levels of this knowledge. Hence it would be foolish for anyone to imagine that H.P.B.'s work is the last word of that knowledge, while it is but the general outline of some of the basic principles thereof.

In the light of existing evidence, both published and traditional, it is therefore obvious that the principal sources of *The Secret Doctrine*—and this applies to many other portions of H.P.B.'s literary output—are collectively the Brotherhood of Adepts whose direct messenger she was, and individually two or more of the Initiates belonging to this Brotherhood, and who chose to unveil in our present era a certain portion of their traditionally hidden knowledge for the benefit of those who were ready to receive it.

Today we have in the world at large many more people ready to receive some of that hidden knowledge, the traditional *Gupta-Vidya*, than was the case when H.P.B.'s *magnum opus* appeared in print. It is to the dissemination of that knowledge that the Theosophical Movement is dedicated. In an age when modern science has proven beyond doubt several of the foundation-thoughts of the Ancient Wisdom, and the world of religious and philosophical pursuits evinces intuitive ideas in close similarity to the teachings of the age-old spiritual traditions, *The Secret Doctrine* is acquiring an ever greater importance as a treasure-house of occult facts and doctrines.

The future of this trend is full of promise, but its realization depends upon our spiritual integrity, our vital sense of brotherhood, our unclouded intuitions and unshakable moral strength. If we live up to these ideals and attend to our sacred duties, then, indeed:

> In Century the Twentieth some disciple more informed, and far better fitted, may be sent by the Masters of Wisdom to give final and irrefutable proofs that there exists a Science called *Gupta-Vidya*; and that, like the once-mysterious sources of the Nile, the source of all religions and philosophies now known to the world has been for many ages forgotten and lost to men, but is at last found.[9]

Notes

1. Original ed.
2. *The Letters of H.P. Blavatsky to A.P. Sinnett*, Transcribed, Compiled and with an Introduction by A. Trevor Barker. New York;

Frederick A. Stokes Co., 1924. Letter No. CXVI, p. 244.
3. *The Path*, New York, Vol. X, January, 1896, pp. 299-300.
4. Barker, *op. cit.*, Letter No. LXXX, p. 194.
5. Wachtmeister, Countess Constance, *Reminiscences of H.P. Blavatsky and "The Secret Doctrine."* London: Theosophical Publishing Society, 1893, p. 101.
6. Wachtmeister, *op. cit.*, p. 101.
7. *Letters from the Masters of the Wisdom*, Transcribed and Compiled by C. Jinarajadasa, Fourth Edition. Adyar: Theosophical Publishing House, 1948. Letter No. 19.
8. *The Theosophist*, vol. IV, May, 1883, p. 182.
9. *The Secret Doctrine*, vol. I, p. xxxviii, orig. ed., vol. I, p. 60, Adyar ed.

3
H. P. Blavatsky and World Thought

GEOFFREY A. BARBORKA

When H.P. Blavatsky received "orders" to go to America, although she had an intimation of the work that she had agreed to undertake, she little realized how it would be inaugurated. She arrived in New York on July 7, 1873. A year passed by without any inkling as to how she should proceed. One autumnal day the first presentiment came: she was instructed to travel to Vermont, to the Eddy farmhouse in Chittenden. So Mme. Blavatsky set out as directed, traveling in company with a French-Canadian woman named Boudreau. There, on October 14, she met Col. Henry S. Olcott, a reporter from New York who was covering the spiritualistic phenomena occurring at the house of the Eddy brothers. She soon learned the reason for being there; remarkable seances were being held. So she stayed for ten days. She also discovered that she was able not only to influence but actually to govern the spirit manifestations that were materialized through the mediumship of the Eddy brothers.

Following H.P. Blavatsky's return to New York City on the 27th of October she read in *The Daily Graphic* the account of Dr. George M. Beard's alleged exposure of the Eddy brothers' seances. This was altogether too much for her. She had been present and there certainly had not been any fraud perpetrated at the gatherings. She sat down and wrote an indignant protest to the *Graphic* under the title

"Marvellous Spirit Manifestations." Little did she realize that this protestation was to be the means of launching her on her life-work. From that moment her pen was to be not only her means of livelihood but the weapon that was to bring about a change in world thought. That she was gifted in superlative degree for this task may be easily determined simply by reading this initial display of her literary work. This inaugural effort was placed before the public by a prominent journal on October 30, 1874.

There must have been joy in Spiritualistic circles to have been so championed. But not so Dr. Beard. He did not respond to the challenge. Because of this, Mme. Blavatsky sent a second missive to the *Graphic*, "About Spiritualism." It was published on November 13. This time her pen awakened a response—but from another source. It came from the editor of the *Spiritual Scientist* of Boston, who wrote to Mme. Blavatsky in part:

> I have read your article in the *Daily Graphic*, and am so much pleased with the statements therein, and the powerful refutations of Dr. Beard's so-called "arguments," that I hasten to acknowledge to you, as editor of the *Scientist*, my gratitude for the service you have done Spiritualism in re-opening the eyes of the skeptical world.[1]

H.P. Blavatsky did not need a second invitation. Immediate recognition was given to this respondent by means of an article, followed by one after another in the *Spiritual Scientist*. The effort to turn a segment of world thought towards "*true* Spiritualism" was off to a good start. This was brought into prominence by her "first occult shot" (as she phrased it) consisting of "A Few Questions to Hiraf," published in two instalments of the journal under the dates of July 15 and 22, 1875. This trenchant article was written in response to an item which appeared in the *Spiritual Scientist* under the title of "Rosicrucianism," signed Hiraf. Many years later (in fact long after the passing of H.P.B.) the significance of Hiraf's article was disclosed.

The name "Hiraf" was actually an acrostic formed of the names of five young men who had formed an intellectual club. Three of the members had gathered together stray items on Rosicrucian data, then the principal literary member of the club worked this material up into an article. This was sent to the journal and it was published. In 1923 Charles R. Flint (1850-1934) published a book entitled *Memories of an Active Life* and divulged the activities of "Hiraf," adding this memorandum:

> . . . parties interested in the theosophic movement have insisted that whatever the origin of the "Hiraf" utterances may have been, the authors were, without their knowledge, inspired by a power over and beyond them, to utter words of weight and possibly prophecy.[2]

Many Theosophists are puzzled as to why H.P.B. should have become associated with the Spiritualistic movement and seances before the founding of The Theosophical Society, when the teachings which she later enunciated clearly indicate that affiliation with seances and their manifestations is undesirable. Study of the printed record by means of her articles demonstrates that she tried to change the thought of the Spiritualists from their erroneous belief in "the spirits of the departed" to the correct explanation regarding materializations. At the same time Mme. Blavatsky was given an opportunity of contacting other avenues of thought by means of the public press. A quotation from Charles Flint shows how he regarded her effort towards changing world thought:

> Whatever adverse opinion may still be entertained as to Madame Blavatsky and her cult, it cannot be denied that her teachings contain much that is interesting, even elevating, and that she has managed to affect many, many thousands, from India in the East to California in the west.[3]

Here also is a paragraph from one of the members of the Hiraf club:

> I have been told by Theosophists here, that we young men had written better than we knew, and that we were probably inspired by higher powers. Of this, I know nothing, *although this may be so*. Certain it is, that "Hiraf" has been quite extensively quoted as authority in various printed publications.[4]

It was in September of 1875 that The Theosophical Society was founded. Unfortunately, not long after that date the journal which had appeared to be so promising, and which had provided an opportunity for H.P.B. to express herself in her effort to revive interest in the Ancient Wisdom, collapsed. The editor, E.G. Brown, declared bankruptcy and the *Spiritual Scientist* was no more (June, 1876).

H.P.B. continued her literary work by submitting articles to other journals—to mention some: the *New York Sun* (which published her occult stories); *The Banner of Light* (Boston); *The World* (New York); *The Religio-Philosophical Journal* (Chicago); *The Spiritualist* (London). However, work had already commenced on *Isis Unveiled* (November, 1875). The first volume of that work had been electrotyped in May, 1877, and the two volumes were published in September, 1877. It is of interest to note that in some places "the Veil of Isis" is alluded to in the Hiraf response article. In fact, this was to have been the title of her first published work, but after a good portion of the running titles of the first volume had been electrotyped the publisher discovered that another book had already been published under that title, therefore an alternate title—*Isis Unveiled*—was submitted and approved by H.P.B.

That *Isis Unveiled* did have an effect upon the thought of the western world may be shown by quoting the reviews which appeared after its publication:

> This monumental work . . . about everything relating to magic, mystery, witchcraft, religion, spiritualism, which would be valuable in an encyclopaedia.
>
> —*North American Review*

> It must be acknowledged that she is a remarkable woman, who has read more, seen more, and thought more than most wise men. Her work abounds in quotations from a dozen different languages, not for the purpose of a vain display of erudition, but to substantiate her peculiar views . . . her pages are garnished with footnotes establishing, as her authorities, some of the profoundest writers of the past. To a large class of readers, this remarkable work

will prove of absorbing interest . . . demands the earnest attention of thinkers, and merits an analytic reading.

—*Boston Evening Transcript*

The appearance of erudition is stupendous. Reference to and quotations from the most unknown and obscure writers in all languages abound, interspersed with allusions to writers of the highest repute, which have evidently been more than skimmed through.

—*New York Independent*

An extremely readable and exhaustive essay upon the paramount importance of re-establishing the Hermetic Philosophy in a world which blindly believes that it has outgrown it.

—*New York World*

Most remarkable book of the season.

—*Com. Advertiser*

To readers who have not made themselves acquainted with the literature of mysticism and alchemy, the volume will furnish the materials for an interesting study—a mine of curious information.

—*Evening Post*

They give evidence of much and multifarious research on the part of the author, and contain a vast number of interesting stories. Persons fond of the marvelous will find in them an abundance of entertainment.

—*New York Sun*

A marvelous book both in matter and manner of treatment. Some idea may be formed of the rarity and extent of its contents when the index alone comprises fifty pages, and we venture nothing in saying that such an index of subjects was never before compiled by any human being. . . . But the book is a curious one and will no doubt find its way into libraries because of the unique subject matter it contains . . . will certainly prove attractive to all who are interested in the history, theology, and the mysteries of the ancient world.

—*Daily Graphic*

> The present work is the fruit of her remarkable course of education, and amply confirms her claims to the character of an adept in secret science, and even to the rank of a hierophant in the exposition of its mystic lore.
>
> —*New York Tribune*

> One of the remarkable productions of the century.
>
> —*New York Herald*[5]

Having received "orders" to go to India in the autumn of 1878, literary efforts were lessened in preparation for the departure from America, which was accomplished in December 1878.

After becoming established in Bombay, H.P.B. resumed her literary work. Articles were written and published in some European journals, as well as a few in India. But a new venture was in the offing: the founding of a monthly journal "devoted to Oriental Philosophy, Art, and Occultism, embracing Mesmerism, Spiritualism and other Secret Sciences." Work on the prospectus announcing the journal was begun in July, articles were prepared, and the first issue of *The Theosophist* came off the press on September 30, 1879.

The inauguration of *The Theosophist* gave H.P. Blavatsky the needed opportunity of being able to broadcast her message without any hindrances. Simply to list the titles of the voluminous articles prepared by her pen for her journal for the years 1879 to 1887 would fill several pages. These articles have been republished and form six volumes in the H.P. Blavatsky *Collected Writings* series.

In spite of all this voluminous writing the crowning work of her career was yet to appear. First broached as an idea to correct and expand *Isis Unveiled*, announced in March 1884, the idea underwent changes as the work on it proceeded. For that matter, more than one draft was prepared in manuscript form—all written in long-hand as H.P. Blavatsky labored in the writing of *The Secret Doctrine*, first in Würzburg, Germany, in the autumn of 1885, then at Ostend, Belgium.

There was a critical period in Ostend, when a physician

from London was called to visit Mme. Blavatsky—in addition to the Belgian doctor who was administering to her. She had collapsed and medical assistance failed to revive her. In fact the Belgian doctor had given up all hope for her recovery. However, a resuscitator of a superior order came to the rescue. Late at night during the interval when her life hung by a thread, her Master arrived and gave H.P.B. a choice: either to leave the world or remain to continue the writing of *The Secret Doctrine.* It was because of her decision to stay and labor on in spite of heartaches, disappointments, and calumnies thrust upon her that the world was given the work which had indeed brought the wisdom of the Orient to the western world—bringing a regenerating influence to the thought-life of the west.

However, the prodigious undertaking which H.P.B. envisioned, that of having *The Secret Doctrine* published in four volumes, was only partially fulfilled. For, just two of the four volumes were published; the first volume comprising Cosmogenesis, the second Anthropogenesis. Notwithstanding this, her efforts to change the current of world thought did not cease; not at all. Even before the two volumes of her marvellous work were published, H.P.B. had founded another journal, this time shocking all crystallized opinion by naming her new periodical *Lucifer* and declaring on the opening page:

> Now, the first and most important, if not the sole object of the magazine, is expressed in the line from the 1st Epistle to the Corinthians, on its title page. It is to bring light to "the hidden things of darkness" (iv, 5); to show in their true aspect and their original real meaning things and names, men and their doings and customs; it is finally to fight prejudice, hypocrisy and shams in every nation, in every class of Society, as in every department of life. The task is a laborious one but it is neither impracticable nor useless, if even as an experiment.
>
> Thus, for an attempt of such nature, no better title could ever be found than the one chosen. "Lucifer" is the pale morning-star, the precursor of the full blaze of the noon-day sun—the "Eosphoros" of the Greeks.[6]

The articles penned for her periodical are not simple ones; they are even more profound than many in her former journal. Even more amazing is their quantity: they comprise four volumes; many had not even been published before her passing. Nor must one fail to mention her superb devotional book *The Voice of the Silence.*

This stupendous literary production, while predominantly appearing for Theosophists, certainly had an impact upon other segments of world thought. In support of this statement reference is made to a work by Emile Burnouf, a Sanskritist, in an article in the *Revue des Deux Mondes* entitled "Buddhism in the Occident." M. Burnouf directs attention to the impact which the Theosophical Society made—primarily because of the literary work of H.P.B. To quote from his article:

> . . . one of the most interesting, if not the most unexpected, phenomena of our day is the attempt which is now being made to revive and create in the world a new society, resting on the same foundations as Buddhism. Although only in its beginnings, its growth is so rapid that our readers will be glad to have their attention called to this subject.[7]
>
> The society is very young, nevertheless it has already its history. . . . It has set itself a moral ideal of great elevation, it combats vice and egoism. It tends towards the unification of religions, which it considers as identical in their philosophical origin; but it recognizes the supremacy of truth. . . .[8]

Mme. Blavatsky quoted these words of Emile Burnouf's and many more in her article entitled "The Theosophical Society: Its Mission and its Future," which every Theosophist would do well to read, not only because of the way in which she responded to the French Orientalist, but because of the potent force of her message, which if followed by Theosophists today would assist in changing world thought.

There need be no doubt about the reason for H.P.B.'s coming to the western world: she declared that she had come to change the molds of mind, for only by accomplishing this may world thought be changed.

Notes

1. Blavatsky, H.P., *Collected Writings*, vol. 1, p. 45.
2. Ibid., vol. 1, p. 99.
3. Ibid., vol. 1, p. 99.
4. Ibid., vol. 1, p. 100.
5. Quoted in *Lucifer*, May 15, 1891.
6. Blavatsky, H.P., op. cit., vol. 8, pp. 5-6.
7. Blavatsky, H.P., op. cit., vol. 10, p. 68.
8. Ibid., vol. 10, p. 68.

4
The Making of The Secret Doctrine

MICHAEL GOMES

Most Theosophists are familiar with the fact that H.P. Blavatsky's magnum opus, *The Secret Doctrine*, was published in 1888, and are aware of the theories of vast cosmogenesis and anthropogenesis contained therein. However, the events which shaped the making of the book are not as well known. Fortunately, a number of eyewitness accounts have survived, making it possible to reconstruct this period. The most fascinating and detailed is Countess Constance Wachtmeister's *Reminiscences of H.P. Blavatsky and The Secret Doctrine* published in 1893 after H.P.B.'s death, and reprinted by Quest Books.

The blonde, blue-eyed countess was a society woman, related to the old French family of de Bourbel de Montjuçon. Her father was the Marquis de Bourbel, and she was born in Florence, Italy, on March 28, 1838. She married her cousin, the Count Karl Wachtmeister, in 1863. He was then stationed in London as the Swedish and Norwegian minister to the Court of St. James. Subsequently they lived in Copenhagen, where he was minister to the Danish court, and in Stockholm, where he was named minister of foreign affairs. After his death in 1871, the countess developed an interest in Spiritualism. But like many titled members of the early Theosophical Society—the Earl of Crawford and Balcarres, Baron Spedalieri, Duchesse de Pomar—her Spiritualism soon developed into occultism. Reading H.P.B.'s *Isis Unveiled* led her to join the British Theosophical Society in 1880.[1]

It was at the London home of the popular Theosophical author A.P. Sinnett, early in April 1884, that Countess Wachtmeister first met H.P.B., who had come over briefly from Paris for the London Lodge elections. The countess saw Mme. Blavatsky later that spring at the chateau of the Count and Countess d'Adhemar at Enghien, France, before returning to Sweden. She was told by H.P.B. that "before two years had passed, I [the countess] would devote my life wholly to Theosophy."[2] At the time, she says, she regarded this idea as an utter impossibility.

When Countess Wachtmeister contacted H.P.B. again at the beginning of December 1885, the situation was very different from the brilliant receptions of London and Paris. Their stay in Europe had culminated with a gala farewell for Col. Olcott and Mme. Blavatsky at Prince's Hall in London on July 21, 1884, attended by 500 people in evening dress. "It's not life," H.P.B. had written to her sister Vera, "but a sort of mad turmoil from morning till night. Visitors, dinners, evening callers, and meetings every day."[3] But now the theosophical leader was under suspicion and felt "abandoned by all and deserted." Letters attributed to her in the September and October 1884 *Madras Christian College Magazine* seemed seriously to compromise the psychic phenomena she had produced, as had her failure to prosecute for libel, as well as her sudden departure from India for Europe in March 1885. An agent had been sent by the newly formed London Society for Psychical Research to investigate the matter, and his soon-to-be-issued report was generally believed to be unfavorable.[4]

The countess had intended to spend the winter of 1885/86 in Italy, and had stopped en route at the home of a fellow Theosophist and student of the occult, Marie Gebhard, in Elberfeld, Germany. Mme. Gebhard, who had been one of the few private pupils of the French Kabbalist Eliphas Levi, urged her guest to see H.P.B., who was now settled in nearby Würzburg. Mme. Blavatsky's response to the countess was a polite refusal; she claimed lack of space and time to entertain a visitor, as she was engaged in writing *The Secret Doctrine.* But while the countess was preparing to leave for Rome, with the cab actually at the door, a telegram arrived saying, "Come to Würzburg at once, wanted immediately—Blavatsky."[5]

Because of the rumors of fraud and deception circulating about Blavatsky, Countess Wachtmeister said she could not help being on her guard as she climbed the steps of no. 6 Ludwigstrasse in Würzburg on the evening of her arrival. She found an unhappy fifty-four-year-old woman who was smarting sensitively under insults and suspicions. An embarrassed H.P.B. told her that she had not initially invited the countess because the small size of her apartment—mainly a bedroom, dining room, sitting room and maid's quarters—might not satisfy someone of her guest's background.

Countess Wachtmeister must have been a remarkably unpretentious person, for she stayed with Mme. Blavatsky for the next five months. A screen separated the bedroom into compartments to provide their only private space. At 6:00 in the morning, their Swiss maid, Louise, would bring a cup of coffee for H.P.B., who then rose and dressed, and was at her writing desk by 7:00. Breakfast was at 8:00 when the day's mail would be read, and then Mme. Blavatsky would return to her writing. Their main meal was served at 1:00, but H.P.B. might not respond for hours to the handbell announcing it, depending how well her writing was going. Finally at 7:00 she put it aside, and after tea the two would spend "a pleasant evening together." H.P.B. would amuse herself with a game of patience, while the countess read her passages and articles from the daily journals. By 9:00 H.P.B. retired to bed, where she would read the Russian newspapers late into the night.

They had few visitors at this time, the routine of their days punctuated only by the weekly visit of H.P.B.'s doctor, who usually stayed an hour, and an occasional appearance by their landlord. Most of H.P.B.'s time was spent working on her new book, which had been advertised in the journal of the Theosophical Society early in 1884 as a "new version of *Isis Unveiled* with a new arrangement of the matter, large and important additions, and copious notes and commentaries." But the work had gone slowly. An attempt at grouping subjects exists from H.P.B.'s 1884 European tour, and before the arrival of the countess she had managed to put together a few chapters.

Like Col. Olcott's testimony for H.P.B.'s writing *Isis Unveiled* and Annie Besant's on the production of *The Voice of the Silence*, Countess Wachtmeister's account tallies with the depiction of Mme. Blavatsky sitting for long hours, writing continuously, stopping only to gaze into vacant space. H.P.B. explained her technique as being able to "make what I can only describe as a sort of a vacuum in the air before me, and fix my sight and my will upon it, and soon scene after scene passes before me like the successive pictures of a diorama, or, if I need a reference or information from some book, I fix my mind intently, and the astral counterpart of the book appears, and from it I take what I need. The more perfectly my mind is freed from distractions and mortifications, the more energy and intentness it possesses, the more easily I can do this."[6]

But soon the peaceful atmosphere the countess had managed to create by relieving H.P.B. from concern about the running of the household was shattered in a most dramatic way. On New Year's Eve 1885 a member of the Germania Theosophical Society, Prof. Sellin, appeared with the finally published report by Richard Hodgson for the Society for Psychical Research Committee on theosophical phenomena. The Committee had judged H.P.B. worthy of permanent remembrance as "one of the most accomplished, ingenious and interesting imposters in history."[7] Hodgson had added his own conclusion that she had done it all as a cover for her being a Russian spy! (H.P.B. was cleared of charges of fraud in April 1986 in an article in the *Journal for the Society of Psychical Research* by Dr. Vernon Harrison, a respected researcher. He concluded that Hodgson was prejudiced against H.P.B. and ignored evidence in her favor, that as an investigator Hodgson was "found wanting." He adds that the Society for Psychical Research owes H.P.B. an apology.)

"I shall never forget that day," the countess records in her *Reminiscences*, nor the look of blank and stony despair that she [H.P.B.] cast on me when I entered her sitting room and found her with the open book in her hands." In the intensity of the moment, H.P.B. turned on her shouting, "Why don't you go? Why don't you leave me? You are a countess, you cannot stop here with a ruined woman, with one held up to scorn before the whole world, one who will be pointed at everywhere as a trickster and an imposter. Go before you are defiled by my shame."[8]

The countess did not go. She stayed on, not only through this crisis, but until H.P.B.'s death in 1891. Her presence did much to alleviate H.P.B.'s suffering, and her personal integrity must be counted toward influencing H.P.B.'s later acceptance by London society. H.P.B. herself acknowledged this, for in writing to a T. S. member in India, she says; "The widow of the Swedish ambassador in London, the ex-visitor at all hours of the Queen, and one who is known in London for twenty years in the highest circles as a woman of unblemished reputation and one who has never uttered a falsehood in her life, is not likely to throw her reputation, her friends and position, to become the most devoted champion of an H.P.B. if there was nothing serious in it."[9]

Still, they had a difficult time, as Countess Wachtmeister's letters to A.P. Sinnett in London show. "We have had a terrible day and the Old Lady wanted to start to London at once," she wrote him on the evening of January 1, 1886.[10] The countess had finally managed to calm H.P.B. down. She had wanted to write a number of indignant protests to all concerned, and in her excited state had developed palpitations of the heart and had required a dose of digitalis. The following days brought rude letters and resignations as the contents of the S.P.R. Report became known, until, the countess says, "my heart used to sink every morning, when the postman's ring was heard at the thought of the fresh insults which the letters would surely contain."[11]

"We are having a horrible time of it here," she informed

Sinnett on January 4.[12] The countess reports how H.P.B. "felt herself deserted by all those who had professed such devotion for her. As she pathetically said one day: 'If there was only one man, who had the courage to come forward and defend me as he would his own mother, if thus scurrilously attacked, the whole current of the Theosophical Society would be changed.' It was a critical moment for the Society, and H.P.B. was left alone in her agony and despair."[13]

Out of this crucial testing period came the nucleus of *The Secret Doctrine* as we know it. The book would no longer simply be a revision of an earlier work, but something H.P.B. felt would serve as her vindication by answering the charges against her. She wrote Col. Olcott, the President of the Society, accordingly on January 6: "*Secret Doctrine is entirely* new. There will not be there 20 pages quoted by bits from *Isis*. New matter, occult explanations—the whole Hindu Pantheon explained, based on exoteric translations (to be easily verified) and explained esoterically proving Xty and every other religion to have taken their dogmas from India's oldest religion. . . . In *four* Parts—Archaic, Ancient, Mediaeval and Modern Periods. Each Part 12 chapters, with Appendices and a Glossary of terms at the end. Countess here, and she sees I have almost *no books*. Master and Kashmiri dictating in turn. She copies all. This *will be* my vindication, I tell you."[14] Thus H.P.B. turned on her critics by producing a book containing one of the most complete outlines of physical and spiritual evolution of her century—a book that has survived a hundred years and is still read around the world.

When H.P.B. returned to the writing of *The Secret Doctrine* at the start of February 1886, it was with a grim determination that would carry her through the next two years and which would triumph over death itself. By the end of the month she had completed 300 foolscap pages of a preliminary volume. This would show "what *was* known historically and in literature, in classics and in profane and sacred histories—during the 500 years that preceded the Christian period and the 500 years that followed it [of the existence of a] Universal Secret Doctrine." The commentary would serve as an introduction to her translation of the Stanzas of Dyzan, the ancient text that she used as the basis of her magnum opus.[15]

As the rent on the apartment at Würzburg was paid only until April 15, H.P.B. decided to pass the summer months at Ostende on the Belgium coast. Her sister Vera and a niece would stay with her, allowing the countess the chance to return to Sweden to settle her affairs. An English Theosophist, Miss Emily Kislingbury, whose affiliation with the Society went back to 1876, would travel with H.P.B. to Ostende. But when they arrived at Cologne to change trains and rest for the day, Gustav Gebhard persuaded H.P.B. to pay a brief visit to his family in Elberfeld. There she slipped and sprained her leg, which postponed her leaving till July, when she was accompanied by her sister and niece.

She arrived in Ostende at the height of the season, to find everything overpriced. With the help of her sister, she managed to find a suite of rooms, first at no. 10 Boulevard Van Isgham, and later at no. 17 Rue d'Ouest, where she passed the winter with the countess. The regularity of their Würzburg days was repeated, the monotony broken only by a few more visitors: the English seer Anna Kingsford and her uncle Edward Maitland; Sinnett gathering material for his proposed biography of H.P.B.; Arthur Gebhard and Mohini Chatterji, who spent their time "studying 'Bhagavad Gita' all day";[16] the Rev. A. Ayton; and K.F. Gaboriau from France.

A manuscript copy of the finished preliminary volume of *The Secret Doctrine* was given to Marie Gebhard to send Col. Olcott from Elberfeld, but she kept it for a month, and it did not reach him in India until December 10. This volume was to be the introductory section to the "real pukka S.D." volume on the Archaic Period, with the seven Stanzas of Dyzan and the commentaries on them. "It is an absolutely necessary one," H.P.B. informed Olcott, "otherwise if they began reading the Archaic vol., the public would get crazy before five pages, *too metaphysical.*"[17]

The countess had been sent to London to attend to a business matter, and H.P.B. passed the New Year into 1887 alone. "The 2nd anniversary in exile &—for what guilt or fault, ye Gods," she wrote to an American member. "Ah, life *is* a hard thing to bear."[18] It was at this time that she made the following important decision about her future. "Either I have to return to India to die this autumn, or I have to form between this and November next a nucleus of true Theosophists, a school of my own. . . . I can stop here, or go to England, or whatever I like," she revealed to Countess Wachtmeister.[19]

Perhaps it was just coincidental, but after the countess's return H.P.B. began receiving letters from a small group of members of the London Lodge who still met on a regular basis. They wrote her for advice on the best way to carry on the work. Dr. Archibald Keightley, who with his uncle Bertram had joined the Society in 1884, was deputed by this group to personally invite H.P.B. to come to England to spend the summer. Since Countess Wachtmeister had to go to Sweden that summer to dispose of property in order to live with H.P.B. on a more permanent basis, the move was decided upon.

A departure date of March 27 had been set, but on the 17th H.P.B., uncharacteristically, lost consciousness in her armchair after dinner. Then she developed a cold, and on the fifth day of her illness, the doctor diagnosed uremic poisoning with inaction of the kidneys. The countess said she became alarmed when H.P.B. began to drift into "a heavy lethargic state; she seemed to be unconscious for hours at a time, and nothing could rouse or interest her."[20]

Mme. Gebhard had come from Elberfeld so that in shifts someone would always be in attendance with H.P.B. As the local doctor could get no results, Countess Wachtmeister telegraphed Dr. Ashton Ellis, a member of the London group of Theosophists, to send a specialist. Dr. Ellis replied that he would come immediately, and upon arrival prescribed a program of massage to stimulate the paralyzed organs, which he proceeded to do for the next three days.

As there seemed no improvement in H.P.B.'s condition, Mme. Gebhard suggested that her will be made out, for if she died intestate in a foreign country there would be no end of complications. A lawyer, the doctor, and the American consul were to come the next day. During that night's watch, the countess says, "To my horror I began to detect the peculiar faint odor of death which sometimes precedes dissolution. I hardly dared hope that she would live through the night."[21]

H.P.B. was anxious about the fate of the manuscript of *The Secret Doctrine*, and gave the countess instructions to send it to Col. Olcott at Adyar to have it printed. She said she was glad to die after what she had suffered in the last years. She drifted into unconsciousness and seemed to grow weaker by the hour. The strain of the last few days also affected the countess, who said a "wave of blank despondency" swept over her, and she too drifted off.

Morning light was already streaming in when Countess Wachtmeister opened her eyes. Her first thought was that H.P.B. might have died as she slept. However, she found an alert and awake H.P.B., who told her that during the night she had the choice of being able to die or to finish *The Secret Doctrine*. "But when I thought of those students to whom I shall be permitted to teach a few things, and of the Theosophical Society, in general, to which I have already given my heart's blood, I accepted the sacrifice."[22]

The lawyer found a joyous group when he arrived to make the will later in the day. The Belgian doctor kept repeating, "But she should be dead . . . she should be dead," and the American consul, who had come as a witness, left with the words, "Well, I think this is enough fatigue for a dying woman."[23] The little party laughed heartily over the events of that day's turnaround.

The countess looked so used up that Mme. Gebhard suggested she leave for Sweden at once, and offered to stay until the Keightleys came to take H.P.B. to London. In spite of bad weather, H.P.B.'s crossing to Dover was without incident, though everyone was concerned as she had not left her heated rooms for weeks. She was housed at "Maycot," a small cottage in Upper Norwood, with Mabel Collins, a member of the London group, on May 1. Before the day's end H.P.B. was back at work on *The Secret Doctrine*.

During Countess Wachtmeister's absence in Sweden throughout the summer of 1887, the narrative for the making of *The Secret Doctrine* is continued by the accounts of two young Cambridge graduates, Archibald Keightley (1859-1930) and his uncle Bertram Keightley (1860-1945). By the end of May, Bertram could write W.Q. Judge—General Secretary of the newly formed American section of the Society and editor of the New York *Path*—that "H.P.B. is fairly well & working away right hard at *The Secret Doctrine*, which is *awfully good*, & I am sure you will be immensely pleased with it."[24]

Soon after her arrival at Maycot, H.P.B. passed her manuscript, now over three feet high, to the Keightleys "to read, punctuate, correct the English, alter, and generally treat as if it were our own."[25] Their summer was spent "reading, rereading and copying." *The Secret Doctrine*, as it came to be published, dates from this time, for it was the Keightleys' suggestion that "instead of making the first volume to consist, as she had intended, of the history of some great occultists, we advised her to follow the natural order of exposition, and begin with the Evolution of Cosmos, to pass from that to the Evolution of Man, then to deal with the historical part in a third volume treating of some Great Occultists; and finally, to speak of Practical Occultism in a fourth volume, should she ever be able to write it."[26]

The material was then rearranged under the headings of "Cosmogenesis" and "Anthropogenesis," with the Stanzas of Dyzan and H.P.B.'s commentaries on them leading off each volume, followed by explanations of the symbolism and science treated therein. The Keightleys were impressed by the paucity of Mme. Blavatsky's personal library. Archibald, who had made the transit with her from Ostende and had helped her unpack, states, "I knew there was no library to consult and I could see that H.P.B.'s own books did not amount to thirty in all, of which several were dictionaries and several works counted two or more volumes."[27] Yet the manuscript edited by them for the press quoted or referred to over 1300 books. Checking the sources alone occupied a group of people, including E. Douglas

Fawcett, assistant editor of the London *Daily Telegraph*, Richard Harte, a member from America, and, it was rumored, even S.L. Macgregor Mathers, who was regularly seen at the British Museum poring over old folios of Kabbalistic lore.

Concurrent with the editorial work on *The Secret Doctrine* were a series of events which revived theosophical work in England. The Blavatsky Lodge of the Theosophical Society (still in existence) was formed May 19 with ten members; by the second meeting a week later, it was decided to publish a magazine that would bring theosophical ideas to a larger public. The Theosophical Publishing Society was started to manage this. By the time Countess Wachtmeister arrived in England in August, a three-story brick building had been leased at 17 Lansdowne Road in London to serve as a residence for the theosophical household.

The Secret Doctrine was to be issued by the London publishing house of George Redway, in which A.P. Sinnett had invested. There was a disagreement on terms, and the work was taken over by the Theosophical Publishing Society, with a release date of October 27, 1888. An advance copy of the first volume (723 pages) exists, bearing the notation by Richard Harte that he received it at Lansdowne Road from the printer on October 20, as he was leaving for India with Col. Olcott. The first edition of 500, bound in light grey and bearing the dedication "to all True Theosophists, in every Country and of every Race," sold out immediately, mainly to subscribers. A second edition was printed before the end of the year.[28] Referring to the day the book was released, Countess Wachtmeister closed her *Reminiscences* with the words, "H.P.B. was happy that day."[29]

The Secret Doctrine was not as widely reviewed by the press as *Isis Unveiled*, though *The Theosophist* reprinted notices from such diverse sources as the *Memphis Appeal*, the New Orleans *Southland*, and the London *Secular Review*. Such was the prejudice against the movement at the time that the New York *Evening Telegram* published a review based only on the prospectus sent out four months before the actual release date. The *Telegram* reported:

> Mme. Blavatsky is undoubtedly an intellectual phenomenon, but because she can soar back into the Brahmin ignorance of the Buddhists and furnish Edwin Arnold with food for thought is no proof that everything she says is true. . . . Ten minutes of Edison and Noah Webster will do more for civilization than all the fine spun immoralities of the Indian poets. However it is a good thing to study history, and Mme. Blavatsky, with her learning and patience, throws the light of her intellectual dark lantern on the monstrosities of the past. Her book is very elaborate and comprehensive in its scope, and will undoubtedly be widely read."[30]

Perhaps the most influential review appeared in London's literary *Pall Mall Gazette*. The anonymous reviewer's closing remarks serve as a fitting conclusion to the making of *The Secret Doctrine* and an introduction to the book itself. "Mme. Blavatsky's views may not meet with acceptance, but they are supported by sufficient learning, acuteness and ability to enforce a respectful hearing. It is indeed the East which, through her, challenges the West, and the Orient need not be ashamed of its champion.

"The book deserves to be read: it deserves to be thought over; and none who believe in the progress of humanity has the right to turn away over-hastily from any contribution to knowledge, however new its form, from any theory, however strange its aspect. The wild dreams of one generation become the commonplaces of a later one."[31]

Notes

1. Biographical information on the countess is given in *The Path*, New York, November 1893, pp. 246-47, and with slight amplification by Boris de Zirkoff in *Theosophia*, Los Angeles, Fall 1957, p. 16. The countess's early psychic experiences are given in her 1897 talk "Spiritualism in the Light of Theosophy," printed by the Mercury Publishing Co., San Francisco, 1897. She applied for membership in the Theosophical Society in London, November 24, 1880, and was elected December 5th.

2. Wachtmeister, *Reminiscenses of H.P. Blavatsky and The Secret Doctrine* (London: Theosophical Publishing Society, 1893, reprinted Wheaton: Quest Books, 1976), p. 9.
3. H.P.B. to Vera Zhelihovsky, July 1884. *The Path*, New York, June 1895, pp. 74-77.
4. For background on this incident, see my article, "The Coulomb Case, 1884-1984," in *The Theosophist*, December 1984, January, February, 1985.
5. Wachtmeister, *Reminiscences*, p. 12.
6. *Reminiscences*, p. 25.
7. *S.P.R. Proceedings* 3 (1885): 202.
8. *Reminiscences*, p. 18.
9. H.P.B. to Judge N.D. Khandalavala, July 12, 1888, Theosophical Society Archives, Adyar. "She would never consciously tell an untruth," remembers another member of the London household, James Pryse. *Canadian Theosophist*, June 15, 1932, p. 126.
10. In *The Letters of H.P. Blavatsky to A.P. Sinnett (LBS)*, p. 270. Letter CXXVI.
11. Wachtmeister, "A New Year's Greeting," *The Vahan*, London, January 1, 1891, and *Theosophical Siftings*, 3: 17, p. 3.
12. *LBS*, p. 272, Letter CXXVII.
13. Wachtmeister, *H.P.B. and the Present Crisis in the Theosophical Society*. Privately printed, London, c. 1895, p. 6.
14. In *The Theosophist*, H.P.B. Centenary Number, August 1931, p. 667.
15. H.P.B. to A.P. Sinnett, March 3 [1886]. *LBS*, p. 195. Letter LXXX.
16. *LBS*, p. 217. Letter XCVII.
17. H.P.B. to H.S.O., September 23, 1886. *The Theosophist*, March 1925, p. 789.
18. H.P.B. to Elliott Coués, dated by her "between 1886-1887." *Canadian Theosophist*, November-December 1984, p. 116.
19. *Reminiscences*, pp. 54-55.
20. *Reminiscences*, p. 59.
21. *Reminiscences*, p. 60.
22. *Reminiscences*, p. 62.
23. *Reminiscences*, p. 64.
24. Letter of May 29, 1887, quoted in Kirby van Mater's "The Writing of *The Secret Doctrine*." *Sunrise*, November 1975, p. 60.
25. B. Keightley, "Writing of *The Secret Doctrine*," in *Reminiscences*, p. 78.
26. B. Keightley in *Reminiscences*, p. 79. In addressing the December

1890 Adyar Theosophical Convention, he revealed that "what would now be the 3rd volume was to have been the first volume. . . ."

27. A. Keightley, "Writing of *The Secret Doctrine*," in *Reminiscences*, p. 84. Marion Meade in her biography *Madame Blavatsky*, 1980, p. 380, notes, "In fact, every person involved with Madame Blavatsky during the writing of *The Secret Doctrine* seems to have gone out of their way to mention the curious lack of reference works." They were genuinely impressed by it.
28. Harte's copy with the October 20, 1888, notation on the flyleaf, now in the Boris de Zirkoff Collection at the Olcott Library, Wheaton, formerly belonged to the Blavatsky Association in London. The note is transcribed in de Zirkoff's exhaustive presentation of the writing of *The Secret Doctrine, Rebirth of the Occult Tradition* (Adyar: T.P.H., 1977), p. 1. A copy of the second edition inscribed December 7, 1888, and presented "to the Adyar Library by its most devoted & humble servant, H.P. Blavatsky," exists in the Adyar Archives.
29. *Reminiscences*, p. 72.
30. New York *Evening Telegram*, June 30, 1888. "Words with Wings."
31. *Pall Mall Gazette*, April 25, 1889, p. 3. "Among the Adepts."

II

Some Secret Doctrine Concepts

5

The Secret Doctrine as a Contribution to World Thought

SRI MADHAVA ASHISH

The world's many religious teachings are human attempts to express mankind's half defined ideas about himself and the world he lives in. As we become richer in our wealth of concepts and more knowledgeable about our environment, we find it necessary from time to time to reformulate our religious ideas. H.P. Blavatsky's contribution to world thought was such a reformulation. It was no new truth that she propounded; she claimed, in fact, that she was only disclosing the secrets of the ancients. And though this was in some measure true, she spoke from the position of a woman of her time, well versed in the science of her time. She produced a reformulation of religious ideas which began to combine the transcendental wisdom of the East with the scientific knowledge of the West.

The Oxford English Dictionary defines Theosophy as: Any system of speculation which bases the knowledge of nature upon that of the divine nature. We may add that knowledge of the divine nature is obtained through knowledge of its manifest qualities in nature. Although H.P.B. rightly tilted at the materialism of nineteenth century science, and though some of her own statements seem to have been extravagantly wrong, she was not so much denying the natural facts discovered by scientists as she was the constructions they built upon those facts. At a time when faith in religious myth and superstition was badly shaken by scientific discoveries, she reintroduced the thinking world to the idea of a nontheistic spiritual path—the path of human evolutionary aspiration. Through the Cosmogenesis of *The Secret Doctrine* she began an attempt to heal the dichotomy between the religio-spiritual and the scientifico-material views of life. Neither did "God" make the world, nor was it made by the random concatenation of energetic particles. And emphatically the world was not limited to the phenomena susceptible to analysis by the scientific method. What the West had regarded as a personal God was the power which sought, as Jacob Boehme said, to find, feel, and behold itself. And to discover that power we have to search with as much realism and urgency in this field of inquiry as does the scientist within the limits of his field.

Although as the Emerald Tablet of Hermes Trismegistus says, our path is analytically to "Separate the earth from the fire, the subtle from the gross, gently and with skill," our view of being must synthetically encompass all things which were "produced from One by the mediation of One." To find the All from which all things come, we must search within the totality of Being with the totality of our being. If in the study of the divine being we ignore the study of its manifest nature, we are rejecting the means by which the divine consciousness itself becomes aware of its own inherent qualities. It is the purpose of a cosmogony to lead us to a perception of the unmanifest power which underlies the world of appearances. This is the purpose of the Stanzas of Dzyan, and this is the purpose of H.P.B.'s *The Secret Doctrine.* Unless we understand the harmonious interrelationships of all things, unless we perceive the divine purpose which gives direction and significance to all events, then we fall into the chaos of meaninglessness.

Many people drew water from H.P.B.'s spring and channeled it into their particular religious schools, but she herself was concerned neither with the founding of a new school nor with the resuscitation of old ones. She taught the timeless truth of man's essential identity with the divine power which, in making manifest its own hidden qualities, discovers itself to itself through the human vehicle of its own awareness. She spoke with the authority of those who stood behind her, the Perfected Men or Masters of the Secret Wisdom who themselves embody the truth she taught. And she expounded their path of compassion through which those men who complete the evolutionary cycle and attain to the goal of self-knowledge, toward which the whole manifest process is directed, remain in their state of utter perfection that the light of their being may shine out as a beacon of love to other men. Love is the unmanifest made manifest. Suffering is its privation. We cannot have the one without the other. Those who reject suffering also reject the demands of love, and for them there is the direct path of self-annihilation in return to the absolute Source of all things.

As we have said, the basic tenets of H.P.B.'s Theosophy were not new. For many centuries the East had known that the Self of man and the Self of the universe are one. But in application this knowledge was restricted to a relatively select number of people, for the reason that it is a truth which can be grasped only by men whose understanding ranks high in the scale of human evolution. In the ancient world the select few raised their level of intelligence and culture at the expense of the many, gaining the physical leisure they needed for active thought by causing others to labor for them. This inevitably led to corruption, for, though it was not true of men of actual spiritual attainment, wherever the inner truth was formulated as a teaching the holders of the teaching denied by their privileges the very unity which by virtue of their privileged position they were able to perceive. The most orthodox of Brahmans would devoutly recite Sanskrit verses in praise of the one divinity manifest in many forms, yet would simultaneously deny other castes access to his knowledge, just as, in another setting, the Roman Catholic priesthood denied the laity access to the secrets of the Church. Nevertheless, it can be maintained that such exclusiveness was justified in that era by the real difficulty of holding to intellectual perceptions against the constant tendency to revert to the level of non-intellectual, tribal man.

As with an individual, the body of humanity simultaneously grows or evolves in all its parts. But, again as with an individual, its parts serve different functions. While the Eastern limb of humanity remained relatively static, holding to its transcendental perceptions, the Western limb set off to adventure in the fields of mundane knowledge. The West's consequent assertion of material values led to a greater separation of the human conscious ego integration from the underlying unity of the Self than occurred in the East. It is this increased separation which gives rise to the West's heightened psychic tension with its consequent expression as available psychic energy.

From the Western viewpoint, the East remains "unconscious" and "primitive," even though it represents the repository of the Secret Wisdom. This is why the Western dreamer, and the novelist who dreams for the collectivity of men, often represent the journey into Self by a recession into primitive or prehistoric surroundings. This is the pattern which led H.P.B. in *The Secret Doctrine* to lay undue stress on the significance of prehistoric races. The dawn that seems to hang permanently over the lands of the rising sun brightens to noon-day glory in the West, so that the brightly wide-awake, outward looking consciousness of the Western man is, as it were, separated from his "Eastern," spiritually perceptive dawn state. Now, having spent his energy and found the product bitter, the Westerner looks toward the East which outwardly represents the dawn state he has lost in himself, while the Easterner begins to summon to the service of his hitherto stagnant life the vitality and persistence which have become second nature to the West. As a generalization one can say that the Westerner typically has difficulty in understanding what the spiritual path is about, but if he once catches onto the idea, he can bring great energy and persistence to its achievement. Knowledge of what has to be done is the Easterner's birthright, but he seldom wants to do anything about it. Theoretical or philosophical knowledge and practical application are two very different things. Knowledge and energy have to be joined; which means, in effect that every individual man has to unite East and West in himself if mankind is to achieve an integral perception of the actual truth, uncolored by racial or sectarian bias.

Whatever our cultural background, we are faced by the same problem: how to bring a realistic attitude to bear on the religious inquiry. Either we do not know what it is all about, or, knowing it, we do not want it. We perform the traditional actions of making spiritual effort, kneeling or sitting cross-legged in meditation, singing devotional hymns, and arguing philosophical problems, but they are ritual automatisms, empty of the fire of true aspiration. The posture is a gymnastic achievement, the meditation is a set exercise instead of being an urgent inquiry, the devotional hymns loaded with sentimentality instead of being the soul's ecstatic agony, and the arguments are set pieces learned by rote.

In this context it may be understood that H.P.B.'s cosmogonic approach to the subject was consonant with her entirely transectarian attitude. The religionist (and the scientist) works within the confines of his creed. The cosmogonist, confronted by the self-evident fact of evolution, perceives the wonder of the divine nature and inquires into its factual source, its purpose, and its goal. Though his system of reference includes much that the scientist would call unproven or even subjective, he is concerned with what to him is rational fact. He is concerned not with "God" but with the power that includes both the world and the awareness by which the world is perceived. The power that raised man from the dust is, in the last analysis, the same as the power that looks through the eyes, hears through the ears, and touches with the hands. Man is at one with the universe; and that is the same as saying that man is at one with God. Man is God, or God is man; it makes little difference which way one looks at it. Nor is it a blank, impersonal power, for what is blank and impersonal could not give birth to the full personality of man.

But to say that the divine power encompasses personality

does not mean that there is a personal God, for the universally diffused awareness does not discriminate between the bliss of one individual and the suffering of another. The undeniable fact of personal grace is to be attributed to the intervention of those Perfected Men at one with divinity whom H.P.B. called the Masters. There can be no two ways about it: the thing we have wrapped up in symbols and called God, Spirit, Atman, Self, or what you will, is the self-nature of both man and the universe. Qualities of being which were so deeply buried as hardly to be called human potentialities were projected out onto the heavens in the form of the God image. This fact finds expression in Hindu ritual worship, where the deity meditated upon in the heart, is breathed out into an image, there to be worshipped, and afterwards breathed in again. Like the Divine Being itself, to know what lies hidden in the darkness of the heart we must first bring it out into the daylight world of form.

When, with the all too slow evolution of man, these potentialities of the Self become realizable, their projection onto the God image is necessarily withdrawn and God seems to die. What was projected outside now has to be found as integral parts of the unity that is man. What previously flowed as external streams of traditional religion must now well up in man's heart as the pure springs of the Spirit. God does not die, but lives where he always was, in identity with the Self of man.

Like everything else, the individual Self must evolve and grow, passing from unrealized potential to a clear focus in the transindividual light. But it is the Self of man—not an Eastern or Western Self. Nor is the distinction between an Eastern and Western psyche any more than that between a peasant and a citizen anywhere in the world. These racial distinctions are not fundamental differences in human types, but are, rather, stages along man's evolutionary path which are reached at different times by different peoples. But neither East nor West is more or less advanced because one has taken a stride with the left leg while another has taken a stride with the right.

This is a point we have to get clear in our minds if the Westerner is to appreciate the full value of H.P.B.'s work and not tend to dismiss it as exotic Orientalism. One has heard of many Westerners blaming their contact with "oriental mysticism" for landing them in psychological trouble of one sort or another, an attitude which is no more intelligent than that of some psychologists in India who trace patients' troubles to their practice of yogic exercises, instead of seeing that the sort of man who is liable to neurosis often seeks relief from his tensions through so-called yoga. Any traveler of the spiritual path ought to know that his road will lead him away from the well-trodden ways of gregarious men and into the deep and unfrequented jungles of the mind. It makes not the slightest difference where one's teaching comes from; one cannot blame the teaching for the beasts that lurk in one's private jungle. By whatever path one goes, sooner or later tensions are going to arise. How one deals with them, and how much tension the individual can stand are matters to be decided between teacher and pupil.

This vexed question of a supposed inherent difference between the Eastern and the Western psyche was propounded by C.G. Jung, the famous psychotherapist, whose apparent failure to come to terms with his own psychic "East" accounts for his theories on the subject and for much of his hesitation on the brink of the spiritual leap. East and West are within each of us. The typically active Westerner needs to find the appreciation of those timeless spiritual values of the East in whose presence the West's technological achievements are as so much dust, while the Easterner needs some of the West's energy. It has to be added, however, that this is a different question from the case of a person who attempts to settle in a foreign environment, such as a Zen monastery or an Indian ashram. The latter person can be courting trouble of a sort that has nothing to do with oriental mysticism but much to do with the ordinary human adjustments to food, climate, language, racial sympathies and customs. He must either be content to remain a foreigner, sticking out from his environment like a sore thumb, or he must submit himself to a reconditioning of his basic habits, equivalent to an intense brain-washing. Resistance to such change, and so the amount of psychic tension involved, varies with individuals. Nevertheless it should be stressed that the only adequate basis for such adaptation is personal and reciprocal affection between teacher and pupil. If this is absent, much of the effort is so much waste.

It is unfortunate that C.G. Jung took the attitude he did toward the Orient and the spiritual path in general. The entry to the path opens inward, and for practical purposes can be equated with the psychological inquiry into the causes of behaviour, emotion, and thought. All real spiritual teachers have been wise in the science of the soul—a science whose modern name is psychology, for the Greek word for soul is Psyche. But Jung, who seems to have come nearer to an affirmation of the spirit than any of the other modern psychologists, sows his doubts in the minds of his readers as he leads them to the point beyond which he fears to go, so that, as he turns away, they turn away with him. The closer to truth a man goes, the more insidious his doubts become.

Unless we are ready to enter the gateway into the subconscious parts of our natures, we never really learn anything about ourselves. Our nature's many aspects cause us to throw many shadows whose basis within ourselves we so much fear to see that we prefer to think them the inferior qualities of our friends. Entry marks the difference between the man who has really begun to work on himself and the one who has vaguely spiritual ideas, has studied philosophy, or performs a few religious observances. We have to unlearn the imposed patterns of childhood's conditioning and, like a deformed plant, be cut back to our roots and grow again—straight. We have to learn a new language, the language of Darkest Africa, that dark continent of all those hidden parts of ourselves of which we are not normally aware. It is the language of feeling: signs, symbols, the primitive sign language of our racial childhood, which we left behind us in the magical East when we set out to discover the material world. Indeed, it is primal rather than primitive, the pictographic ideograms from which language derives, basic to man as man. He who can read this language aright has the key to many mysteries. It is the gateway to the East, the return path to psychic wholeness, the path which is truly open only to the strong, for, as Kipling said:

> But there is neither East nor West,
> border, nor breed, nor birth,
> When two strong men stand face to face,
> though they come from the ends of earth!

Mankind is one. If we cannot see this, if we are so identified with the material accidents of our racial environment that we cannot recognize the common bond of humanity which bridges all differences of culture, language, symbolic vocabulary, and psychic attitude, then we should at least have the humility to admit our inferiority in the scale of human evolution.

To many of us, and in particular to the younger generations who know nothing of H.P.B.'s work, some of the main ideas disseminated by Theosophy are now so much of a commonplace that we may fail to appreciate our debt to the person who made them available in popular form, just as few of us appreciate our debt to Martin Luther for our freedom to write of these things, unhindered by fear of the Catholic Inquisition. People who are unwittingly indebted to H.P.B. for the mystical road to the East which she opened to them ignorantly side with the detractors of her controversial personality. In fact, one finds it hard to imagine what it was like before such ideas were commonly available, and the only way offered was through the seemingly empty and meaningless posturings of orthodox religion.

Perhaps every generation feels that it stands at a vitally significant turning point in human evolution. In our present age the fate of mankind seems to turn less on good or bad works than on how many of us can get a direct grasp on those basic values of being which make it matter whether people do or do not do anything at all. It is the loss of such values, with the consequent sense of life's meaninglessness, that has led to the present position in which society seems bent on plunging into undirectioned chaos. When, however, the significance of life seems to disappear, it is not really lost; the old formulation of life's meaning has become inadequate, the light has gone out of the form, and an attempt must be made to reformulate the light of meaning in a somewhat more meaningful manner.

The God image, with its associated creeds and dogmas, has been an effective means of guiding human evolution for several centuries. Under the influence of its projected potency the general level of mankind has been raised from tribal law to the democratic concept in which each individual is supposed to have developed a sufficiently rational control of his baser instincts to enable him to achieve some sort of personal fulfillment while contributing to the common good. In other terms: the individual has developed a conscience which tempers his egotistic desire. But his conscience, when examined, turns out not to derive from direct perception of the eternal verities but from reflexes conditioned by childhood's indoctrination. When a society learns to challenge the validity of its conscience, its ethic tends to collapse into amorality. At such a moment mankind's continuing health depends on the appearance of a reformulation of the eternal truth in such a form as can be readily understood by the averagely intelligent man. And that, we repeat, is what we feel to have been the significance of H.P.B.'s contribution to world thought.

6
Man—the Miracle of Miracles

HELEN V. ZAHARA

> We are the miracle of miracles—the great inscrutable mystery.
> —H. P. BLAVATSKY

Anyone who takes a close look at *The Secret Doctrine* cannot but be overwhelmed by the enormous erudition and knowledge displayed by its author, H.P. Blavatsky. It is an outline of a vast metaphysical system embracing both cosmogenesis and anthropogenesis, which H.P. Blavatsky affirmed she received from her spiritual teachers. It has been supplemented by material drawn from many sources, including the sciences, philosophies, and religions of East and West, of the past and present, as well as from the mystery teachings of antiquity, and—in particular—from an archaic Eastern manuscript *The Book of Dzyan*, on which it is a commentary. Although more than eighty years have passed since the work was first published, its value has not diminished with time, for it is based on universal principles which continue to be valid.

These universal principles are deeply meaningful and are relevant to the present moment. Therefore, anyone who is searching for an understanding of life's purpose, who cannot accept the ready-made, pat answers which orthodoxy has so long offered, and yet who rejects materialistic values, will find in *The Secret Doctrine* much inspiration and help. Even if he does not accept all that is written he will find it deeply thought-provoking, for it is a work which shows that it is possible to draw on all sources of knowledge—scientific and religious, physical and metaphysical, learning and intuition—in order to discover for oneself a wider vision of what life is all about, here and now.

One of the most important keys which *The Secret Doctrine* offers the student is that which leads to a deeper understanding of the mystery of man's nature, his occult history, his hidden sources, his place on the evolutionary ladder, his relationship to the universe and all that it contains, his present situation, and his future possibilities.

We can all agree that man is wondrously made. The developments of science—anatomy, physiology, anthropology, biology, psychology, psychiatry, and other fields of research—have built up a fantastic amount of knowledge of man as a product of nature's evolutionary processes, although there is much about him which is still far from being understood. If we add the teachings of most religions, we find an attempt to explain another dimension of man's being which includes the assumption of the existence of a soul and a spiritual cause of his existence.

If we go still further and draw on the vast amount of material derived from the traditions of occultism, which H.P. Blavatsky has presented in *The Secret Doctrine*, we are staggered at the immensity of the task of understanding the complexity and depths of man's nature, his roots in the eternal, and the forces and entities which have participated in the fashioning of his vehicles of expression and consciousness. *The Secret Doctrine* does not set this out in easy lessons, and we have to thread our way through hundreds of pages of abstruse and baffling material. But for anyone who is really serious in seeking this deeper knowledge, it is well worth the effort.

One way to undertake this study is to begin by considering some of the underlying principles concerning man and his relationship to the universe, and then try to fill in the details. It is an exciting, stimulating, satisfying, and illuminating quest.

As we begin our search through the pages of *The Secret Doctrine* we quickly find in the Proem a basic law enunciated.

This is the statement that there is "ONE LIFE, eternal, invisible, yet omnipresent, without beginning or end . . . the one self-existing Reality."[1] This concept is repeated in what is called the first fundamental proposition of *The Secret Doctrine*, which speaks of "An Omnipresent, Eternal, Boundless, and Immutable PRINCIPLE, on which all speculation is impossible, since it transcends the power of human conception."[2] It is stated that this "one infinite and unknown Essence exists from all eternity, and in regular and harmonious successions is either passive or active."[3]

This brings us to the second fundamental proposition of *The Secret Doctrine*, which affirms "The Eternity of the Universe *in toto* as a boundless plane; periodically 'the playground of numberless Universes incessantly manifesting and disappearing.' . . . This second assertion of the Secret Doctrine is the absolute universality of that law of periodicity, of flux and reflux, ebb and flow which physical science has observed and recorded in all departments of nature. An alternation such as that of Day and Night, Life and Death, Sleeping and Waking, is a fact so perfectly universal and without exception, that it is easy to comprehend that in it we see one of the absolutely fundamental laws of the Universe."[4]

With this introduction of these great underlying principles governing the one boundless existence and the law of periodicity which is evident throughout nature, we come to the third fundamental proposition, which relates to man and arises naturally from the first two. This is "The fundamental identity of all Souls with the Universal Over-Soul, the latter being itself an aspect of the Unknown Root; and the obligatory pilgrimage for every Soul—a spark of the former—through the Cycle of Incarnation, or Necessity, in accordance with Cyclic and Karmic law, during the whole term."[5]

Very quickly have these tremendous principles been presented, and we have already come to man himself and his relationship to—or we should say his actual identity with—the universal Oversoul, which is an aspect of the Unknown Root.

Yet despite this identity of every soul with the Oversoul, the One Divine Consciousness, it is clearly stated that every individual is embarked on a pilgrimage, and is governed by the law of karma, of action and reaction, cause and effect. Each one is evolving by the process of reincarnation in an ever increasing spiral toward a state of complete unfoldment which can only be won by personal effort. Says *The Secret Doctrine*: "No purely spiritual Buddhi (Divine Soul) can have an independent (conscious) existence before the spark which issued from the pure Essence of the . . . Over-Soul has (a) passed through every elemental form of the phenomenal world of that Manvantra,[6] and (b) acquired individuality, first by natural impulse, and then by self-induced and self-devised efforts, checked by its Karma, thus ascending through all the degrees of intelligence, from the lowest to the highest Manas,[7] from mineral and plant, up to the holiest Archangel (Dhyani-Buddha)."[8]

Here we have in these short statements the description in outline of a tremendous panorama of evolution, which includes all kingdoms of nature—mineral, plant, human and angelic. What profound concepts are stated so succinctly and what great philosophical questions are touched upon! One which is immediately apparent is that which relates to the problem of destiny and free will. The pilgrimage for every soul is said to be obligatory, and we read that at first evolution is governed by natural impulse. But then suddenly we are introduced to the idea of self-induced and self-devised efforts, which each soul makes after having acquired individuality. There then enters the action of free will, the results of which, however, are subject to the law of karma. "The pivotal doctrine of the Esoteric philosophy admits no privileges or special gifts in man, save those won by his own Ego through personal effort and merit throughout a long series of metempsychoses and reincarnations."[9]

This then is the basis of *The Secret Doctrine* philosophy insofar as man is concerned. Within the cycle of evolution, in which all forms are evolving and the One Life is thrilling, man is experiencing his own particular journey of forthgoing and return. He is in his essence a fragment of divine consciousness, pure spirit, termed a Monad. Furthermore, it is said that "Man contains in himself every element that is found in the Universe. There is nothing in the Macrocosm that is not in the Microcosm."[10] From this point of view the dimensions of man's spiritual nature are limitless and beyond our possible imagining. In order to unfold his god-like powers, however, the Monad, which has its roots in the Universal Spirit, projects into the denser fields of matter on its long evolutionary pilgrimage. This is a process requiring vast eons of time, which began in a previous field of existence and which embraces other levels of being. It involves the building and unfoldment of vehicles of consciousness which are not only physical, but psychic and spiritual as well.

The Secret Doctrine postulates that the universe is manifest according to a septenary law. From the One emanate seven primordial rays. There are seven basic forces in nature, seven principles or differentiations of matter which form seven planes of existence, and corresponding to these are seven states of consciousness. This septenary law is also manifest in man, in whom the seven rays are reflected. Man is described as a *saptaparna*, a seven-leaved lotus. Each petal is a principle which must be fully unfolded in order to come to the flowering of the perfect man. One of the classifications given for these principles is as follows: Atman (Spirit, man's universal principle), Buddhi (intuition), Manas (the mind principle), Kama (desire), Prana (the life principle), Linga-Sharira (the model or etheric body), and Sthula-Sharira (the physical body). The first three principles are three aspects of the Monad and represent the immortal part of man; the remaining four principles make up what is called the lower quaternary. They are aspects of the personality and perish after each incarnation.

The Secret Doctrine speaks also of the triplicity of nature, the trinity, which too is reflected in man in many ways. One of the most mysterious aspects of this law is that which relates to a triple evolutionary process which, it is said, is occurring and interblending in both the universe and man.

It is summarized as follows: "There exists in Nature a triple evolutionary scheme for the formation of the three periodical Upadhis;[11] or rather three separate schemes of evolution, which in our system are inextricably interwoven and interblended at every point. These are the Monadic (or Spiritual), the Intellectual, and the Physical Evolutions. These three are the finite aspects, or the reflections on the field of Cosmic Illusion of Atma, the seventh, the One Reality." The statement goes on to say that the Monadic evolution "as the name implies, is concerned with the growth and development into still higher phases of activity of the Monads."[12] This works in conjunction with the intellectual and physical evolutionary processes.

The Secret Doctrine now introduces a marvelous concept which is quite outside the realm of science and is difficult to comprehend. It is stated that these schemes are guided and represented by creative hierarchies of beings who participate in the different processes. To the Western reader they are strangely described and named, but this should not deter the student, for the whole idea is worth pondering. We read that the intellectual evolution is represented by beings called "The Manasa-Dhyanis (the Solar Devas, or the Agnishvatta Pitris), the 'givers of intelligence and consciousness' to man." The physical is represented by the Chhayas (that is shadows or images) of beings called the Lunar Pitris, "round which Nature has concreted the present physical body. This body serves as the vehicle for the 'growth,' to use a misleading word, and the transformations through Manas—and owing to the accumulation of experiences—of the Finite into the *Infinite*, of the Transient into the Eternal and Absolute."[13]

Each of these three systems is said to have its own laws and is guided and ruled by different sets of great beings called Dhyanis or Logoi. "Each is represented in the constitution of Man, the Microcosm of the great Macrocosm; and it is the union of these three streams in him, which makes him the complex being he now is."[14]

Although the above references may be very difficult for the reader to comprehend at first, they are given because they introduce a very important aspect of metaphysical teaching, that in the building of man, as well as the universe, there are not only many forces involved, but also myriads of beings. Some of these are themselves evolving and experiencing through man, and man in turn is evolving and experiencing through them. There is thus a close interrelationship of which most of us are quite unaware.

For man to reach his present state of growth, as has already been mentioned, has taken vast eons of time, both in a previous scheme and in the present scheme of existence. In our present field of evolution there occurred, along with the densification of matter, the densification of physical forms for man to inhabit, for these were at first etheric and formless. Gradually, during long ages, came the separation of the sexes and then, 18,000,000 years ago, according to *The Secret Doctrine*, physical man as we know him today was developed. Humanity is said to pass through seven great phases of unfoldment which are related to the awakening and action of different levels of consciousness in man. This process, it is said, is now just beyond the half-way mark.

At the point when man's individuality became established and he was awakened at the level of mind, he began to exercise choice and his karma became self-induced. Free-will now came into play and he became responsible for the working out of his own evolutionary unfoldment and destiny. This idea has great importance for each one of us, for it means that we ourselves have created the conditions in which we find ourselves today, and the way we act now will determine the conditions of the future. Says H.P. Blavatsky: "Those who believe in *Karma* have to believe in *Destiny*, which, from birth to death, every man weaves thread by thread around himself, as a spider his web." This destiny, we are told, is guided either by the heavenly voice of the invisible Prototype (Monad), or by our astral (desire) nature. "Both these lead on the outward man, but one of them must prevail; and from the very beginning of the invisible affray the stern and implacable Law of Compensation steps in and takes its course, faithfully following the fluctuations of the fight. When the last strand is woven, and man is seemingly enwrapped in the network of his own doing then he finds himself completely under the empire of this *self-made* Destiny."[15]

It can thus be seen that through reincarnation and karma, operating within the field of evolution (despite the myriads of beings involved in the building of the forms and the long eons of time which have passed in the process), man is a self-determining individual who is a god in the becoming. Many more eons must pass before all achieve their divine potentiality, yet even now, in the present time of strife and turmoil in world affairs, we can envisage the possibility of a more glorious humanity which, when it begins to understand nature's laws, will work in cooperation with them. We can see a foreshadowing of this goal if we consider the fact that some individuals have already reached a fully awakened spiritual state. They are the great teachers and guides of humanity who themselves have trodden the same road on which we are struggling, and they are ready to help us along the way.

The metaphysical system of *The Secret Doctrine* has been described as an algebraic formula of cosmology. In addition to the description of man's occult history and nature, which we have touched on only in barest outline, this great work deals with the emanation and periodic activity of universes, and the unity of all life in the visible and invisible worlds. Included in this vast scheme of cycles within cycles are the hosts of creative forces, the hierarchies of being which we have briefly mentioned, and all life in all kingdoms of nature. Each unit, including man, is part of a great evolving whole, each is an expression of and subject to the same universal laws. All are links in an endless chain of existence with no apparent beginning and no apparent end. As H.P. Blavatsky says, "From Gods to men, from Worlds to atoms, from a Star to a rush-light, from the Sun to the vital heat of the meanest organic being—the world of Form and Existence is an immense chain, the links of which are all connected."[16] This has the greatest relevance and meaning and practical implication for all of us, for we can see that all are part of the one hierarchical ladder of being. Since all are rooted in and expressions of the One Life, the unity of life is a fact in nature.

This, when it comes down to mundane every day existence, means that all men are truly brothers, that to injure another is to injure oneself, and that our responsibility toward life in all its forms, in all kingdoms of nature, is much greater than we may have realized. H.P. Blavatsky tells us that many of the difficulties which beset mankind, which many people attribute to Providence, would disappear if men would work in brotherliness and harmony, instead of in disunity and conflict. She says: "Were no man to hurt his brother, Karma-Nemesis would have neither cause to work for, nor weapons to act through. It is the constant presence in our midst of every element of strife and opposition, and the division of races, nations, tribes, societies and individuals into Cains and Abels, wolves and lambs, that is the chief cause of the 'ways of Providence.' . . . If one breaks the laws of Harmony . . . one must be prepared to fall into the chaos oneself has produced."[17]

Although linked to all others by the One Life, each man exists at the same time as an individual Self, a partial expression of the One Infinite Reality. We may thus raise our eyes not to an external far away Creator but to the spark of God within. "The ever unknowable and incognizable *Karana* alone, the *Causeless* Cause of all causes, should have its shrine and altar on the holy and ever untrodden ground of our heart—invisible, intangible, unmentioned, save through 'the still small voice' of our spiritual consciousness. Those who worship before it, ought to do so in the silence and the sanctified solitude of their Souls; making their Spirit the sole mediator between them and the Universal Spirit, their good actions the only priests, and their sinful intentions the only visible and objective sacrificial victims to the *Presence*."[18]

Anyone who even scratches the surface of the profundity of wisdom contained in *The Secret Doctrine* cannot but realize what a great debt is owed to H.P. Blavatsky for her remarkable work. Vilified, ridiculed, and misunderstood as she may be by some, her writings continue to stand as a monument to her erudition, courage, and wisdom. They are the source for teachings flowing through many movements and other works and teachers, and their influence in leavening modern thought is therefore incalculable. All who realize their value are filled with respect and gratitude. In time history also will give them the honor they deserve.

Notes

1. Blavatsky, H.P., *The Secret Doctrine*, Adyar ed., vol. 1, p. 70.
2. Ibid., vol. 1, p. 79.
3. Ibid., vol. 1, p. 71.
4. Ibid., vol. 1, p. 82.
5. Ibid., vol. 1, p. 82.
6. A world period said in Hindu philosophy to last 617,000,000 years.
7. The level of spiritual intelligence.
8. Ibid., vol. 1, p. 82.
9. Ibid., vol. 1, p. 83.
10. Ibid., vol. 5, p. 556.
11. Base or vehicle.
12. Ibid., vol. 1, p. 233.
13. Ibid., vol. 1, p. 233.
14. Ibid., vol. 1, p. 233.
15. Ibid., vol. 2, p. 364.
16. Ibid., vol. 2, p. 328.
17. Ibid., vol. 2, p. 368.
18. Ibid., vol. 1, p. 323.

7
The Pattern and the Law

CHRISTMAS HUMPHREYS

I have been invited to write on *The Secret Doctrine* and the contribution made by its author to world thought. As this involves an approach illustrated by personal experience rather than the usual objectivity of scholarship, I have chosen as material the twin doctrines which most appealed to me when I read the two volumes of the first edition just fifty years ago. These interrelated themes are what I call the purpose or meaning of life, and the living and intelligent law which pervades and controls the smallest part of it.

These are but two doctrines from the great store of such to be found in these volumes, yet the whole work is but an outline-drawing of the Tree of Wisdom of which all religions, large and small, are but the branches and the leaves.

How vast indeed is the "accumulated wisdom of the ages" which H.P. Blavatsky gave to the world just eighty years ago, being as much as might be told! As she herself wrote, it would be for the twentieth century to prove the claims therein set out, and she claimed no more authority for them than is inherent in the system itself, and the intuition of the student who finds it to be true.

For my double theme but a few quotations will suffice, and all these passages are preserved in *An Abridgement of the Secret Doctrine* which I helped to edit two years ago. In these 250 pages is to be found enough for a lifetime's study and application and, in the two volumes together, more, as I have found, than in all the scriptures of the world available in English.

None of *The Secret Doctrine* is to be viewed as revelation, either revealed by H.P.B. or by the Masters who taught her all she knew. This body of teaching is indeed the "accumulated wisdom of the ages," tested and verified by generations of those who have mastered it. All these truths have been checked and re-experienced, in principle and in detail, by the independent research of hundreds of self-perfected men. These Masters of the Wisdom form what H.P.B. called a guardian wall about humanity, and they, its servants, teach such men and groups of men, as the centuries go by, those portions which they may be trusted to use in the service of mankind. We have much of the teaching in the very words of two of them, in *The Mahatma Letters to A.P. Sinnett*, from which we glean not only an outline of the Wisdom but the life which must be led to gain it and the sacrifice of self which this entails. For them the wisdom is the law. For them wisdom and compassion are one, to know and to teach, to experience and to apply.

What did they teach, through their chosen instrument H.P. Blavatsky, to the Europe of eighty years ago? That the universe is totally a manifestation, projection, expression or, in oriental imagery, a breathing out of That which can never be known to human faculty nor fully described. In the Proem to *The Secret Doctrine* the author called it "Be-ness," for Being is its child. For lack of better words she wrote of "an Omnipresent, Eternal, Boundless and Immutable Principle, on which all speculation is impossible since it transcends the power of human conception and could only be dwarfed by any human expression or similitude." Yet if we may not know it as Be-ness, we know it as that which it becomes, the One, the penultimate but not the ultimate goal of spiritual aspiration. As a Zen master put it, "When all is reduced to the One to what is the One reduced?" The Theosophist would answer, "the Absolute"; the Hindu, "That"; the Christian mystic, in the words of Eckhart, "Gottheit, 'Godness' beyond God"; and the Buddhist metaphysician-mystic, "Sunyata, the Void."

Only then comes the first shadow of twoness, when the "nonduality" (Not Two, Not One) of Zen Buddhism descends to be Two. It follows, of profound importance, that even "absolute, abstract Space," pure subjectivity, and "absolute abstract Motion," the primordial opposites, are illusion, and when That breathes in, the universe it once breathed out will cease to be.

For one young reader this was a light blazing in the darkness, deep satisfaction for the questing mind and food for a heart that yearned, it knew not why, to serve the Masters of the Wisdom in their service of mankind. It refused—I look back with amusement at my fierce announcement—to begin a new life without at least some understanding of what it was all about. Why make a living, have a family, be successful among men, grow old and die unless the whole round of tedious activity made sense? When I learned that this was a part, however small, in a process of infinite becoming whose end and conscious purpose was a return to That from which, with all the universe, it came, I had my answer in *The Secret Doctrine*, and was and am content.

For if all in manifestation is One then men are one, and I did not need the Stanzas of Dzyan to tell me how and why. And the smallest form of life, whether seen or unseen, of the size of an atom or a solar system, is equally and all of it alive—all me, all other-me, all no-me in its own unique, supernal purposes.

But One is static, and I saw why Two was needed. For "God" as Absolute could not know himself as "God" unless he ceased to be God, the All. To be consciously whole he had to be less than whole. Two-ness was the visible witness to the One and the proof of it; and the tension of two-ness, with all the hell of suffering which its very existence entails, is essential if the One is to begin to move consciously on the journey back to its essential nonduality.

But two is literally inconceivable; no man can conceive just two. There must be relationship, and Fohat, the aspect of the one Life-Principle which applies, as it were, life to form, is an ancient name for the third of that Trinity which is the basis of manifestation.

For me much followed from these premises. There is tension in the universe; there must therefore be tension in me. The god in the animal has its noble desires and the will to ascend; the animal prefers its animality. But here was good and evil for me to understand and the mutual need of both. That there is absolute truth unattainable as yet, and relative truth to be known here and now was also apparent; and that the universe in its unborn essence alone is Real, and that all that we know by the senses and the thinking mind, *samsara*, is *maya*, illusion.

But all this, though to me a living reality of vision, was still remote, a plan or pattern dimly perceived but not yet usable. It needed the second affirmation in the Proem of *The Secret Doctrine* to set the vast machinery in motion, to turn a blackboard design into dynamic use. This is "the absolute universality of the law of periodicity, of flux and reflux, ebb and flow" or, in Buddhist terms the alternation of the opposites, which move in an infinite, that is, unmeasurable round of cycles large and small, from the breathing out and in of That to the "birth, growth, decay and death" of an amoeba. Even as my own life moved in a daily and yearly rhythm within the larger cycle of youth, maturity, and decay, so empires rose and fell, worlds were made and unmade, the unmeasured units of astronomical science moved in their own brain-staggering round of evolution and involution, "world without end."

But I was still unsatisfied. I still felt negative. I was a unit, albeit an essential part of the whole, to which things happened in the course of a process I could dimly perceive but in no way influence. I needed some other truth, some fresh proposition which the intellect would seize from the grasp of intuition and make its own. I found it in the Hindu-Buddhist doctrine, reproclaimed by H.P.B. at its own supernal level, of karma, the living, intelligent, all-pervading law of justice absolute.

Karma is a truth of many meanings. The word means action, in the sense of action/reaction as equal and opposite, and was already old in the Buddha's time. In the *Brihadaranyaka Upanishad* it is spoken of as a mighty secret which only the initiated might safely know. But the Buddha, as with much more of the ancient wisdom, made it available to all mankind as the law of moral responsibility, involving retribution for evil deeds and merit for good. In the Pali Canon the whole process by which the one life-force uses a succession of forms is described as karma in action; and the "self," which to the Theosophists is the unreal not-self, has been called by Pali scholars "a discrete continuum of karmic impulse."

All this is of vital value on the Way, but it is on a much higher plane that H.P.B. includes it in the plan and process of the universe. According to the Wisdom it is "the Ultimate Law of the Universe, the source, origin and fount of all other laws which exist throughout Nature. Karma is the unerring law which adjusts effect to cause, on the physical, mental and spiritual planes of being; . . . Karma adjusts wisely, intelligently and equitably, each effect to its cause, tracing the latter back to its producer. Though itself unknowable, its action is perceivable." Later, in the same passage from *The Key to Theosophy* she adds, "though we do not know what Karma is *per se* we do know how it works." There are long portions of *The Secret Doctrine* in which its application is described. But these sentences alone, amplified with inspired comment, would fill a volume and for me they had dynamic value. They set in motion a Plan too wide for the intellect to grasp and turned a static picture into an equally vast machinery of involution evolution. Here were cycles of motion too large to follow and within them others too small to see, and somewhere within them all a place for the complex entity, at once supremely real and utterly unreal, which we, with a blend of deep humility and arrogant pride, call Man.

This concept of karma is far more than ethical causation, than the fact that "it pays to be good." If karma is indeed the ultimate and total "Law of Laws," then all things, all events and every particle of man *is* karma and karma-made. It further follows that no man can escape the consequences of his thoughts and actions, whether he calls them "good" meaning pleasant, or "bad" meaning unpleasant. There is indeed no such thing as good or bad karma; the Law is neutral, utterly impersonal, and must be so accepted. It is "an impersonal, yet ever-present and ever-active Principle," and no man can interfere with it. Why not? Because we are made of it, are making it, *are* it. We can no more interfere with it than we can interfere with the law of gravity.

It is intelligent, one of the most tremendous concepts in the whole of *The Secret Doctrine*. The Unmanifest Absolute comes forth as a Life-force which is deathless. It has a million million forms, each changing without pause, but none is dead. There is no death; only the coming-to-be and ceasing-to-be of the forms in which Life manifests. A dead law, therefore, has no meaning, and law itself is only our feeble concept for one aspect of the Life-force in the world of form.

It is utterly just, the impersonal process of harmony broken and restored. Harmony is indeed a key word in the understanding of karma. "The only decree of Karma—an eternal and immutable decree—is absolute Harmony in the world of matter as it is in the world of Spirit." When the Master K.H. wrote, "we recognize but one law in the Universe, the law of harmony, of *perfect* equilibrium" he was followed by H.P.B. herself in the translations which form *The Voice of the Silence*: "Compassion is no attribute. It is the Law of Laws—eternal Harmony, the light of everlasting right. . . ." He who meditates on the interrelation of these three aspects of one law, harmony, compassion and karma, will learn a great deal. Note the word "adjusts," so often used in H.P.B.'s long passages on karma, meaning to make just, by the law of justice, karma, that the disturbance of nature's harmony by the claim of self put forward by some foolish man may be, and must be, adjusted by that man.

Seen from below, karma is in one way destiny, fate. Seen from above it is but harmony disturbed and the disturber "fated" to "adjust" the status quo. But the total creation of karma, of effects produced by man and any man, is changing every moment of time, as man and every man is changing too. This is a swift, perpetual process, a million million causes meeting to produce some new effect; a million million effects on the existing state of circumstance produced by every cause. The total result is such a brain-reeling interrelation of cause/effect as few have the courage to face. There can be no such thing as chance, no "mere coincidence," and no more talk of luck whether good or bad. All is as it must be; all is, though the thought is staggering. "*right*"!

And who is at the heart of this intelligent, ever-living process which exceeds our concepts of both space and time, save man, save each of us? "Since each disturbance (of Harmony) starts from some particular point, it is clear that equilibrium and harmony can only be restored by the reconverging to that same point of all the forces which were set in motion from it." That point is each of us. Hence utter and complete responsibility of every man for all that each man thinks and wills and does. There is therefore no escape from karma and it is useless to project our insufficiency beyond the ambit of our skin. We are self-responsible and everyself-responsible, with the enormous dignity for every individual which flows from that tremendous truth. For if I seem to be at times the plaything of fate, a pawn being played by a force I cannot control, this is, in the wider view, illusion. I made things as they are or helped to make them so. I can unmake them as and when I choose to begin, and no power on earth or God in heaven can stop me. Asked by a pupil, "Master, what shall I do to be free?" a Zen master replied, "Who puts you under restraint?"

Karma, then, is the law which binds each living thing, and in that bondage sets it free. There is no freedom save within limits, and the argued conflict between law and freedom is an illusion of the human mind. In the enlightened man the will is servant to the total Will and there is no self to intervene. We struggle but for self; where self is thrust aside the power of the opposites, the tension of good/evil, part and whole, is ended. The mind steeped in awareness of the Absolute accepts the limitations of the part within the Whole. He accepts the law, is the law, and in that wisdom uses the law to the world's enlightenment. He is no more troubled about his own.

If the Plan be firmly viewed, if the law of which it is the moving force be utterly accepted, then man is free. The rest is treading the Path, in joy now, not in fear or with a sense of blind frustration. Here is meaning and purpose in life and every hour of it, and the next job to be done. Now, with his destiny in his own hands he is at peace within and has for the first time the courage to face the immortal challenge of Thoreau, "I know that the enterprise is worthy; I know that things work well. I have heard no bad news."

This is, in my view, the contribution made by H.P. Blavatsky to world thought. Her *Isis Unveiled*, and to a lesser extent *The Secret Doctrine*, was a double-barreled attack on current religion and science, and the war between them. In this she succeeded for a while, but the rapid advance in the twentieth century of materialistic science has nearly killed out organized religion; and it is a curious practice of modern science that it flatly ignores all previous discoveries on the subject under review and looks for proof of non-material knowledge within methods of proof which to higher Knowledge are quite impossible.

But the pendulum of karma never stops; and in London today, where alone I can speak with personal knowledge, there are scores of small, unorganized, nameless groups of men and women who seek for meaning in a form of life which seems to have no meaning, and to penetrate to the beyond of the physical where truth at a higher level may be found. Some of these are content with discoveries on the psychic plane; some look to the science of psychology, the nature and workings of the instrument by which the scientist accumulates his views on science; a few seek the beyond of all of these, and care not in what form or name it may be found. These are unfrightened by the word mysticism, and view metaphysics at its actual worth of *meta*-physics. Even the heart and its need of ritual and devotion is no longer despised.

What material have these few in their inquiry? There is a widespread, and to me illuminating, interest in comparative religion; so much so that every college and high school must have a series of lectures on this theme. But these brief courses avoid the depths of thought and feeling at which alone they would be worth while, and the reason is surely obvious; that none provides a Plan of the universe from its birth to dissolution, nor the proper place of Man within its finite yet immeasurable scheme. And only Buddhism teaches karma as the force which made us what we are, and enables us, without delay, to become what we would be, "just so much nearer to the heart's desire."

In all this welter of ill-digested doctrine and rootless ethics *The Secret Doctrine* of H.P. Blavatsky stands supreme and, though it is difficult to believe, unique. Of course there are those who decry the author, hurling upon her beloved memory every form of abuse, and I am surprised that the Theosophical Movement as a whole has not yet seen the importance of *Man, the Measure of all Things*, which was the result of twenty-five years study by the late Sri Krishna Prem, whom I knew well at Cambridge University as Ronald Nixon. Here is an independent commentary on the same Stanzas from the Book of Dzyan which complements and illumines H.P.B.'s own commentaries and surely proves that whatever else the "S.D." was, it was not its author's invention!

If *The Secret Doctrine* is indeed unique in its depth and range of teaching, it is not surprising that it has sold increasingly in various editions since 1888, and that the Abridgement, selling in its thousands, should have actually stimulated the sale of the original work. Although the author prepared the way for her major work with *Isis Unveiled*, and added a new presentation of some of its themes in *The Key to Theosophy*, it is *The Secret Doctrine* by which she will be indefinitely remembered; this is her contribution to world thought and her supreme gift to mankind. For here is a work in which, for the student willing to stretch the intellect to its limits and to add the light of the intuition, is to be found as nowhere else a reasonable, coherent, all-embracing outline of the origin and ceasing-to-be of the universe, the laws which dominate the process, and the part played in it by Man.

8
The Celestial Laboratory

EDWARD L. GARDNER

"One Omnipresent Essence"

The Eternal Parent, awakening from the slumber of eternities, is the theme of the first Stanza of Dzyan. Another vast cycle of manifestation is here envisaged—for the awakening is of Parabrahman, the One Reality, Boundless Space,[1] the Divine Plenum.

This statement that the Eternal Parent is Space, that the Divine Plenum *is* the One Life of the whole universe, may seen to many at first strange and somewhat disconcerting. But our everyday familiar views of space are limited to little more than one-half of a single plane, the physical! Now, however, that the unit of physical matter is known to be an expression of energy, difficulty should vanish.

All life and energy, says *The Secret Doctrine*, is of one homogeneous absolute and omnipresent Essence, the all-inclusive Kosmos, infinite Space. In "Him" indeed we live and move and have our being, though "He"—the Divine Plenum (Neuter)—is not a God but Parabrahman—All.[2]

A synonym also used in the Stanzas is the "Great Breath," the implication then being that manifestation is about to begin. The Breath, being an emanation of the Plenum, is also neuter—in perfect equilibrium, neither conscious nor unconscious, neither benevolent nor malevolent, in absolute poise—and therefore "knows itself not."[3]

To achieve knowledge, the Breath becomes focused in Adi and then, as "a spark of the Flame," is prepared to "journey through the worlds." Thus, the focused Breath, the original Monad, journeys forth, sharing the omnipotence of the Plenum—"Thou art myself, my image and my shadow. I have clothed myself in thee."[4]

The "Withins" and the "Without"

The Secret Doctrine speaks of the Divine Plenum as "The eternal within, within two other withins"[5]—a somewhat cryptic saying. The "eternal within" is the Plenum of Space, unmanifest while in slumber; the "two other withins" are Adi and Anupadaka, Samskrit words which mean "first" and "parentless." The Adi plane is the highest and first of the seven planes and the Adi atom provides for the parentless Monad "the most tenuous vesture compatible with objectivity." Thus, the "eternal within" is the Plenum of unmanifest Space. The "two other withins" are the Adi vesture and the Monad, the focused Breath.

In occultism, the terms *within* and *without* are often used as being more suitable than *above* and *below*, and their aptness will be clear to all who are familiar with radio or television broadcasting. Speech, music, and pictures on the air flow around and about us nowadays continually, but are unheeded unless a receiving set is tuned in. All such wavelengths are "within" and must be transformed to those "without" to which our sense-organs can respond. The receiving set is an artificial *chakram* that does exactly that—it links within and without.

The marvelous properties of Space are such that vast numbers of wave-lengths are farther, and still farther, within, constituting the varying fields of force called the subtler planes, also around and about us here and now. These inner extensions of matter, as H.P.B. called them, must not be confused with a fourth dimension; a misnomer itself though plausibly convenient to use. There are but three *dimensions* and to speak of a fourth is as inaccurate as to describe the sun as "rising" or "setting."[6]

During the "slumber of eternities," the Plenum is in

equilibrium, balanced, in unison, poised. After awakening, every variation in the field of absolute motion, any change whatever means obviously a difference in rates of motion —and therefore friction. Hence the birth of opposites and their result—a distinction between spirit and matter. Opposites are a property of motion.

> Motion is eternal in the unmanifested, and periodical in the manifest.[7]

The balanced equilibrium of the One Life of the Plenum can be divided and broken into many lives only by the creation of form-structures. Separations accompany the birth of opposites and when the Breath functions through forms and is limited by them the differing rates of motion give rise to an awareness of living—through *friction* consciousness is born. The Monad, a focused unit of the Breath thus may awaken gradually amid the play of opposites to a knowledge of itself.

A Web—For the Creation of Forms

A medium for form-building, the means whereby the One may become Many, is a necessity. Thus the third Stanza of Dzyan:

> Father-Mother spin a Web whose upper end is fastened to Spirit . . . and the lower one to its shadowy end, Matter; and this Web is the Universe, spun out of the Two Substances made in One.[8]

In what sense it may be asked can the Web *be* the universe? The answer seems to be that it is a necessity for the building of forms in the same sense, to name a very simple correspondence, that paper is a necessity for the writing of a letter. Strictly speaking the letter itself is of language symbols traced in ink but these need and must have the support of the paper. The paper carries the letter, and reasonably enough, we speak of the *carrier* as *being* the letter. Similarly, the Web, though strictly speaking not a form itself, serves to separate the One Life into many and then carries the forms.

A striking example of the use made of a web to break one into many is provided by the modern spectroscope. In this instrument, made for the analysis of light, a plate is used on which some thousands of fine lines have been cut, side by side, within the narrow spacing of one inch. A light-ray, striking this, is deflected by the web of parallels and is displayed as a long spectrum—a multitude of lines and colors. The web of straight lines, called a grating, is by way of being a two-dimensional copy of the three-dimensional Web of the Universe. Like the strings of a harp which create and sustain the sound waves of music though not themselves "sound," the Web is the medium and supporting carrier of the vibrations that we know as forms. That which we call material, therefore, is motion that is caused by the play of the Breath.

Three modes of motion may be traced. Thought moves as do electric pulses through wire; emotions are wavelike and undulatory; physical matter is shaped in rings and spirals. These latter units are probably those that are hardened by Fohat.[9]

All formal shapes, whether of thought pulses, astral waves, or physical spirals, play through the Web as waves through water, wind flowing over grass or corn, or as the circling lights of a pictorial advertisement. None of these carriers—the water, the grass, the light bulb—moves forward though all appear to do so. The forms, carried similarly by the Web, are all of motion and may vary in an infinite complexity. The means are thereby afforded for every conceivable mode of manifestation—from the content of the humblest planet to the glories of the loftiest stellar manifestation. From its creation till its transcendence, the Web serves as a radio network linking all life, in the worlds of form, at the mid-mental level. In its rectangular mesh we may perceive too the secret of harmonic spacings and rhythms, the positional and related orbits of planets in the solar system and electrons in atoms, the cause of quanta (units) of energy, and geometric patterns in simple forms.

The Builders work on "a mathematical and geometrical scale of progression."[10]

The Creations

The earliest creations are at that highest and subtlest of regions, the Adi and Anupadaka planes; these are the "two other withins" as stated above and are designated the first and second creations. In addition to being the birthplace of Monads, about to begin their journey through the forms of the Web, the Adi plane is the domain of the Architects, Designers and Builders of worlds, who have made the journey successfully and returned. It is the realm too of the ministers of the Solar Lord, His *shaktis*—great creative centers of force, the Devic Dhyanis.

These two planes of the "within" are described as of Light, and the planes of the "without," carried by the Web, are described as of Life.

> Above Light; Below Life: . . . the former is ever immutable, the latter manifests under countless differentiations.[11]

The undifferentiated Light of the Plenum enters the Web at all levels. Within the forms therein created, it functions as the Life side. For three vast cycles and on to the fourth, the rupa-devas skillfully build the "bodies" of the kingdoms of nature—mineral, plant, animal, human—under the supervision of the Builders and the inspiration of the Dhyanis. The Monads of our hierarchy pass in succession through them, arrested for a while by some but ever gaining experience and expanding in consciousness. At length, during the fourth cycle of the Chain, and the mid-way point of its fourth round and on its fourth globe, the Monad attains self-consciousness as man with the prospect and promise of freedom and self-responsibility.

Humanity and Freedom

The Monad is of the Plenum and therefore of the Light, all-powerful but, as such, "knows itself not." On attaining the dual-mind in man, the monadic ray at this, the very dawn of self-awareness, finds itself between the "above" and the "below" and very insecure. This balanced, unbiased condition of consciousness still knows nothing of good and evil; such qualities are non-existent.

> Nature is destitute of goodness or malice; she follows only immutable laws. . . . Evil has no existence *per se* and is but the absence of good.[12]

The monadic ray, reaching self-consciousness in man, is thus "naturally" innocent though on attaining manhood, he is free, for the freedom of man's will, his absolute freedom of choice, is the bequest of the Plenum. Man is of the unbiased neutral parentless Breath. The limitations to the exercise of that will are due to the protective veils, the bodies, that he wears—and are well worth their limiting effect, for the will, in ignorance, can destroy as readily as it may build. The determinist, with his "irresistible logic of cause and effect," fails to trace causes to their root-source in the Causeless Cause, the One Reality, the Divine Plenum. Therein and therein alone is the foundation of free will and freedom. With the awakening, however, of free will, at the mid-way point of human evolution, the lure of the new selfhood gained in the personal bodies with their keen taste for sensation, the monadic ray is as prone to lose itself in the shadows of matter as to find the light of wisdom and immortality.

But the innocence of the newly-born personal self can win knowledge only through experience gained amid opposites: and the clamor of the bodies for sensation forces the pace to the very borders of the "without." Though knowledge at first hand is acquired in that outward direction, if pursued too far it leads eventually to the loss, maybe the annihilation, of the personality. Knowledge of good and evil, the "pearl," is of "great price" only if it be lifted from the depths.

In the exercise of free will, the risk attending an exclusive pursuit of sensation is terribly real—because it is based and founded on that very freedom of action which is the birthright of every human being. The monadic ray, though awake and self-conscious, is still of the neuter, unbiased, Breath. The risk and the dangers are emphasized in *The Secret Doctrine* and *The Mahatma Letters*:

> The potency for evil is as great in man—aye, greater—than the potentiality for *good* . . . the *origin* of every evil is in

> human action, in man whose intelligence makes him the one free agent in Nature.[13]
>
> Unless drones . . . who refuse to become co-workers perish by the millions.[14]

In the all-embracing majestic economy of the Solar System, a safeguarding provision is made by the creation of that which may be called a celestial laboratory.

A Celestial Laboratory

A definition of the Samskrit term Avatman, or Atma, implies that the plane serves as a bridge-like medium, a crossover. It is in this sense that Atma may be regarded as the site of the third creation, called "the organic." Broadly speaking, it may be said that thereon the subjective forces of the "within" are linked to the objective field of the "without," to the forms of the Web.

In the third creation, a special task is undertaken by the great Dhyanis and the Builders—that of endowing a part of the Breath with a certain quality. By some process of spiritual alchemy, a specific bias is imparted; and the modified Breath then pervades the Web to the mental level, no further, and is known as *buddhi.* By the joyous sacrifice of those who operate the atmic laboratory, the quality with which the neutral Breath is inspired is "Goodness." When responded to, buddhi makes for righteousness and its goal of immortality. Buddhi is therefore called wisdom. "The third creation . . . termed the organic creation . . . begins with buddhi . . . abounding in the quality of goodness."[15] As archetypal forms are concealed in the Ideal World (Atma)[16] and buddhi is said to be the vehicle of Atma,[17] the influence of buddhi is idealistic and inspiring.

The change that is thus effected in the Breath, its modification, and endowment, are of the greatest significance. They are illuminating. As an emanation of the Plenum the Breath is in equilibrium; though all-powerful it is neutral, hence the significance is in the specific bias imparted. Though we may know little or nothing whereby this poignant change is made, it is clear and obvious that no addition can be made to a Plenum. Hence the modification must be by a diversion or deletion of part.

A correspondence with that of sunlight will be familiar to all. Nothing can be added to that light but, with a screen-filter, part of the light can be diverted and the rays of a single color are allowed to pass. The sunlight has then been modified and specialized. In some similar way, we can surmise, the Breath is modified and informed by the spirit of Atma.[18] The enigmatic phrase that "Buddhi is neither a discrete nor an indiscrete quantity but partakes of the nature of both"[19] is clarified. The Breath, homogeneous and indiscrete, becomes modified by union with Atma and issues as buddhi, discrete and specialized.

Mirrored in Atma are the archetypes of the plan of the Earth-Chain. Contact with buddhi, therefore, through the higher mind, inspires the future. Buddhi illumines those who respond to its influence. Man alone, with the attainment of self-consciousness, can do this. And, abounding in the quality of goodness, buddhi makes for right living, right behavior, for righteousness—and leads to the mastery of the "personal" ego.[20]

Though it may appear that we treat here of that which is transcendental and may seem academic—the broad principles of the vast Solar economy may be stated quite simply and plainly, however involved and intricately complex are their workings.

The Light of the Unmanifest and the Life of the Many in the manifest are of the Plenum, the One Reality. The Breath of the Plenum permeates the Web as the Life of its forms and, though still homogeneous and a continuum in itself, "destitute of goodness or malice," functions under immutable laws. Through the cycles of involution and evolution on and up to the awakening of the higher mind and self-consciousness, the human monad is subject to the same immutable laws of environment and heredity, and is innocently unaware of any distinction between good and evil. With the awakening, however, to self-consciousness, the monadic ray plays through into activity as the Breath itself, with freedom won. Yet, under the veils of forms the birthright of freedom of the will may be overwhelmed amid the strains of the environment and the claims of the elemental life of the bodies worn. The temptations of personal acquisitiveness and sensual experience are severe to an extreme.

Hence, the third creation, known as "the organic," which "begins with buddhi," and results in the Breath, in considerable measure, becoming modified and "abounding in goodness." Moral and ethical behavior arise in human consciousness by contact with buddhi—though may be of the slightest. Every Avatar of the Gods, every sage, saint and great Teacher of mankind, founding a philosophy or religious system that fosters neighborliness and love of one's fellows, has spread the light of buddhi. And the source, fount and origin of that which we call spiritual inspiration and illumination—all is of that reservoir of wisdom. Man, the one free agent in nature, possessed of mind, alone can respond consciously to buddhi.

> The function of buddhi? On this plane it has none, unless it is united with manas, the conscious Ego.[21]
>
> Buddhi becomes conscious by the accretions it gets from manas.[22]
>
> Manas is the *upadhi* (vesture) of buddhi.[23]

The choice before every human being, in the long run, is between a self-incurred dispossession of his birthright and hardly won consciousness, on the one hand, and a self-won immortality, on the other.

Assistance in the choice is abundantly offered but the decision and acceptance by oneself is a necessity because based on the very fact of free will and a consequent freedom of action.

At-one-ment, made vicariously by another, is a vain and cruel delusion. Advice that is given in moral admonition, in the confessions and analyses of the different branches of psychotherapy, may be of real value if voluntarily sought and voluntarily accepted—but vicarious shrivings and absolutions given by another are as valueless as a life-belt to a fish. Man, by virtue of his status, is free to ignore the Wisdom offered, and ultimately vanish in oblivion, or to accept its guidance and inspiration and achieve immortality.

In one of the last messages of instruction and advice that were written by H.P.B. is the following passage:

> Keep ever in mind the consciousness that though you see no Master by your bedside, nor hear one audible whisper in the silence of the still night, yet the Holy Power is about you, the Holy Light is shining into your hour of spiritual need and aspiration.[24]

Notes

1. The term "space" as used in this article refers to an occult concept and is not to be confused with the meaning of the word as understood in modern science.—Ed.
2. Blavatsky, H.P., *The Secret Doctrine*, Adyar ed., vol. 1, pp. 73-81.
3. Ibid., vol. 1, p. 124.
4. Ibid., vol. 1, p. 309.
5. Ibid., vol. 2, p. 396.
6. Ibid., vol. 1, pp. 295, 296.
7. Ibid., vol. 1, p. 160.
8. Ibid., vol. 1, p. 148.
9. Ibid., vol. 1, p. 150.
10. Ibid., vol. 4, p. 301.
11. Ibid., vol. 5, p. 492.
12. Barker, A.T. ed., *The Mahatma Letters to A.P. Sinnett*, p. 56.
13. Ibid., pp. 130, 57.
14. Blavatsky, op. cit., vol. 5, p. 501.
15. Ibid., vol. 2, pp. 172, 173.
16. Ibid., vol. 2, p. 95.
17. Ibid., vol. 1, p. 178.
18. Ibid., vol. 2, p. 291.
19. Ibid., vol. 2, p. 172.
20. Ibid., vol. 1, p. 187.
21. Ibid., vol. 5, p. 494.
22. Ibid., vol. 1, p. 289.
23. Ibid., vol. 1, p. 163.
24. Ibid., vol. 5, p. 504.

III

The Theosophical View of Consciousness

9
H. P. Blavatsky and the Timeless Wisdom

ALFRED TAYLOR

In all ages there are those who, with little fanfare and though little known, bring to bear powerful influences on human affairs. An outstanding example of such a relatively silent force in our civilization is exemplified in the life and works of H.P. Blavatsky. Her contribution has certainly been little recognized; nevertheless, there is evidence that the ideas she introduced to the modern world toward the end of the last century are slowly but persistently permeating human thought and viewpoints.

Mme. Blavatsky did not bring something new to mankind. In fact, her offering was something very old. She succeeded in the great task of communicating wisdom as ancient as mankind. Her first serious work, *Isis Unveiled*, was published in 1877. This extensive introduction to esoteric philosophy accomplished several important objectives. In the first place, it served to expose the irrationality that permeated prevailing theologies and, at the same time, revealed the doctrine of materialism as equally unrealistic. The result was to invite the wrath of the followers of both these opposite fields of dogma or belief. *The Secret Doctrine*, H.P. Blavatsky's major work, was published in 1888. These two publications, *Isis Unveiled* and *The Secret Doctrine*, gave to the world as much of the Ageless Wisdom as seemed wise at the time they were published. In addition to these two comprehensive works, H.P. Blavatsky translated an ancient teaching under the title of *The Voice of the Silence.* This little book, first published in 1889, is deeply occult and mystical in nature, but carries the same metaphysical message as does *The Secret Doctrine.* It has attracted many readers and is still widely read. It is reported that a copy of *The Voice of the Silence* was on the bedside table of the poet Lord Tennyson at the time of his death.

The Secret Doctrine contains the most comprehensive account of esoteric wisdom, or Theosophy, available to the public. The preparation of the work was a most difficult task, since the author not only had the responsibility of explaining theosophical concepts and principles as clearly as possible, but also had the further assignment of demonstrating the presence of this wisdom in religion, philosophy, science, and other fields of knowledge. This involved deep appreciation and understanding of wide areas of human thought and investigation. Also, it was necessary for the author to be able to penetrate to the inner meanings of various religious scriptures, myths and legends.

H.P. Blavatsky spent many years in intensive study and contemplation under the guidance of Master Teachers in training for her work. In addition, she was unusually gifted with intuition, high intelligence, and the capacity for vivid, exquisite communication of metaphysical ideas.

At the time Madame Blavatsky gave to the world her illuminating works on theosophic philosophy, materialism was well entrenched in the western world among scientists, philosophers, and leaders of thought generally. Another segment of the public was swayed by primitive religious dogmas. Theosophy gave to the few independent minded people an alternative to the deadly, depressing materialistic doctrine on the one hand and, on the other, the even more pernicious insults to reason of the prevailing theologies. In Theosophy, the aspirant for understanding was introduced to a wisdom in accord with the basic principles of all the great religions, and also in agreement with the data of science. Further, the Ageless Wisdom provided a realistic, undogmatic approach to truth, free from authoritarianism and self-evident as it was understood.

Throughout past ages, theosophical teachings have helped people to solve the problems inherent in human life. And since they are founded upon realities within us, around us, and in our experience, they are timeless or ageless truths. Those who have been able to respond to the Ageless Wisdom have experienced a transformation into more vital, confident and effective living. However, in our modern world there are few who seek this knowledge, though the need for it is very great. Why is this so? The answer seems to be that most people are unable to throw off established ideas and beliefs to which all of us are subjected during a lifetime. Added to this type of conditioning is the fact that throughout the history of man, there has always been a drift toward a materialistic viewpoint of man and nature. This is to be expected, since the world we contact through our sense organs seems so real, so vivid, that we tend to accept it as it appears. We note this tendency for forms and appearances to become overemphasized among the followers of both religion and science. In Christian beliefs, the Christ principle becomes identified with a particular individual, and the birth of the Christ consciousness has become the birth of a baby. Also, western funeral procedures reveal underlying tendencies to associate a person with the physical body. Even in Buddhism, the statues of the physical form of the Buddha tend to become more important than the teachings. The same materialistic trend is present in all religions.

In our modern civilization the brilliant achievements in the field of science have made a tremendous impression on most people. As a result, world opinion has been influenced by the viewpoints and ideas expressed by scientists and materialistically oriented philosophers. When we add to this the fact that scientific research is conducted strictly on a materialistic basis, we can appreciate the reason for the dominance, at the present time, not only of materialism, but of materialism with a scientific flavor. It is this kind of materialism that now prevails, and because it is linked with the brilliant achievements in the field of science it is a most powerful influence on human thinking.

In order to evaluate the importance of H.P. Blavatsky's contribution to humanity, it is necessary to have in mind just what is involved in some of the basic assumptions of materialism and to compare them with some of the concepts set forth in *The Secret Doctrine*. In this way we can decide for ourselves the relative merits of these completely opposite approaches to the understanding of ourselves and the world around us. We can note how each harmonizes with reason, intuition, and experience.

Modern materialism is based upon a few relatively simple principles. The main idea, of course, is that the reality of beings and things is matter or energy. A human being is the physical body. Thoughts and emotions arise from actions and reactions in the cells, tissues, organs, and systems that make up the body. According to the materialistic viewpoint there is nothing other than matter or energy as the ultimate reality of a human being.

Certain consequences are implicit in the materialistic idea. The universe is assumed to have evolved from a space-time continuum as the source of all that is. And since brain tissue had not evolved in the unruffled, or unevolved, space-time continuum, no intelligence or mind was present. So, the unthinkably complex world of the present was evolved by chance or by the random play of forces inherent in the original energy sources. Today, there are chemical elements and compounds, planetary systems, plants, animals, and human beings. According to the materialistic hypothesis, all this vast accumulation of meaningful organizations has developed by accidental actions and reactions. There is no instance in human experience of *order* issuing from no order on the basis of accidental, mindless play of forces, but the principle of evolution by chance is vital to materialism.

Bertrand Russell, in his book *Mysticism and Logic*, realistically reveals some of the implications of this strange doctrine when he states that "man is the product of causes which had no prevision of the end they were achieving;

that his origin, his growth, his hopes and fears, his loves and his beliefs, are but the outcome of accidental collocations of atoms. . . ."[1]

The basic principles set forth in *The Secret Doctrine*, as they relate both to man and to nature, are also quite simple. The reality from which all has evolved is an unknowable Absolute, "an Immutable Principle on which all speculation is impossible." From this Absolute emerges Spirit, or Pre-Cosmic Ideation, and Pre-Cosmic Root-Substance. The combination of these two aspects of the Absolute results in the evolvement of the universe. The present universe is one of an endless series of universes that emerge from and are reabsorbed by the Absolute. All nature, including our own cycle of rest and activity, reflects this sequence of action and inaction. "The Secret Doctrine teaches the progressive development of everything, worlds as well as atoms; and this stupendous development has neither conceivable beginning nor imaginable end. 'Our Universe' is only one of an infinite number of Universes, all of them 'Sons of Necessity,' because links in the great cosmic chain of Universes, each one standing in the relation of an effect as regards its predecessor, and of a cause as regards its successor."[2]

Cosmic Ideation is channelled through Beings evolved in past universes and who will a new universe, sound the keynote of what it is to be and work through myriads of lesser intelligences to bring the Word, or keynote, into manifestation. The concepts and principles set forth in *The Secret Doctrine* are revealed in human experience. This is true because man is a reflection of the total reality. "The Universe is worked and guided from within outwards. As above, so it is below, as in heaven so on earth, and man the microcosm and miniature copy of the macrocosm is the living witness to the mode of its action."[3]

The unreality of materialism becomes evident when we really appreciate human affairs. All human productions are a combination of ideation and the material necessary for their manifestation. The simplest example of this is a written message or a book. The physical book serves to manifest ideas which are not in space or time but require a material form for their communication from one person to another. The physical book wears out in time and finally ceases to exist, yet the message it conveys is not affected by the passage of the years. We note the same principle where a machine such as an automobile is concerned. The car grows old, disintegrates and is scrapped, but the plan, the design, remains unaffected by time and can be embodied in a new model. The evolution of the automobile since its appearance about the beginning of this century is in accord with the evolution of plants, animals, and human beings. The inventor worked out a plan and built a car to its specifications. Then as a result of experience with this kind of machine, the plan was improved and used for the construction of better models. In this way, automotive engineers gradually evolved the present cars. In the process, car design, or the blueprint, has been passed through millions of car bodies.

In these areas of human production, the fact that the physical form serves as a means of manifestation of thought or ideation is beyond question. But what about living organisms? Here again, as with human constructions, there is the plan, or design, that is brought into manifestation through physical matter. An acorn carries oak tree information for the tremendous complication of development, growth, and maintenance of the tree form. If we dissect an acorn, there is no evidence of a tree in it, just as there is no trace of an automobile in a set of automobile blueprints. In both instances the physical manifestation embodies a particular ideation. The same is true for the germ cells of all living forms in relation to the plant or animal forms that develop from them.

Man proceeds through the spiritual qualities of will, wisdom, and intelligence in all his works. He first wills to do something, next he determines what it shall be, and finally, by intelligent effort he materializes his thought or ideation. The outer form is a necessary part of the process of bringing an idea into its practical application, but it is a secondary value, just as the paper and ink of a letter are secondary to the message it carries. All man's constructions are materialized thought. The reality of a machine, a cathedral, a symphony, is in that which is contributed by mind or intelligence. If the plan of a house were to be removed there would remain a meaningless pile of materials. The same is true for all meaningful forms.

The Secret Doctrine extends this principle, so evident in human affairs, to the total universe. "The most distinct and the one prevailing idea, found in all ancient teaching, with reference to Cosmic Evolution and the first 'creation' of our Globe with all its products, organic and *inorganic* . . . is that the whole Kosmos has sprung from the *Divine Thought*."[4]

The question arises why then are not all the affairs of nature characterized by perfection? The Plan comes forth from Universal Mind in completeness, but it comes into manifestation through the cooperation of evolving intelligences that only gradually learn how to carry out the work. A musician may have before him a musical composition of great perfection and value, yet he must spend much time in practice before he can begin to bring out its real merit as he plays it on his musical instrument.

In a brief paper, only a few of the ideas that characterize *The Secret Doctrine* can be considered, but enough has been given, perhaps, to reveal that it is in accord with reason, intuition and, above all, with human experience. The accompanying table may be helpful in clarifying a few of the fundamental differences that exist between the materialistic hypothesis and the Secret Doctrine, or Theosophy.

Table of Contrasts between Materialistic and Secret Doctrine Concepts and Principles

Materialism

1. The universe has evolved from One Source the unruffled space-time continuum, or more specifically, electromagnetic energy.
2. The One Source of the universe, electromagnetic energy,

is lifeless, and evolution began in the absence of will, wisdom, or intelligence.

3. Since there was no intelligence in existence when the universe began, evolution began and continued on the basis of accidental or chance actions and reactions in matter and energy.
4. Man and all other living forms are the physical bodies we perceive through the sense organs. Everything in the universe can be reduced to matter or energy.
5. Biological evolution has proceeded on the basis of chance changes, or mutations, in the germ cells. These changed germ cells resulted in variations in the adult forms that developed from them. The principle of natural selection eliminated some of these adult forms and preserved others. In this way have evolved environmental adaptations and new species, culminating in man.

Secret Doctrine

1. The universe has evolved from One Source, the Absolute, which works through its two aspects, Pre-Cosmic Ideation and Pre-Cosmic Substance.
2. All that exists is a manifestation of the One Life, or Spirit, and evolution began and has continued through will, wisdom, and intelligence.
3. Since this universe is one of an endless series, Intelligences from previous evolutions were present to will, plan, and guide its beginning and continuance.
4. Every meaningful form is an embodied Plan or Soul. This is true even for atomic and sub-atomic matter. Hence, it follows that the total universe can be resolved into thought, ideation or spirit.
5. A living form is essentially soul and body. The body evolves in accordance with the inner urge of the soul to fulfill its place in the Divine Plan of the Universe. Natural selection and gene mutation are secondary to the power and purpose of the Divine Plan that permeates every manifestation.

* * *

H.P. Blavatsky has brilliantly presented in her writings truths that are in accord with reason, intuition, and experience, truths which form the heart of all the great religions and truths that are implicit in nature as revealed through the facts and principles of science. Her *The Secret Doctrine* has been a source of inspiration and information to a growing number of seekers for understanding ever since its publication. In spite of numerous attempts to discredit the work by slanderous attacks on its author, its influence on world thought has steadily increased. Through this wisdom, the aspirant for truth receives illuminating insights into basic realities of man and nature. Further, these teachings do not rest upon authority, since they are self-evident as they are understood. In the light of the Secret Doctrine, modern materialistic concepts are recognized as crude dogmas unrelated to the facts of science and to ordinary human experience.

Invisible currents of thought shape the destinies of mankind. Today, the doctrine of materialism hangs like a cloud over human hopes and aspirations. But in the present, as in the past, the power of truth quietly and persistently forces its way ever deeper into human consciousness. This has been the experience of man throughout history. The seemingly enduring misconceptions of one age are forgotten in succeeding eras. In bringing to the modern world the realism and the light of the timeless wisdom, H.P. Blavatsky has made a monumental contribution to the progress of human enlightenment and welfare. She has reactivated ideas that are cleansing the mind of man of the superstitions that are now, in this age, the main source of human misery and desolation, and at the same time giving to mankind growing confidence in himself and in the universe.

Notes

1. *Mysticism and Logic*, Doubleday & Co., Inc., Garden City, New York.

2. H.P. Blavatsky, *The Secret Doctrine*, vol. 1, p. 113.
3. Ibid., p. 317.
4. Ibid., p. 53.

10
The Nature of Consciousness

CORONA TREW

Consciousness is the primary fact of our human experience and yet it is not susceptible to scientific proof; it can only be realized as a personal awareness. It stands like an axiom in mathematics, the starting point of all experience. Each of us is aware that he is conscious, that he is here and awake, and yet cannot prove this awareness directly to anyone else. At some time or another in his life every thoughtful person has asked himself the questions: "What is consciousness? What is life? Is the 'I' immortal and eternal, or does it perish at the death of the body?" In thoughtful mood we have all asked questions such as these, and thinkers down the ages have attempted to supply answers.

Using the analytical scientific method, Erwin Schrödinger, the physicist, in *What is Life?*[1] has analyzed the nature of life in terms of the energy laws of the universe. Even from this somewhat restricted standpoint he has shown that living organisms have certain unique characteristics which enable them to overcome for a time the universal disintegrating and randomizing forces of nature (known to science as entropy). Finally he deals with the problem of consciousness and in the concluding chapter comes face to face with two incontrovertible contradictory facts of experience for each human being. Each of us can say as a fact of experience "My body functions as pure mechanism according to the laws of nature"; but yet "I know also by incontrovertible direct experience, that I am directing its motions, of which I foresee the effects, and feel and take full responsibility for them." The paradox that faces us is that of a deterministically controlled body, yet a conscious sense of freedom, motivation and responsibility. Schrödinger then resolves the problem, much as do the Zen Masters, by moving to a deeper dimension with an assertion beyond the rational processes of logic. "I—I in the widest sense of every conscious mind that has ever said or felt 'I'—am the person if any who controls the motion of the atoms according to the laws of nature." To clarify this he recalls the ancient statement of the Brahmans, "Thou art That," "Atman is Brahman" or, in the words of the Christian philosopher, "Deus Factus Sum." Although we may have learnt to pronounce this with our lips, he continues, few in the West have learned "really to assimilate in their minds this grandest of all thoughts." We remain "curiously rooted in plurality" and feel that there are many separate minds, consciousnesses and monads inhabiting the world. Yet "consciousness is never experienced in the plural, only in the singular, and the only possible alternative to the philosophical absurdity of the pluralistic hypothesis is to keep to the immediate experience that consciousness is a singular of which the plural is unknown." So starting from an analytical scientific point of view, the wholeness and singularity of consciousness and the unity of the self of man with the whole has been recognized. We are the total process itself and are responsible for it.

This truth, as old as the Upanishads, was however first set out for the West eighty years ago by H.P. Blavatsky in metaphysical and philosophic terms in the Proem of *The Secret Doctrine.* In the now well known three fundamental propositions of that Proem we find the "a priori" axioms of, first, an "Absolute Reality which antecedes all manifested, conditioned, being." This is said to be the "Essence of which conscious existence is a conditioned symbol." Secondly, within this Eternity there emerges a "periodicity of flux and reflux, ebb and flow, which physical science has observed and recorded in all departments of nature." This results in the universal "cycles of opposites" of conscious conditioned experience. "An alternation such as that of Day and Night, Life and Death, Sleeping and Waking, is a fact so common, so perfectly universal and without exception, that it is easy to comprehend that in it we see one of the absolutely fundamental Laws of the Universe." The third proposition of "the fundamental identity of all Souls with the Universal Over-Soul, the latter being itself an aspect of the Unknown Root," leads to the "obligatory pilgrimage for every Soul . . . through the Cycle of Incarnation (or 'Necessity') in accordance with Cyclic and Karmic Law."[2] In these three fundamental propositions lies the resolution of the paradox of our conscious experience as stated by Schrödinger in our own time.

The Secret Doctrine is based upon the ancient *Stanzas of Dzyan*. In *Man, the Measure of All Things*, a recent commentary on the *Stanzas of Dzyan*, Sri Krishna Prem and Sri Madhava Ashish point out the importance of the kind of "symbolic correspondences" which the *Stanzas* and thence *The Secret Doctrine* present to our consciousness. "We and the universe are interdependent elements of psychic process in consciousness. Looking outwards we fill the universe with values taken from within ourselves. Looking inwards we find that the patterns of the psyche correspond to the patterns of the outer world. Through the understanding of these symbolic correspondences we are enabled to reach a deeper understanding both of ourselves and of the universe, of the relationship between the two, and of our common source." At this point where the self meets the problem of matter we have to "find an integral understanding of all experience which will resolve the dilemma and the interdependence of conscious observer and content of experience." Pointing out that neither the teachings of conventional religion, of theoretical philosophy, nor of material science can help us here, the authors tell us that "only when we turn to the evidence of mystical vision do we find accounts written by men in whose experience the duality of self and matter was resolved."[3]

We may believe that H.P. Blavatsky was inspired and guided by Those who had indeed effected this resolution. The unity of the One and the Many, of Man with the Universe, of the inner and outer poles of manifested being is, according to H.P.B., "the One fundamental law in Occult Science." The Stanzas on Cosmogenesis in the first volume of *The Secret Doctrine* describe symbolically the basis of this law. Stanza 3 deals with the movement of the Cosmos from a state of latency into active emanation, and its cryptic but beautiful language contains the essence of our problem. Thus ". . . the last Vibration of the Seventh Eternity thrills through Infinitude. . . . The Vibration sweeps along, touching with its swift Wing the whole Universe and the Germ that dwelleth in Darkness. . . . Darkness radiates Light, and Light drops one Solitary Ray into the Waters, into the Mother-Deep. . . . The Root of Life was in every Drop of the Ocean of Immortality. ". . . Where is the Spirit of the Flame that burns in thy Lamp, O Lanoo?" Even at this early stage of cosmic unfoldment, Man is evoked within the whole in that last phrase. Although immediately following Stanzas deal with the organization of the multidimensional Cosmos, and Man only comes on the stage in the last slokas of Stanza 7 of this set, there is no break in the scheme. Man emerges as part of that Solitary Ray which has impregnated the Mother-Deep. In *The Secret Doctrine* commentary on this Stanza 3 H.P.B. says that "The Solitary Ray" dropping into the "Mother-Deep" may be taken to mean Divine Thought, or Intelligence, impregnating Chaos.[4] Rather later she explains that this results in a "World of Truth, or Sat (Be-ness) through which the direct energy that radiates from the ONE REALITY—the Nameless Deity—reaches us."[5] Then, quoting the ancient Occult Catechism, the mystical insight is given that this "World of Truth" can be described only as "A bright star dropped from the Heart of Eternity, the beacon of hope on whose Seven Rays hang the Seven Worlds of Being."[6] This is almost immediately followed by a quotation from the Occult Catechism, in which the Master tests the knowledge of the pupil as to his realization of the ethical consequences of this teaching.

"Lift thy head, O lanoo, dost thou see one, or countless lights above thee, burning in the dark midnight sky?"

"I sense one Flame, O Gurudeva, I see countless undetached sparks shining in it."

"Thou sayest well. And now look around and into thyself. That light which burns inside thee, dost thou feel it different in anywise from the light that shines in thy Brother-men?" "It is in no way different, though the prisoner is held in bondage by Karma, and though its outer garments delude the ignorant into saying, 'Thy Soul and My Soul.' "

H.P.B. then explains the profound basis of this realization. "The radical unity of the ultimate essence of each constituent part of compounds in Nature—from star to mineral atom, from the highest Dhyan Chohan to the smallest infusorium, in the fullest acceptation of the term, and whether applied to the spiritual, intellectual, or physical worlds—this unity is the one fundamental law in Occult Science."[7]

This has been expressed in more immediate personal terms which have a telling impact. "The flame of consciousness that burns in our hearts is the Flame which shines so brilliantly within the Universal Mind, the one consciousness that shines in all beings, the 'Light that lighteth every man that cometh into the world.' "[8]

The realization of this is surely the most important task of our times, for it will liberate from duality and unite the individual consciousness with its source in Universal Mind. "Divided by separative desire we are our lower selves. Dominated by our perception of the universal harmony we become our higher selves. This is as true of our physically embodied state as it is of any subtle state of being."[9] Such is the consequence stated by Sri Krishna Prem and his co-author. Here then lies the solution of the riddle and paradox of our human consciousness, and if we would repay the debt owed to H.P.B. we should seek to realize this in meditation in the heart.

The state of conscious being to be attained is the subject of H.P.B.'s last writing, the mystical *Voice of the Silence*. "Thou hast estranged thyself from objects of the senses, travelled on the 'Path of seeing,' on the 'Path of hearing,' and standeth in the light of Knowledge." Then she describes the one who has attained: "He standeth now like a white pillar to the west, upon whose face the rising Sun of thought eternal poureth forth its first most glorious waves. His mind, like a becalmed and boundless ocean, spreadeth out in shoreless space." His consciousness at one with the Whole, all Nature is attuned and sings the triumph of the Pilgrim back "from the other shore." The method of attainment is simple, to listen to the inner voice, see with the inner vision and just touch the inner life, yet it may well take a lifetime or many lives. We can all but try. Seeking a quiet place, not easy to find in these days, a comfortable seat and, with quiet and rhythmic breathing, a stilled and withdrawn mind is directed to the pure Being of the Self—the "Flame within the Universal Mind." Like the coming of the morning sun there arises a dawning awareness of the Self which brings a growing recognition, as a fact of conscious experience, of unity with all. This must inevitably have consequences in daily life and in time become a habitual mode of being. It must issue forth as a quality of spirit and a new refinement in living and, as *The Voice of the Silence* tells, in that "Compassion" that "is no attribute. It is the Law of Laws—eternal Harmony . . . the law of Love eternal."[10] The attainment of this is the highest state of human consciousness.

Notes

1. Schrödinger, Erwin, *What is Life?* 1945.
2. Blavatsky, H.P., *The Secret Doctrine*, Adyar edition, vol. 1, pp. 79, 82.
3. Prem, Sri Krishna and Ashish, Sri Madhava, *Man, the Measure of all Things*, pp. 3, 4.
4. Blavatsky, H.P., op. cit., vol. 1, p. 133.
5. Ibid., p. 178.
6. Ibid.
7. Blavatsky, H.P., op. cit., vol. 1, p. 179.
8. Prem and Ashish, op. cit., p. 176.
9. Ibid., p. 407.
10. Blavatsky, H.P., *The Voice of the Silence*, Fragment III.

11
The Basis for the Unconscious in The Secret Doctrine

SEYMOUR D. BALLARD

During the nineteenth century, interest in the West in human consciousness steadily mounted. Men had been suspecting for a long time that there were uncharted, mysterious areas of the mind, "the twilight realms of consciousness," S.T. Coleridge called them. Since the latter part of the eighteenth century the term, "the unconscious," had come into use. (See *The Unconscious Before Freud*, by Lancelot L. Whyte.) About the end of the nineteenth century a milestone was passed with the findings of Freud and the other great pioneers who followed him.

The nature of consciousness is one of the major topics in the theosophical synthesis and is a great theme in H.P. Blavatsky's works, especially in *The Secret Doctrine*, published in 1888, three years before her death. Thus she did not live long enough to know of Freud's work, nor of that of his contemporaries.

If one is not acquainted with H.P. Blavatsky's writings, the question might be raised: Was she aware of this developing interest in the unconscious? One finds that there are many references in *The Secret Doctrine* to European thinkers' speculation on the subject, for example, men such as Schopenhauer, E. von Hartmann, Charcot, Ficthe, Hegel, and earlier philosophers such as Spinoza and Leibnitz. Indeed, there are at present theosophical students with training in the field of psychology who think that if *The*

Secret Doctrine had been written, say, a generation later, the ideas of a number of men, especially those of Carl G. Jung, would have been drawn upon.

Here, for example, is a passage from *The Secret Doctrine* (as indeed are all the quotations in this article), which indicates quite definitely an interest in and knowledge of the hidden areas of human consciousness:

> In these fantastic creations of an exuberant subjectivism there is always an element of the objective and real. The imagination of the masses, disorderly and ill-regulated as it may be, could never have conceived and fabricated *ex nihilo* so many monstrous figures, such a wealth of extraordinary tales had it not had, to serve it as a central nucleus, those floating reminiscences, obscure and vague, which unite the broken links of time to form with them the mysterious dream foundation of our collective consciousness.[1]

One wonders if it would be too much to suggest that these thoughts tend to parallel those of Jung—some of his, at least. The affirmative seems to be indicated when one bears in mind the basic ideas relating to the nature and extent of human consciousness as set forth in *The Secret Doctrine*. These ideas formed a touchstone for the author when she was examining the progress of Western explorers of the subject who, she must often have felt, were groping and not intuiting the profound occult concepts from the East which she maintained were the answer to the rising tide of materialism in her era.

At the beginning of *The Secret Doctrine*, H.P. Blavatsky outlines a few broad premises or principles upon which the book is based. She observes that the variety and interplay of dualities which abound in the universe are, indeed, the warp and woof of the universe. All of these dualities may be seen to be engendered by the ultimate duality of spirit and matter; and this primary duality is, she says, "to be regarded not as [two] independent realities, but as the two symbols or aspects of the Absolute, Parabrahman. . . ."[2] She comments that the contrast of these two aspects, or poles, is "essential to the existence of the manifested universe."[3] And this duality of spirit and matter is the means whereby consciousness emerges. "There can be no manifestation of consciousness . . . except through a vehicle of matter . . . it is only through some molecular aggregation or fabric that Spirit wells up in a stream of individual or subconscious subjectivity."[4] In another place she puts it this way: ". . . it is only through a vehicle of matter that consciousness wells up as I am I."[5]

It must not be thought that consciousness is the product of a kind of friction between the poles of spirit and matter because, she says, reading again the above quotations, consciousness *manifests* as a result of the juncture of spirit and matter. The welling up of "I am I" is, she says, "a conditional symbol" of Parabrahman, which in turn she qualifies as "the field of Absolute Consciousness."[6] And the sense of self, of self-awareness which can assert I am I, is really a thrusting of a "ray of the Universal Mind"[7] through the great duality.

What seems to be the reverse or opposite of this cosmic action is the reaching into and through the limited sense of self which occurs during the mystic experience—that moment out of time and space, when there is a profound awareness of union with all other selves, with everything in the universe. The reports of these experiences show that they unfold in many and ever deepening stages. But what is common to them is knowing that what is thought of as one's own mind, one's own self, is a part of a vaster, a total mind, an all-inclusive self or being. In such a self-transcending experience the unconscious is no longer unconscious. One is awake and not aware of having "gone" anywhere.

"When my readers once realize the fact," she writes, "that this grand universe is in reality but a huge aggregation of various states of consciousness, they will not be surprised to find that the ultimate state of consciousness is considered as Parabrahman by the Advaitis."[8] In the same passage, she says, "There is only one permanent condition in the universe, which is the state of perfect unconsciousness, bare Chidakasham (the field of consciousness) in fact."

The heights of the self-transcending experience would thus bring about or show a dissolving of the sense of a plurality of selves, however glorified, and an absorption into Chidakasham/Parabrahman. Metaphorically it is as though the self-transcending experience were a bird flying upward toward a great source of light, whose wing tips brush the two pillars of spirit and matter. But as he flies higher and higher, the pillars thin out and the feathers feel nothing, and all criteria evolved in the dual-conditioned world as to whether there is light or darkness, self or not-self, fullness or emptiness, vanish along with the two pillars. And the bird and the light grow together, are one.

We find H.P. Blavatsky explaining it in this manner:

> The Ego, progressing in an arc of ascending subjectivity, must exhaust the experience of every plane. But not till the Unit is merged in the All, whether on this or any other plane, and Subject and Object alike vanish in the absolute negation of the Nirvanic state—negation, again, only from our plane—not until then, is scaled that peak of Omniscience, the knowledge of things-in-themselves, and the solution of the yet more awful riddle approached, before which even the highest Dhyan Chohan must bow in silence and ignorance—the Unspeakable Mystery of that which is called by the Vedantins, Parabrahman."[9]

One function of the unconscious she states is to give guidance to the unfolding forms and life in nature. This is what she says:

> The Universe was evolved out of its ideal plan, upheld through Eternity in the Unconsciousness of that which the Vedantins call Parabrahman. This is practically identical with the conclusions of the highest Western philosophy, the innate, eternal, and self-existing Ideas of Plato, now reflected by von Hartmann.[10]

Von Hartmann was the author of the much read *Philosophy of the Unconscious* first published in 1868. Of the author she wrote that he, "despairing of unaided Natural Selection, regarded Evolution as being intelligently guided by the Unconscious—the Cosmic Logos of Occultism."[11]

Now it is hoped that all the foregoing has succeeded in conveying something of the position H.P.Blavatsky maintained with regard to the nature of consciousness. Actually, much more is said about it in the pages of *The Secret Doctrine* than can be brought into this brief article. The quotations offered here serve to indicate that the concept of consciousness is very much a part of the theosophical synthesis. It was natural, then, for her to take a keen interest in Western thinking on the subject, especially since that thinking seemed in some instances to be similar to the Eastern sources to which she had access.

For ". . . there is One Absolute Reality," she says, "which antecedes all manifested, conditioned Being. This Infinite and Eternal Cause [is] dimly formulated in the 'Unconscious' and 'Unknowable' of current European philosophy. . . ."[12]

Notes

1. Vol. 3, p. 295.
2. Ibid., vol. 1, p. 80.
3. Ibid., vol. 1, p. 81.
4. Ibid., vol. 2, p. 42.
5. Ibid., vol. 1, p. 81.
6. Ibid., vol. 1, p. 80.
7. Ibid., vol. 1, p. 81.
8. Ibid., vol. 4, p. 170.
9. Ibid., vol. 2, p. 43.
10. Ibid., vol. 1, p. 324.
11. Ibid., vol. 4, p. 219.
12. Ibid., vol. 1, p. 79.

IV

Science and The Secret Doctrine

12

Theosophy and Science: Some Parallels and Differences

DOSS McDAVID

The following parallel passages may be of interest to students of *The Secret Doctrine*. In the left column are some descriptive phrases from the book *Until the Sun Dies* by Robert Jastrow, founder and director of NASA's Goddard Institute for Space Studies. They set forth, in very general terms, the current scientific ideas about the birth of the Universe and the evolution of living organisms. In the right column are some passages from *The Secret Doctrine*. Reading these passages, the student of theosophy may well rejoice at the modern rediscovery of some of the truths of cosmogenesis known to esotericists for centuries. Science still has lots to learn, however, and the passages dramatically show the other side of the coin.

Jastrow	The Secret Doctrine
Picture the radiant splendor of the moment of creation. Suddenly a world of pure energy flashes into being; light of unimaginable brightness fills the universe;	Darkness radiates light. . . . Behold . . . the unparalleled refulgent glory: Bright Space Son of Dark Space . . .

This article first appeared in *The Theosophical Research Journal*, December, 1984.

the cosmic fireball expands and cools;	The Mother swells, expanding from within without, like the bud of the lotus. It expands when the breath of fire is upon it . . . when it is cooling it becomes radiant.
after a few minutes, the first particles of matter appear, like droplets of liquid metal condensing in a furnace.	The Mother is the fiery Fish of Life. She scatters her spawn . . . The Sons dissociate and scatter . . .
The scattered particles collect into nuclei first, and then into atoms;	The grains (of spawn) are soon attracted to each other and form the curds in the Ocean (of Space). The larger lumps coalesce and receive new spawn.
the searing heat and blinding luminosity of the early Universe fade into the soft glow of a cooling cloud of primordial hydrogen. Giant galaxies form in the hydrogen cloud;	He (Fohat or "Cosmic Electricity") separates the sparks of the lower kingdom (mineral atoms) that float and thrill with joy in their radiant dwellings (gaseous clouds) and form therewith the germs of wheels.
in each galaxy stars are born, one after the other, in great numbers. Many of these stars are surrounded by planets.	He builds them in the likeness of older wheels . . . the Central Sun causes Fohat to collect primordial dust in the form of balls . . . those that survive become worlds.
on one planet—the earth—life arises; at the end of a long chain of development, man appears.[1]	Make thy calculations . . . if thou wouldst learn the correct age of thy small wheel. The spark (of life) . . . stops at the first (kingdom) and is a metal and a stone; it passes

into the second (kingdom) and behold—a plant; the plant whirls through seven forms and becomes a sacred animal.

From the combined attributes of these manu (man) the thinker is formed.[9]

Nearly five billion years ago, in one of the spiral arms of the Milky Way Galaxy, a cloud of gaseous matter formed *by accident* out of swirling tendrils of the primal mist.[2]

The "fiery Wind" is the incandescent Cosmic dust which . . . follows magnetically, as iron filings follow the magnet, the directing thought of the "Creative Forces."[10]

How our planet accumulated out of that halo of tiny, orbiting grains is one of the minor mysteries of science. Probably the accumulation resulted from *random collisions* occurring now and then between neighboring particles in the course of their circling motion.[3]

They (planets) evolve into Manvantaric life from primeval Chaos . . . by aggregation and accumulation of the primary differentiations of the eternal matter, according to the beautiful expression in the Commentary. "Thus the Sons of Light clothed themselves in the fabric of Darkness." They are called allegorically "the Heavenly Snails" on account of their (to us) formless INTELLIGENCES, inhabiting unseen their starry and planetary homes, and so to speak, carrying them as the snails do along with themselves in their revolution.[11]

Perhaps the appearance of life on earth is a miracle. Scientists are reluctant to

The expression employed by Science, "inorganic substance" means simply that accept that view, but their choices are limited; *either* life was created on the earth by the will of a being outside the grasp of scientific understanding, or it evolved on our planet spontaneously, through chemical reactions occurring in nonliving matter lying on the surface of the planet.[4]

Several billion years have gone by since the first chapter was written in the history of life, and still the seas contain only soft-bodied animals . . . But six hundred million years ago the first animals with external skeletons appeared, and the fossil record exploded into a variety of forms—corals, starfish, snails, trilobites, sea scorpions, and many others . . . Soon another form of life appeared in the oceans, possessing little or no external armor but equipped instead with an internal skeleton and a backbone . . . They were the first fishes . . . But early in the history of the fishes . . . some individuals crawled out of the water and became the vanguard of a new development . . . that would lead to man.[5]

No direct proof exists for the evolution of man out of the

the latent life slumbering in the molecules of so-called "inert matter" is incognizable. All is LIFE, and every atom of even mineral dust is a LIFE . . .[12]

. . . the zoological relics now found in the Laurentian, Cambrian, and Silurian systems, so-called are the relics of the Third Round. At first astral like the rest, they consolidated and materialized pari passu with the new vegetation. Once, however, the prototypes are projected out of the astral envelope of the earth, an indefinite amount of modification ensues.[13]

. . . the differentiating "causes" known to modern science only come into operation after the physicalization of the primeval animal root-types out of the astral.[14]

Owing to the very type of his development man cannot

lower animals, but the circumstantial evidence for this view of human origins is very strong. The fossil record reveals a continuous chain of development in land animals, stretching from the air-breathing fish through the amphibian to the reptile, the first mammal, the tree dweller, the ape, and finally to man.[6]

The early tree dwellers were small animals with pointed faces and long tails, similar in appearance to the modern tree shrew of Borneo. These unimpressive creatures were singled out by the circumstances of their tree-dwelling existence, to be the ancestors of man.[7]

Bone by bone, the anatomist has been able to trace the changes in fossil skeletons, and observe how the body of the fish was transformed into the body of man by imperceptible degrees over a period of 350 million years. The fin of the fish became successively the sprawling limb of the reptile, the paw of the mammal, and the hand of man; part of the reptile's jaw was transformed into two delicate bones in the

descend from either an ape or an ancestor common to both, but shows his origin from a type far superior to himself. And this type is the "Heavenly Man"—the Dhyan Chohans, or the Pitris so-called . . . all the forms which now people the earth, are so many variations on basic types originally thrown off by the MAN of the Third and Fourth Round.[15]

The first race of men were, then, simply the images, the astral doubles, of their Fathers, who were the pioneers, or the most progressed Entities from a preceding though lower sphere, the shell of which is now our moon.[16]

The economy of nature does not sanction the co-existence of several utterly opposed "ground plans" of evolution on one planet. The fact is that . . . the human type is the repertory of all potential organic forms, and the central point from which the latter radiate. So far as our present Fourth Round terrestrial period is concerned, the mammalian fauna are alone to be regarded as traceable to prototypes shed human ear; and every one of the 28 bones in the human skull originated in the bony mask of our fish ancestor.[8]

by Man. The amphibia, birds, reptiles, fishes, etc. are the resultants of the Third Round, astral fossil forms stored up in the auric envelope of the Earth and projected into objectivity subsequent to the deposition of the first Laurentian rocks . . . the Third Round terrestrial animal forms were just as much referable to types thrown off by Third Round man, as that new importation into our planet's area—the mammalian stock—is to the Fourth Round Humanity of the Second Root-race.[17]

With respect to the beginning of the universe, in its physical aspect at least, the conclusions of modern science are in many ways consistent with the teachings of the Esoteric Philosophy. While there still exist major discrepancies, especially with regard to the time-scale and the role of superphysical forces, there are many aspects of modern cosmology which appear to run parallel with the propositions set forth in *The Secret Doctrine*. It is in the realm of those branches of science which are, so to speak, closer to home—notably geology and biology—that the greatest discrepancies are to be found. While contemporary geology, in its current infatuation with the theory of continental drift, rejects the existence of Lemuria and Atlantis, modern biology clings as tightly as ever to the evolution of man from the animal.

It is somewhat ironic that it has been within the realm of physics, which has always been regarded as the model "nuts and bolts" science, that the greatest breakthroughs have occurred. Probing deep into the heart of matter in an attempt to discover its inner structure and underlying nature, the physicists of our century have witnessed the "solid" world of everyday perception and "common sense" disappear before their very eyes. This has come about largely through the development of the theories of relativity and quantum mechanics. The former called into question the traditional ideas of space, time, energy, and matter while the latter broke down the belief in determinism and the independence of the observed and the observer. Add to these developments the discovery of the world of subatomic particles and the mysterious interaction processes which link them together, and it is no wonder that modern physics begins to sound more and more like occultism. While physicists as a whole are still cautious about the metaphysical implications of their science, some of them have been quite outspoken in this regard. David Bohm, for example, who is recognized as one of the leading authorities on quantum mechanics, has recently set forth a theory which treats the totality of existence, including both matter and consciousness, as an unbroken whole.[18] Bohm's ideas about the "implicate order" which, he maintains, underlies the "explicate" order of observable phenomena constitute a great step toward the Esoteric Teaching. Struck by the parallels which seem to exist between the "new physics" and Eastern mysticism, other physicists have begun to write books pointing out these correlations. Fritjof Capra's *The Tao of Physics*[19] is a prime example of this trend.

Biology, on the other hand, the science which attempts to elucidate the nature of life itself, remains, for the most part, staunchly anchored to a mechanistic, reductionist approach. While there now exist theoretical approaches which appear to have the potential of leading biologists away from reductionism—notably the work of Ilya Prigogine on non-equilibrium thermodynamics,[20] Erich Jantsch's theories on "co-evolution,"[21] and Rupert Sheldrake's controversial theory of "morphogenetic fields"[22] —these are yet in their infancy and it is yet too early to tell where these trends will lead. In the meantime, biology remains mechanistic and the idea of a "vital force," a cardinal dogma of occultism, remains taboo. Life is "defined" as the possession of a genetic program, evolution occurs by chance alone, and man's ancestry, as we have seen earlier, is traced back in a continuous line through mammals, reptiles, amphibians, and fish. As these ideas are in direct conflict with the teachings of *The Secret Doctrine* we seem to be at an impasse. One can only hope that the growing weight of evidence will finally force biologists to reconsider their assumptions just as physicists were prompted nearly a hundred years ago to re-think theirs. There is some hint that this is beginning to take place. Evidence against the accepted ideas of evolution does exist and is gradually coming to the surface as, for example, in Gordon Rattray Taylor's *The Great Evolution Mystery*.[23] Taylor writes:[24]

> The evidence is accumulating that chance alone is insufficient to explain the appearance of marvelously coordinated structures and perfectly adapted behaviour that biologists are uncovering. . . . In short, the dogma which has dominated most biological thinking for more than a century is collapsing. This marks a turning point in the history of science, one of those "paradigm shifts" (to use a current term) which transform our world view.

If this turns out to be the case, it seems more than likely that the biologists of the future will begin to talk more and more like occultists, just as some of their physicist colleagues are doing now.

A discussion of geology, time-scales, and continental drift has been intentionally omitted, as this would require a depth of knowledge in these areas beyond that of the present writer. Suffice it to say that this is another area in which the discrepancies with *The Secret Doctrine*, for the time being, appear to outweigh the correlations. However, the field is in such a flux that it seems premature to become overly concerned about any correlation or lack of it which may be found to exist. The theory of continental drift, which forms one of the cornerstones of modern geology, was anathema only a few decades ago. So are Lemuria and Atlantis today. For the time being, it seems best to wait and see what happens.

In closing this brief survey of science and its relationship to *The Secret Doctrine* it is well to remember the inherent limitations of science. Spiritual Reality must be spiritually discerned. Since today's science is confined by the limitations of physical instrumentation, even the most advanced theories and conjectures of that science must necessarily fall short of Reality. Like the blind men in the fable who try to make sense out of the elephant, scientists are limited by their perceptions. To transcend these limitations they would have to be "initiated into perceptive mysteries."[25] In the words of H.P.B.:[26]

> Science cannot, owing to the very nature of things, unveil the mystery of the universe around us. Science can, it is true, collect, classify, and generalize upon phenomena; but the occultist, arguing from admitted metaphysical data, declares that the daring explorer, who would probe the inmost secrets of Nature, must transcend the narrow limitations of sense, and transfer his consciousness into the region of noumena and the sphere of primal causes. To effect this, he must develop faculties which are absolutely dormant—save in a few rare and exceptional cases—in the constitution of the off-shoots of our present Fifth Root-race in Europe and America. He can in no other conceivable manner collect the facts on which to base his speculations.

Notes

1. R. Jastrow, *Until the Sun Dies* (New York: Warner Books, 1977). 19.
2. Ibid., 63.
3. Ibid., 65.
4. Ibid., 76.
5. Ibid., 85-6.
6. Ibid., 167.
7. Ibid., 133.
8. Ibid., 170.

9. H.P. Blavatsky, *The Secret Doctrine* (1888; reprint, Los Angeles: The Theosophy Company, 1942), I:28-34, 97, 201.
10. Ibid., I:107.
11. Ibid., I:103.
12. Ibid., I:248.
13. Ibid., II:712.
14. Ibid., II:649.
15. Ibid., II:683.
16. Ibid., II:115.
17. Ibid., II:683-5.
18. D. Bohm, *Wholeness and the Implicate Order* (Boston: Routledge & Kegan Paul Ltd., 1980).
19. F. Capra. *The Tao of Physics* (Berkeley: Shambhala Publications, 1975).
20. I. Prigogine, *From Being to Becoming: Time and Complexity in the Physical Sciences* (San Francisco: W.H. Freeman and Co., 1980).
21. E. Jantsch, *The Self-Organizing Universe* (New York: Pergamon Press, 1980).
22. R. Sheldrake, *A New Science of Life* (Los Angeles: J.P. Tarcher, 1981).
23. G.R. Taylor, *The Great Evolution Mystery* (New York: Harper and Row, 1983).
24. Ibid., 15.
25. Blavatsky, op. cit., I:326.
26. Blavatsky, op. cit., I:477-8.

13
The Nights and Days of Brahma: The Oscillating Universe

HUGH MURDOCH

Introduction

In this article I shall discuss Mme. Blavatsky's view of the main features of the universe as described in her chief work *The Secret Doctrine*, particularly in the Proem to that work.[1] I shall also discuss modern scientific theories of the universe and I hope to show that there is considerable common ground. Blavatsky drew heavily on the philosophy of the ancient Hindus and other ancient sources, some generally available, others not. *The Secret Doctrine* is chiefly a commentary of these sources, together with her own interpretation and her views on the many topics raised. She is at her best when staying close to the original sources.

Before discussing Blavatsky's views I shall discuss the main scientific theories in order to provide a convenient basis for comparison. To put the matter in perspective it will be necessary to give a brief historical review of the development of modern scientific cosmology.

Scientific Cosmology

Bondi gives a popular public lecture entitled "Why is it dark at night?" This refers to what is commonly known as Olbers' paradox,[2] but in his 1967 Halley lecture, Sandage[3] points out that the question was first asked by Halley in 1720. The problem was that if the universe extends to an infinite distance, the night sky should be uniformly bright due to the combined light of the very distant stars. The problem remained unsolved for 200 years after it was posed by Halley. Blavatsky was certainly able to point out in *The Secret Doctrine* that science had no real knowledge about the nature of the universe.

Modern Cosmology dates from 1917 when Einstein applied his newly developed General Theory of Relativity to the universe at large. Einstein assumed along with all his predecessors that the universe was static and he was able to satisfy this condition by introducing a new term into his equations involving what is called the cosmological constant. This term fitted neatly into the mathematical framework of the theory but it implied a new physical law to the effect that the farther apart two objects are, the greater is their mutual repulsion. This would not be detectable for objects as close as those in the solar system. For the universe as a whole, the cosmical repulsion of distant objects would cancel the gravitational attraction of nearby ones and keep the universe from expanding or contracting. The cosmological constant would have just the necessary critical value to achieve this balance. That an expanding universe was not only possible but would solve the Halley-Olbers paradox does not appear to have occurred to him at the time. The currently available evidence on the velocities of distant stars seemed to suggest a static universe.

Others soon discovered non-static solutions of Einstein's equations and it was shown that Einstein's original solution was a universe in unstable equilibrium. It could not remain static indefinitely; either cosmical repulsion would eventually win out over gravitation and the universe would expand or the reverse would happen and it would contract. No permanently stable solutions of Einstein's equations are possible. The universe must expand or contract. The full range of possible solutions or models (of the universe) as they are sometimes called, both with and without a cosmological constant, was discussed by the Russian mathematician Friedmann in 1922. Unfortunately he died soon afterwards.

About this time Hubble, using the 100-inch telescope at Mt. Wilson observatory, was accumulating experimental evidence about the expansion of the universe. In 1924 he obtained photographs of the so-called nebulae of sufficient resolution to show that they were composed of stars and were thus galaxies like our own Milky Way. By 1929 he had observed the shift of spectral lines towards the red end of the spectrum in sufficient galaxies to establish that the observed red shift was proportional to their distance. As the red shift is a measure of the recession velocity according to the well-known Doppler effect, this showed that the galaxies are receding from us with velocities proportional to their distance from us. The constant of proportionality is known as Hubble's constant.

The fact that all distant galaxies are observed to be receding from us can be simply understood without placing ourselves in any position of special privilege by assuming that the whole universe is expanding. Observers on any other galaxy would also see all distant galaxies receding from them. It is most important that no significant blue shifts (indicating velocities of approach) have ever been discovered. Only a very few nearby galaxies have a slight velocity toward us and this is easily understood as a random motion superimposed on the general expansion of the universe. No distant galaxies are moving toward us.

As well as being consistent with Relativistic Cosmology the expansion of the universe solved the Halley-Olbers paradox. Even if the universe is infinite the most distant galaxies would be receding at greater than the velocity of light and their light would never reach us.

But which of the many possible solutions of Einstein's equations gives the correct model which represents our real universe? After Friedmann's work, Einstein flatly rejected the idea of a cosmological constant which he himself had introduced. He regarded it as an unnecessary *ad hoc* addition to the theory which spoils its logical simplicity. Gamow[4] quotes him as saying that its introduction was the greatest blunder he had ever made.

There are powerful philosophical arguments in favor of simplicity or economy of hypotheses but they can never be conclusive. Experimental evidence must be the final arbiter. Most cosmologists, until about 1950, insisted on retaining the cosmological constant, as models without it gave an age estimate for the universe less than that obtained for the age of the earth from radiological dating techniques.

Eddington always favored a model proposed by the Belgian Abbe Lemaitre in 1927 in which the universe began in the original Einstein unstable state and expanded from there. It would continue expanding forever. Lemaitre himself later adopted a modified version of this model in which the universe began in a superdense state which he referred to as the "primeval atom." It then expanded until it reached the Einstein unstable state, when expansion virtually ceased. After a long time close to this region it again began to expand more rapidly. These two closely related models appeared to be the only ones which could give an age for the universe which was sufficiently great to account for the age of the earth. They achieved this by retaining Einstein's original critical value for the cosmological constant so that the universe could remain for a long time in or close to the Einstein unstable equilibrium.

In the early 1950's Baade and Sandage, using the recently completed 200-inch telescope at Mt. Palomar, showed that the astronomical distance scale was wrong by an appreciable factor.[5] The distance of all other galaxies was found to be substantially greater than previously supposed. Consequently their light has taken longer to reach us and the universe is much older than previously supposed. As a result of this discovery it is possible for the universe to be older than the earth without recourse to the cosmological constant.

Shortly before Baade's discovery, Hoyle proposed a somewhat different modification of the Einstein equations. Instead of the cosmological constant he introduced a term involving continuous creation of matter. In this model the universe expands indefinitely but is saved from "thinning out" by the continuous creation of new matter so that the universe presents the same general appearance to any observer, not only anywhere in the universe but at any time in the past, present, or future. For this reason it is known as the Steady State Theory. Distant galaxies become unobservable when their recession velocity exceeds the velocity of light and their place is taken by new galaxies which form from the newly created matter. A similar theory was proposed by Bondi and Gold.

The Steady State Theory not only avoided the problem of the age of the universe but avoided entirely the question of a beginning of the universe in time. This was considered an attractive feature and the theory was retained by its supporters long after Baade's discovery removed the problem of too short a time scale for the age of the universe. Radio astronomers have suggested in recent years,[6] that sources of radio emission must have been either stronger or more numerous in the distant past. This is quite inconsistent with the Steady State Theory. This theory has also suffered from the discovery in recent years of a universal low temperature background radiation as predicted by the theories which involve an initial superdense state.[7]

In the meantime, revision of the distance scale, and hence the time scale of the universe, opened up for serious consideration the solutions of the Einstein equations without a cosmological constant, the only solutions accepted by Einstein himself after 1930. If one rejects the cosmological constant, then there are certain potentially observable properties of the universe, any one of which, together with Hubble's constant, completely determines a particular solution of the Einstein equations and hence the main properties of the universe. All such models represent a universe which has expanded from a superdense state and the rate of expansion has been slowing ever since, due to mutual gravitational attraction. There is no cosmical repulsion to counteract gravitation. If the amount of matter in the universe is sufficient, the expansion will eventually slow to a standstill and contraction will follow. The whole process will then be repeated indefinitely. In other words the universe will oscillate with alternate phases of expansion and contraction. On the other hand, if there is insufficient matter, the universe will never cease expanding although the expansion will be at a slowly decreasing rate.

Only upper and lower limits can be set to the present mean density of matter in the universe. The upper limit is above and the lower limit is below the critical density which marks the dividing line between endless expansion and oscillation. A more precise estimate of the mean density of matter would determine the issue but this is difficult, one of the major uncertainties being whether there is any undetected matter between the galaxies.

Another approach is to seek the present rate of slowing down of the expansion. Hubble's red shift measurements have been extended to vastly greater distances and Sandage believes that the latest measurements favor an oscillating universe with 80,000 million years for a complete cycle of expansion and contraction. The observations are not adequate to determine this figure at all precisely. The present age of the universe on this model is about 10,000 million years. These measurements also provide evidence against the Steady State Theory.

An oscillating universe has the same philosophical advantage as the Steady State Theory, in that it avoids a beginning or end in time. Furthermore, it does so without requiring continuous creation of new matter accompanied by endless expansion.

Although the cosmological constant is no longer necessary, there are many who feel that it is an essential part of the theory and should still be seriously considered as a possibility. On this view the issue is not as clear-cut. For example one would need to observe *both* the mean density of matter *and* the rate of slowing down of expansion. The possibility of a definite conclusion is then more remote, but the choice still lies between a universe which will expand indefinitely and an oscillating universe.

We cannot entirely overlook the possibility that new experimental discoveries will require further modification of all existing theories in ways not yet even envisaged. Nevertheless one important fact which emerges from the present discussion is that the oscillating universe is a serious contender among current theories and perhaps even the most serious contender on present evidence. Furthermore as already noted it has considerable philosophical appeal. The astronomer Opik has written a book entitled *The Oscillating Universe* in which, apart from reviewing the facts, he makes his personal preference very clear.[8]

In summary, some of the outstanding developments in scientific cosmology this century have been:

1. On the theoretical side the application of general relativity to the universe and the consequent identification of the universe with space (discussed in the final section) and the prediction of expansion or contraction.
2. On the experimental side, (a) the discovery of the expansion of the universe, and (b) the revision of the distance scale which opened up the theory of an oscillating universe for serious consideration.
3. On the philosophical side, the recognition of an oscillating universe without beginning or end as an appealing philosophical concept.

We shall see in the remainder of this article that all of these developments lead to views expressed by Mme. Blavatsky during the last century which were then in conflict with current scientific belief.

The Universe as Seen by Mme. Blavatsky

Mme. Blavatsky's conception of the universe runs much wider and deeper than the material which we have just been discussing. I have not attempted to discuss scientific views on such matters as mind, life, consciousness. Suffice it to say that on the really fundamental issues, science is on even less sure ground than in theories of the nature of the material universe.

It was possible to discuss the physical universe without mention of life or consciousness because, to most scientists, these arise from physical matter and could not exist without it. On the other hand it will readily become apparent that such dichotomy is not possible when considering Blavatsky's view of the universe.

Her views are well summarized in her Proem to *The Secret Doctrine* in which she sets out three fundamental principles. The first of these is "An Omnipresent, Eternal, Boundless and Immutable PRINCIPLE." The following is a compound quotation consisting of several extracts from her explanation of this first postulate.[9] I have chosen parts which seem relevant to the present discussion.

"There is One Absolute Reality which antecedes all manifested, conditioned Being. It is symbolized in the Secret Doctrine under two aspects: on the one hand, absolute Abstract Space, representing bare subjectivity; on the other, absolute Abstract Motion, representing Unconditioned Consciousness. This latter aspect of the One Reality is also symbolized by the term 'the Great Breath.'

"The Great Breath assumes the character of Pre-cosmic Ideation. On the other hand, Pre-cosmic Root-Substance is that aspect of the Absolute which underlies all the objective planes of Nature. Just as Pre-cosmic Ideation is the root of all individual Consciousness, so Pre-cosmic Substance is the substratum of matter in the various grades of its differentiation.

"Apart from Cosmic Substance, Cosmic Ideation could not manifest as individual consciousness. Again, apart from Cosmic Ideation, Cosmic Substance would remain an empty abstraction and no emergence of Consciousness could ensue. From Spirit, or Cosmic Ideation, comes our Consciousness from Cosmic Substance, the several Vehicles in which that Consciousness is individualized and attains to Self-consciousness. Spirit (or Consciousness) and Matter are, however to be regarded, not as independent realities, but as the two symbols or aspects of the Absolute."

It is the current fashion in western science and philosophy to regard such dual concepts as spirit-matter, mind-brain, soul-body as misleading and unnecessary. Blavatsky would obviously agree on the *fundamental* unity of such opposites but in her view the unity occurs at a much deeper level. Furthermore, in current western thought the emphasis is always on the material side, e.g., mind cannot exist without a brain or consciousness without matter. In

Blavatsky's view, both poles are given equal importance at the deepest level of abstraction, but at any level closer to everyday reality, pre-eminence is given to the spiritual side, e.g., as often stated in theosophical literature, "Man *is* a soul and *has* a body" rather than the other way around.

This leads us naturally to the third postulate[10] which begins "The fundamental identity of all Souls with the Universal Over-Soul and the obligatory pilgrimage for every Soul—a spark of the former—through the Cycle of Incarnation or Necessity."

Note that the existence of souls is here taken for granted and given pre-eminence. It is the soul which incarnates in a body. All souls are expressed to be fundamentally united. This is the basis for the concept of Universal Brotherhood which is the main plank of the theosophical platform.

It is, however, the second fundamental postulate which concerns us most in the present article.[11] "The second assertion of the Secret Doctrine is the absolute universality of that law of periodicity, of flux and reflux, ebb and flow, which physical science has observed and recorded in all departments of nature. An alternation such as that of Day and Night, Life and Death, Sleeping and Waking, is a fact so perfectly universal and without exception, that it is easy to comprehend that in it we see one of the absolutely fundamental Laws of the Universe."

This idea is established at the spiritual as well as the material level, as for example the cycles of incarnation of the soul as expressed in the third postulate.

Most important, however, is the application of the law of periodicity to the universe itself. "The appearance and disappearance of Worlds is like a regular tidal ebb of flux and reflux."[12] This idea is expressed more clearly elsewhere in the Proem where Mme. Blavatsky quotes from what she calls "The Occult Catechism." I will again abbreviate the following quotation by selecting the most relevant parts:[3]

"What is it that ever is?—Space. What is it that is ever coming and going?—The Great Breath. That which ever is, is one, that which ever was is one, that which is ever being and becoming is also one and this is Space. It proceeds from without inwardly, when it is everywhere, and from within outwardly, when it is nowhere. It expands and contracts (exhalation and inhalation). When it expands, the Mother diffuses and scatters; when it contracts, the Mother draws back and ingathers. This produces the periods of Evolution and Dissolution, Manvantara and Pralaya."

There are two very important ideas in the above quotation (recall also the quotation from the first postulate). The first is the predominant role of Space, which is considered further below, and the second is the idea of expansion and contraction of Space, also referred to as the Great Breath.

Although at the philosophical level, the concepts expressed here go rather deeper than the ordinary scientific ideas of the material universe, there is a very strong affinity with some of the important concepts of scientific cosmology. The expansion of the universe was first seriously considered about 35 years after *The Secret Doctrine* was first published in 1888. As already mentioned, Einstein, as late as 1917, introduced the cosmological constant (which he later regretted) to keep the universe static. The concept of an oscillating universe, which on present evidence has as good a chance as any other theory of proving correct, bears a remarkable resemblance to the ideas put forward in the above quotations from *The Secret Doctrine.*

Mme. Blavatsky was well aware that she was running counter to the scientific views of her time.[13] She says, "Among many other objections to the doctrine of an endless evolution and involution (or reabsorption) of the Kosmos, a process which, according to the Brahmanical and Esoteric Doctrine, is without beginning or end, the Occultist is told that it cannot be since 'by all the admissions of modern scientific philosophy it is a necessity of Nature to run down.' "

The idea of a universe without beginning or end is today highly regarded among scientists. It was one of the ideas which prompted the Steady State Theory but this idea now seems more likely to be fulfilled in the oscillating universe.

In referring to the Hindu concept of the Nights and Days of Brahma, Mme. Blavatsky points out that Brahma "is derived by some from the root Brih, to grow or to expand."[14] In this rather poetic concept the whole universe is but the outbreathing of Brahma during an expanding phase, and when Brahma breathes in again the universe contracts. Opik is at least aware of the Hindu concept as he refers briefly to "the Day of Brahma" when discussing the oscillation of the Universe.[15]

Elsewhere Mme. Blavatsky quotes from an ancient Tamil calendar[16] which gives the period of each Day and Night of Brahma as 4,320 million years or 8,640 million years for a complete cycle. The Night is regarded as a period of Pralaya or rest when no life is manifest. It is not at all clear whether this should be equated to the contracting phase of the universe, or whether, to agree with Blavatsky's ideas, we should pose a long period of Pralaya at the point of maximum collapse. This would be difficult to explain scientifically but the period of maximum collapse is so difficult to deal with in any case that such an idea cannot be completely ruled out.

The Tamil calendar gives the present age of the universe as about 2,000 million years although Blavatsky says this should apply only to the earth. These figures are far from being in accord with scientific estimates of about 5,000 million years for the earth and 10,000 million years for the universe. The lowest reasonable time for a complete oscillation is also longer than the combined time of a Day and Night of Brahma. Sandage's estimate[17] is about ten times as long. I wonder, however, whether we should be more impressed with this discrepancy or with the fact that all the relevant figures in both the Hindu and scientific systems are measured in thousands of millions of years. These figures are certainly very different from the estimate of some thousands of years given by certain sections of the Christian church in Mme. Blavatsky's time. They are also very different from the scientific estimate of about ten million million years for the age of our galaxy which was current during the 1920's. One can expect the present estimates to change somewhat as new knowledge comes to light, but it would be surprising if precise agreement were ever obtained with the Tamil calendar. This should not be regarded as detracting from the similarity of the concepts of the oscillating universe.

The Nature of Space

Further interesting comparisons can be made regarding the nature of space. In scientific cosmology the properties of *space* are intimately bound up with the *matter* which occupies it. The one is inconceivable without the other. Space is all that exists. The universe does not expand *into* a pre-existing space. There is no space, nothing, outside the universe. It is space which expands. This is very different from Newton's concept of absolute space which would exist irrespective of whether or not it were occupied by matter. Space and the universe are synonymous, just as they are to Mme. Blavatsky in the quotation already cited, though to her of course the universe is more than just matter.

She says further, "Parabrahman[18] is simply the all-inclusive Kosmos—or rather the infinite Cosmic Space—in the highest spiritual sense of course."[19] And "Locke's idea that 'pure space is capable of neither resistance nor motion' is incorrect. Space is neither a 'limitless void' nor a 'conditioned fulness' but both; being, on the plane of absolute abstraction, the ever incognisable Deity, which is void only to finite minds."[20]

A very important property of space in scientific cosmology is its curvature. It is very difficult for us to conceive of a three-dimensional curved space since there is no fourth dimension which would render its comprehension easy. To understand it we must work by analogy and step down one dimension. Examples of a dimensional curved space are the surface of a sphere (positive curvature) and a saddleback (negative curvature).

The surface of a sphere represents a closed two-dimensional surface of positive curvature. Let us imagine some hypothetical flat creatures confined to such a surface who know neither up nor down. Light for them travels along the surface of their sphere. If their sphere is very large it is hard for them to appreciate that it is curved or to realize that if they go far enough in the same direction they will come back to where they started. Because we know three dimensions, their situation is very clear to us.

For certain models of the universe, and in particular for an oscillating universe with zero cosmological constant, our three-dimensional space has positive curvature and is bounded just like the surface of a sphere. Such a space is very interesting in that though it is finite, it is not limited in the sense that one could ever come up against a boundary. If it were possible to travel thousands of millions of light years in the same direction we would eventually come back to where we started just as on the surface of a sphere.

We can consider such a space by the two-dimensional analogy of a sphere or even the one-dimensional analogy of a circle which represents a one-dimensional bounded space of positive curvature. In this respect, a further quotation from *The Secret Doctrine* is interesting. Once again this is a composite quotation which puts together extracts from several related paragraphs. Mme. Blavatsky is discussing the symbolism of the World Egg and says,[21] "The World-Egg is, perhaps, one of the most universally adopted symbols, highly suggestive as it is, equally in the spiritual, psychological and cosmological sense. It is a true symbol for it suggests the idea of infinity as an endless circle. It brings before the mind's eye the picture of Kosmos emerging from and in boundless Space. It is the symbolical circle of Pascal and the Kabalists 'whose center is everywhere and circumference nowhere.' "

In a further reference to the subject[22] she says, "The Eastern Occultists agree entirely with Pascal who says that 'God is a circle, the center of which is everywhere and the circumference nowhere.' Whereas the Kabalists say the reverse." In other words the Kabalists are saying that God is a circle whose circumference is everywhere and center nowhere. Blavatsky goes on to say that the idea came originally from Hermes Trismegistus. She also says that the original inscription read, "The Cosmic Circle is a circle whose center is everywhere and the circumference nowhere" and that Pascal substituted "God" for "Cosmic Circle." She further states that these terms were in any case synonymous to the ancients.

If we can interpret the Cosmic Circle as space, we have once again the concept of the identity of the deity with the universe and with space. The expressions "center everywhere, circumference nowhere" and "circumference everywhere, center nowhere" are at first puzzling, but a little thought will show that they are very suggestive of the scientific concept of curved space. Every observer, on whatever galaxy he lives, sees the universe expanding away from him as though he were at the center of the universe; thus everybody appears to be at the center while nobody appears to be at the circumference. However the Kabalistic reversed version is rather more profound. There is no center for our space, just as there was no center of the sphere for our imaginary surface dwellers because to them only the surface existed. Likewise any center of our space would be in a fourth dimension of space which does not exist. Hence "circumference everywhere, center nowhere" very aptly describes our curved space.

At this point it is worthy of mention that to Mme. Blavatsky, and to Theosophists, the existence of souls implies the existence of superphysical realms which they may inhabit. It has sometimes been suggested that these may be four-dimensional. It is possible that our physical space may be a cross section of a four-dimensional space and that our souls may have extension at all times in the fourth dimension and even be able to exist right away from the physical world altogether. This can be seen more clearly by analogy with our imaginery two-dimensional creatures whose *physical* world would be the surface of their sphere. Their souls would have extension into the third dimension, i.e., into the inside and outside of the sphere. When in contact with a physical body they would have to reside at the surface of the sphere. At other times they might have the whole of the inside or outside of the sphere in which to roam. Step this up one dimension and our physical world is the surface of a curved hypersphere in four dimensions, our souls being confined to that surface (the physical world) only when in contact with a physical body. These ideas should be regarded only as interesting speculation. I merely want to point out that to my mind the concept of spherically curved space renders the concept of higher dimensional superphysical worlds more feasible. The previous remark that a fourth dimension of space does not exist, whilst certainly true for physical space, does not necessarily apply to superphysical space.

As a final thought, I want to note that many times we have come across the concept of the identity of the deity with the universe in the quotations I have cited from Mme. Blavatsky. I suggest that this is the kind of deity in which a scientist can readily believe if he is not satisfied with a purely materialistic philosophy. Most scientists are materialists because to them the universe is all that exists. They dislike the idea of a God who can create a universe from outside and, if He chooses, interfere with its natural laws. Once God is no longer outside the universe but synonymous with it, the natural laws are His laws, and the question of interfering with them does not even arise. There is no creation of the universe. It exists in perpetuity but has periods of active life and periods when life as we know it does not exist, the Days and Nights of Brahma.

Notes

1. Blavatsky, H.P., *The Secret Doctrine*. All page references are to the Adyar edition.
2. Bondi, H., *Cosmology*, 2nd edition, 1961. Much of the material on scientific cosmology is obtained from this book.
3. Sandage, A., *Observatory*, June 1968, p. 91.
4. Gamow, G., *Scientific American*, September 1956, p. 136.
5. The reason for the previous error is a little too involved to be discussed adequately here, but the evidence in favor of a revision of the scale was overwhelming.

6. Ryle, M. and Shakeshaft, J., *Science Journal*, Oct. 1966, p. 56.
7. Dicke, R.H., *Science Journal*, Oct. 1966, p. 96.
8. Opik, J., *The Oscillating Universe*, 1960.
9. Blavatsky, H.P., op. cit., vol. 1, pp. 79-81.
10. Ibid., vol. 1, p. 82.
11. Ibid., vol. 1, p. 82.
12. Ibid., vol. 1, p. 77-78.
13. Ibid., vol. 1, p. 204.
14. Ibid., vol. 1, p. 75.
15. Opik, E.J., op. cit., p. 122.
16. Blavatsky, H.P., op. cit., vol. 3, pp. 77-79.
17. Sandage, A., op. cit., p. 91.
18. The Hindu term for the Absolute.
19. Blavatsky, H.P., op. cit., vol. 1, p. 73.
20. Ibid., vol. 1, p. 75.
21. Ibid., vol. 1, pp. 133-134.
22. Ibid., vol. 4, p. 115.

14

The Evolutionary Cycles and Their Chronology

The Secret Doctrine and Science Compared

JEAN RAYMOND

When Mme. Blavatsky wrote *The Secret Doctrine* in 1888, her expressed aims as given in the preface were "to show that Nature is not 'a fortuitous concurrence of atoms,' and to assign to man his rightful place in the scheme of the Universe; to rescue from degradation the archaic truths which are the basis of all religions; to uncover, to some extent, the fundamental unity from which they all spring; finally, to show that the Occult side of Nature has never been approached by the Science of modern civilization."[1]

Although her views were widely divergent from those of the science of her day, she still expressed the view that "Chemistry and Physiology are the two great magicians of the future, which are destined to open the eyes of mankind to great physical truths."[2] In the intervening years, scientific concepts have altered considerably, and although there is much in *The Secret Doctrine* with which they would not agree, in general they share an increasing amount of common ground. One would expect this to be so, if science is indeed the key which will unlock the door to many of the secrets she propounded.

Mme. Blavatsky claimed that the system of cosmogenesis and anthropogenesis as outlined in her book was taken from certain records kept by the spiritual leaders of the human race since its inception. To support her thesis, she also quoted from innumerable works of ancient scripture and modern science, and it is interesting to read the descriptions of reliable witnesses to her method of writing. The work, as we know, was written in the town of Würzburg, with no reference books at hand, and only her faithful friend the Countess Wachtmeister to attend her. The story of its writing is almost as fascinating as the contents of the book.[3,4]

Of the many interesting lines of study which one may follow in *The Secret Doctrine*, a particularly interesting one is the chronology of the evolutionary cycles on this earth. It can be related favorably to the developing ideas of geology, paleontology, and anthropology at a number of points. Since the book was written, there has been a revolution in the scientific concepts of the age of man and the earth. In the late nineteenth century, the periods allotted to the various geological eras were considerably shorter than they are now, and this must be remembered when reading the work. For example, Mme. Blavatsky refers to a certain geological upheaval as occurring during the Miocene epoch, by which she means 850,000 years ago.[5] Today, we date the Miocene at 25-13 million years ago. Modern methods of dating, based on the decay of radioactive elements, have increased our accuracy enormously although they are subject to certain variables, especially to the amount of disturbance to which the specimens have been subjected since their deposition.

A brief outline of the generally held scientific views is as follows. The earth is thought to be about 4,600-5,000 million years old. However, the date for the first appearance of "life" on the planet has long been a vexed question. Fossilized remains of single-celled microorganisms resembling blue-green algae dated as 2,100 million years old have been found in rocks in Canada. More recently, fossil evidence of rod-shaped bacteria-like organisms, dating back to 2,800-3,000 million years has been found in Africa, but the evidence for these is not so conclusive. Various workers have been trying to show through chemical analysis that rocks 3,000 million years old contain organic compounds which could only have originated from living organisms. They have indeed demonstrated certain soluble hydrocarbons here, which are characteristic by-products of organic metabolism, but there have been some inconsistencies in the results which cast doubt on whether the compounds actually originated in these strata or seeped into them at a later date. There is still also the question of whether such compounds could possibly have an inorganic origin, as related compounds can be synthesized in the laboratory, but this appears to be unlikely.[6]

The fossil record is poor until the Cambrian era 600 million years ago. There are some fossils of primitive aquatic plants, and also evidence of early animal life in the form of jellyfish, worms, and sea pens all soft-bodied. In 1965, fossils of a clam-like brachiopod found on Victoria Island, Canada, were dated at 720 million years old. These finds have shown that the earth's atmosphere contained sufficient oxygen at that time, and for probably a much longer period, to allow the development of animals with specialized organs of respiration, digestion, etc.[7]

Immediately prior to the Cambrian era, there was an extensive glaciation of almost the whole planet, known as the Infra-Cambrian Ice Age. During this there was an abrupt break in the fossil record and many forms of life appear to have been blotted out. With the coming of the Cambrian period, however, we see a sudden flowering of a remarkable variety of multicellular animals, which already showed a high degree of specialization. In fact, they included representatives of nearly every major phylum or division within the animal kingdom, except the group which includes the vertebrates. This did not put in an appearance for another 100 million years or so.[8]

The next 400 million years or so has been called the age of fishes and amphibians, because it was during this period that they reached their peak. Following an extensive glaciation about 230 million years ago, large numbers of marine animals became extinct. Then came the age of the reptiles—the dinosaurs and their relatives, who flourished for a period of close to 200 million years. Some early mammals appeared in this era.

About 63 million years ago there occurred another of those strange breaks in evolution: the large reptiles suddenly died out, and there was a rapid flowering of all the basic orders of the placental mammals, including the primates. No new orders have evolved since that time, although much variation has occurred within the existing ones.[9]

About 25-35 million years ago, there was yet a further development—the appearance within the primate order of the catarrhines ("hook-nosed")—the group which is thought to have led to both man and the anthropoid apes. The fossils of this group still seem to be definitely ape-like, and the earliest record of a being who could be considered as an ancestor of modern man is from two fragments of upper jaw, one found in North India, the other in Kenya, and dated at about 14 million years, called respectively Ramapithecus and Kenyapithecus. No other parts of the skeleton have yet been found, but these two are almost identical and reveal a foreshortened face and a dental curve and small canine tooth which are characteristic of man, but not of the ape. Another interesting feature is that the Kenyapithecus fossil possesses a fossa or depression above the canine tooth which exists only in man, and acts as an anchor for some of the specialized lip muscles he uses in speech. The ape does not have this. Were these men?[9,10] This would be a revolutionary idea from the standpoint of anthropology. At any rate, the current opinion is that man and the ape deviated from a common ancestor at least 14 million years ago, and probably closer to 20 million. So far, the earliest unquestionable remains of a tool-making being who walked erect and who could be called "man" date back two million years.[10,11]

From this outline, we see that life seems to evolve in sudden spurts, not gradually. There is a period of quiescence, such as during an Ice Age, after which nature takes a spurt and a whole new group of forms appears, of which there was no sign earlier.

Now, it is of interest to consider the chronological tables quoted by Mme. Blavatsky in *The Secret Doctrine*, which have been in existence among the Hindus for thousands of years. She states that they correspond fairly well with those to which she had access, although she enumerates several points of difference. One fundamental tenet of both is the doctrine of cycles—of activity and quiescence, both universal and particular. Another is the doctrine of the duality of life and form, the unfolding of the life being emphasized, while the form evolves under pressure of the life desiring to express itself. The evolution of form is taught, from mineral to vegetable to animal to man, but in this context.

In Hindu cosmogony, the beginning of the major evolutionary cycle for this earth, known as a Kalpa, is given as 1,960 million years ago. In theosophical terminology, this would be identified as the arrival of the life wave on this earth at the beginning of what is called the earth chain. (In *The Secret Doctrine* Mme. Blavatsky postulated that the physical earth is the densest of seven foci or "planets" collectively called a chain, around which the life wave travels seven times in this particular evolutionary cycle.) In some Hindu calendars, it is said that this date is the beginning of cosmic-evolution, but in occult chronology it refers only to our earth chain.[12] Now the first scientific evidence of life on this planet, as has been mentioned, dates from 2,000 to 3,000 million years ago, the older dates still being in doubt. Mme. Blavatsky, in speaking of various cycles in the *Doctrine*, makes several points which may be taken into consideration here, with the dates mentioned later. She remarks that, although definite periods of years are given in the chronology of cycles, there are individual variations, some taking longer than others. She also states that there is considerable overlapping,[13] and that it takes hundreds of millions of years to prepare for a cycle.[14] Keeping these points in mind, it is interesting to note the relationship between the figures.

The actual mineral structure of the earth, as mentioned earlier, is considered to be about 4,600-5,000 million years old. From the occult point of view, it is also considered to have been in preparation for many hundreds of millions of years to receive the life wave. Although we are supposed to be 1,960 million years from the beginning of this Kalpa, its total period is said to last for 4,320 million years, and to have been preceded by an equal period of quiescence or "obscuration," called in Hinduism a Pralaya. In fact the cycle is said to repeat itself endlessly, within larger cycles. I would suggest that if the preparation of the earth commenced from the mid-point of the preceding Pralaya, its date would fall on 4,120 million years ago.

Within the major evolutionary cycle, or Kalpa, there are said to be seven minor cycles known as Manvantaras (in theosophical literature called Rounds), lasting about 308½ million years each and followed by an equal period of quiescence. Thus each new Manvantara begins every 617 million years or so. (The length varies slightly with different calendars.) The dates of commencement of these Manvantaras, starting with the first about 1,960 million years ago, would give us the second as beginning about 1,340 million years ago, the third beginning about 730 million years ago, and the fourth, in which we are now, beginning only about 110 million years ago.

The second Manvantaric period corresponds roughly with the geological era known as the Proterozoic which extended from about 1,000 million to 600 million years ago. It is thought that quite a profusion of life existed at this time, but the fossil record is poor as most of the organisms were soft-bodied, as I mentioned previously in my outline.

Regarding the third Manvantara, I mentioned that geologically there was the great Infra-Cambrian Ice Age over 600 million years ago, followed by the sudden flowering of the lower animals; and that this was the era of the fishes and amphibians, followed by that of the giant reptiles. In the occult chronology, the lower animal forms are said to have appeared at the beginning of the third Manvantara or Round.[15,16] It is also said that the emphasis was on the element water in this cycle.[17]

The fourth Manvantara has been in existence for approximately 100-110 million years. Mme. Blavatsky records that in this cycle, the emphasis is on the element earth, and that the planet reaches its densest and most solid state. Can we find any abrupt alteration in the paleontological record which may correspond with the beginning of this cycle? About 70 million years ago, we find another rapid alteration in the fauna of the earth, when the giant reptiles died off, and the placental mammals put in an appearance. Once again we can correlate this with the statement in the *Doctrine* that the placental mammals appeared some time after the beginning of the fourth Manvantara—probably about 50 million years ago.[18,19]

Finally, there is the Hindu and occult contention that the appearance of physical man as we would recognize him was 18 million years ago. Compare this with the scientific theory that man started his independent evolution close to 20 million years ago.[20]

We can see that there is a definite correlation between the introduction of the successive evolutionary forms as traced by science and as stated in the *Doctrine*. We must always remember that these points of comparison can only be made with regard to *physical* evolution—the time scale of appearance of the various physical forms. From the occult point of view, the age of humanity is much older than 18 million years; in fact, Mme. Blavatsky states that supraphysical man long antedates the *physical* forms of the vegetable and animal kingdoms. However, the precipitation of the forms onto the physical plane followed the order which has been discovered by science. She also describes how the forms of all the major subdivisions or root types of the animal kingdom are precipitated within a relatively short period, already having evolved somewhat on superphysical levels; and how the further evolution of these forms occurs within these major divisions.[21] This is supported by the fossil records which I mentioned earlier, wherein all the major phyla seem to make their appearance together and already exhibit considerable differentiation.

In the Eastern doctrine, the commencement of new cycles is accompanied by either volcanic upheaval or flood (caused by the melting of glaciers following Ice

Ages?). Associated with this is a tradition of the shifting of continents. (Sometimes Mme. Blavatsky describes the continents as sinking or rising, while elsewhere she speaks of them as "breaking up," "shifting" and of their "geographical change of place," bringing to mind the current idea of continental drift.)[22] Geologically, we have noted evidence of evolutionary changes which have followed extensive glaciations, but there have been other changes, such as mass extinctions, which have no obvious link with the Ice Ages.

Another possible explanation for these is the periodic reversal of the earth's magnetic field, first discovered in 1906 which, it is suggested, by permitting greater penetration of cosmic rays through the atmosphere, causes a higher incidence of mutation. It is estimated that reversals of the field take about 5,000 years to complete and occur approximately every 100,000-500,000 years.[23] In *The Secret Doctrine*, Mme. Blavatsky makes frequent mention of the inversion of the earth's poles and states that the process is always accompanied by cataclysms and continental displacements. She states that the poles have been thrice inverted since 850,000 B.C.[24] According to current paleomagnetic findings, there have been reversals of the earth's magnetic field three times in the past 900,000 years, the last one being about 500,000 years ago.[23]

Mme. Blavatsky also states that the reversal of 850,000 B.C. caused a great flood, and that there was a lesser flood about 11,000 years ago.[25] We know geologically that we have had four glaciations in our present era, the first and major one 800,000-plus years ago, and the last one finally ending 11,000-12,000 years ago, which would have caused a considerable rise of sea level as the ice melted. From the discovery of ancient shorelines it has been estimated that the level of the sea has varied as much as 600 feet at different times.[26,27]

The whole subject is most complex, but also fascinating, and I have touched on only a few aspects of it. If one bears in mind that the *Doctrine* was written in 1888, and that its author claims further antiquity for its contents of many hundreds of thousands of years, one begins to suspect that modern science is in fact rediscovering that which has been known to earlier civilizations whose very existence we have forgotten. Even though there are some aspects of the work which appear to be inconsistent in the light of modern science, possibly due to the misinterpretations or mistranslations of the author or to our own lack of insight, we still find that the broad tenets are today widely accepted, and there is much—such as the scheme I have outlined above—which has been vindicated by science.

Notes

1. Blavatsky, H.P., *The Secret Doctrine*, Adyar ed., vol. 1, p. 8.
2. Ibid., vol. 1, p. 305.
3. Barborka, Geoffrey, A., *H.P. Blavatsky, Tibet and Tulku,* Theosophical Publishing House, Adyar, 1966.
4. Heindel, Max, *Blavatsky and The Secret Doctrine*, Phoenix Press, Los Angeles, 1933.
5. Blavatsky, H.P., *The Secret Doctrine*, Adyar edition, vol. 3, p. 431.
6. Eglington, Geoffrey and Calvin, Melvin, "Chemical Fossils," *Scientific American*, January 1967.
7. Glaessner, Martin, "Pre-Cambrian Animals," *Scientific American*, March 1961.
8. Harland, W.B. and Rudwick, M.J.S., "The Infra-Cambrian Ice Age," *Scientific American*, August 1964.
9. Simons, Elwyn L., "The Early Relatives of Man," *Scientific American*, July 1964.
10. Leakey, Louis B., in *The National Geographic*, September 1960; October 1961; January 1963; February 1965.
11. "The Great Ideas Today," 1963, p. 231, *et. seq. Encyclopedia Brittanica, Ltd.,* U.S.A.
12. Blavatsky, H.P., *The Secret Doctrine*, Adyar edition, vol. 3, pp. 78-79.
13. Blavatsky, H.P., *The Secret Doctrine*, Adyar edition, vol. 3, p. 431.
14. Blavatsky, H.P., ibid., vol. 3, pp. 78-79.
15. Blavatsky, H.P., *The Secret Doctrine*, Adyar edition, vol. 3, p. 78; vol. 4, p. 281.

16. Preston, E.W., *The Earth and its Cycles*, Theosophical Publishing House, Adyar.
17. Blavatsky, H.P., op. cit., vol. 1, p. 301.
18. Preston, E.W., *The Earth and its Cycles*, Theosophical Publishing House, Adyar.
19. Blavatsky, H.P., *The Secret Doctrine*, Adyar edition, vol. 4, p. 187 *et seq.*, p. 245 *et seq.*, p. 303.
20. Ibid., many references.
21. Ibid., vol. 4, pp. 219, 282.
22. Blavatsky, H.P., *The Secret Doctrine*, Adyar edition, vol. 1, p. 316; vol. 3, p. 263; vol. 4, pp. 268, 274.
23. Cox, Allan; Dalrymple, G. Brent; and Doell, Richard R., "Reversals of the Earth's Magnetic Field," *Scientific American*, February 1967.
24. Blavatsky, H.P., op. cit., vol. 3, pp. 153, 352, 360.
25. Blavatsky, H.P., *The Secret Doctrine*, Adyar edition, vol. 3, pp. 22, 154.
26. Fairbridge, Rhodes W., "The Changing Level of the Sea," *Scientific American*, May 1960.
27. Leakey, Louis B., in *The National Geographic*, September 1960; October 1961; January 1963; February 1965.

15
Man before Ape, or Ape before Man?

ADAM WARCUP

One of the more radical propositions to be found in *The Secret Doctrine* is that "man, in this Round, preceded every mammalian—the anthropoids included—in the animal kingdom" (SD II 1). This article seeks to explore this idea, and to evaluate its impact on modern thought.

Mme. Blavatsky was well aware of the ideas of Darwin and his contemporaries. Thus the radical position adopted in *The Secret Doctrine* was taken in the full knowledge of the then current biological thinking. It is interesting to note that Darwinian theory has not changed dramatically during the last 100 years. The same issues that were addressed in *The Secret Doctrine* are still relevant issues today. It is true that neo-Darwinists have refined the theory, and that much more empirical information is now available. But does any of this invalidate the claim put forward by Mme. Blavatsky?

The basic Darwinist position is that the higher species have evolved from the lower through mutation, and the processes of natural selection and survival of the fittest. It would thus postulate that the mammals evolved from preceding amphibian and reptile stocks, and that the higher mammals have evolved from the lower, and similarly that man and presentday ape have evolved from a common ape-like ancestor. Man is thus the apex (though not by design, for there is none) of the mammalian branch of the animal kingdom.

The evidence on which the theory is based is the familial similarity of related species and on the fossil record. Mme. Blavatsky did not deny the basic similarities of related species. The variations on a basic theme do indeed come about through purely physiological mechanisms, but this does not by itself prove that the same means can produce new orders. The fossil record, to be found in geological strata, is inconclusive. Though it does ostensibly show a progressive development of species, the record is still extremely incomplete. By its very nature, it is likely to remain so. Much is totally inaccessible, being either under the oceans or buried deep within the earth. It is only where older strata are exposed through geological action that fossils can be found at all.

The genealogy of man is still under discussion in scientific circles. Until recently it was generally accepted that the branch leading to homo sapiens resulted from the split between the new world monkeys and those of the old world, which occurred about twenty million years ago. At subsequent points, this line diverged again from what later became gibbons and orangutangs, and later still from what became gorillas and chimpanzees. This picture was based almost wholly on fossil evidence, though, in truth, there was little enough of this. The fossil remains, it has been said, would fit comfortably into two shoe boxes! This picture has somewhat changed recently on the basis of evidence from molecular biology, which has shown that the DNA of man, gorilla and chimpanzee are 99 percent identical. This points to a much more recent divergence than had been previously assumed. In general, though, the evidence from molecular biology is seen as confirming the whole Darwinist position.

The theoretical framework put forward in *The Secret Doctrine* depends on premises that are admittedly outside the scope of a materialistic science. These include an astral as well as a physical world, and the influence of intelligences other than man on the whole evolutionary process. *The Secret Doctrine* states that an astral prototype of man's physical form preceded its physical appearance.

Moreover, this prototype was to become the blueprint for all mammalian stocks before the emergence of physical man.

The Secret Doctrine divides life on Earth into seven major periods or Rounds. We are currently said to be in the fourth such Round which began in Cambrian times. (Estimates of timescales differ. Science says that the Cambrian era was about 600 million years ago; *The Secret Doctrine* suggests it was about 320 million years ago.) Animal evolution had proceeded in the third Round, albeit in an astral condition, and this formed the basis for all animal species in the fourth Round, up to and including the reptiles. During the early stages of this Round, those species gradually became physical, and thus were capable of leaving fossil remains.

Human evolution in the fourth Round is also divided into seven sequential stages, somewhat misleadingly referred to as *Races* or *Root Races*. The first two and a half Races were entirely astral, in terms of their external form. These astral Races existed for hundreds of millions of years. Exact figures are not given.

The forms pertaining to the first Race were derived from a superior class of beings referred to as the Lunar Ancestors or Lunar Pitris (Fathers). It is they who provided the prototypal form in which was contained not only the seed for the development of all human forms throughout the Round, but also the seed for all mammalian forms. Both the first and second Races were sexless, and reproduced by fission and budding. The third Race was initially hermaphrodite, becoming male and female towards its close. This hermaphroditic stage accounts for the vestigial traces of characteristics of the opposite sex in contemporary men and women.

Seven offshoots from the second Race became the root stocks for the subsequent development of the different species of mammal. At first, these root stocks would have been astral in character, as was the parent human stock. But gradually, over a long period of time and probably at different rates, these stocks became physical. Details of this process are not given, but an analogy can be found in the materialization of forms during a spiritualist seance. Once the root stock had become physical, it would then have been subject to the processes of differentiation, as described by Darwin.

The major point to notice at this stage is that mammals do not evolve from some preceding and lower order animal stock, but as an offshoot from the prototypal human stock. This is a reflection of a general principle that nature proceeds from within outwardly, from the spiritual to the material, and that evolution follows a plan or pattern.

During the third Race, human forms also began to change from a purely astral condition towards a physical state. But they did so later than the mammals. This means that mammals became wholly physical before man did, and thus left remains to become fossilized before the appearance of physical men. It is this fact which creates the misleading appearance of mammals preceding man altogether.

The Secret Doctrine states that, through lack of innate intelligence, certain human stocks in the later third Race interbred with ape-like mammalian stock. As both man and animal were still close to the original type, the union was invariably fertile. This interbreeding produced an offshoot or hybrid race which, ages later, during the fourth Race, culminated in what are now referred to as the lower apes. Thus the anthropoid apes, according to *The Secret Doctrine*, are even more directly descended from man than are the other mammals.

The process of the descent from an astral to a physical state was completed by the beginning of the fourth Race. *The Secret Doctrine* says, and tradition repeats, that this was a race of giants. The stories concerning Atlantis relate to this time, but it has to be understood that this Race existed for perhaps ten to fifteen million years. At least in principle, there is no reason why human remains from this period should not be found. However, as cremation was apparently a universal practice during this phase, this may never happen.

Towards the end of the fourth Race, a second interbreeding occurred. This time it was between Atlantean men and females of the intermediate anthropoid stock just mentioned. It was this cross-breeding which resulted in the gorilla and the chimpanzee. It is said that such apes are, in fact, part of the human kingdom, and are animated by primitive human, as opposed to animal, entities. Thus from the occult standpoint, man not only preceded all the mammals, albeit in an astral condition, but preceded the apes even in purely physical terms.

How does occultism account for the evidence which scientists claim supports their case? In truth, there is not a great deal of evidence which does support the scientists' case. There are two general points to be made before examining the evidence, such as it is. The first point is that the Darwinist explanation of evolution is a theory, and no more. Darwin himself merely deduced some principles based on his own field work. Later on, these were woven into a theory concerning the generality of life on earth. However, this is not good science. The scientific method is based on experimental data, which is repeatable, and on prediction. By its very nature, the evolution of life on earth is non-repeatable. It is certainly possible to draw some inferences from the data, but this does not elevate it to the status of a fact. To test the theory as now stated would require biologists to make a series of predictions based on present knowledge, theory and data. We would then have to wait for tens of thousands, if not hundreds of thousands of years to see if the predictions proved correct. Until this is done, the evolutionists' ideas are no more than a theory.

The second point concerns the whole materialist viewpoint. Life on earth is assumed by scientists to have developed from simple forms to more complex forms, in a relatively straight line. Most do not even concede that the term *life* is anything more than a verbal convenience. They would argue that what is commonly referred to as *life* is nothing more than the complex interaction of atoms and molecules. This contrasts sharply with the occult standpoint, as exemplified by *The Secret Doctrine*, which states that matter, and hence all form, is derived from life itself, and that life is universally present. Furthermore, the forms through which life is expressed are said to evolve in a cyclic, as opposed to a linear, pattern. Although occultism would agree that man has indeed evolved from more primitive stages, it would not agree that this has happened during man's tenure on earth. Thus the very assumptions on which the biologists' case rests tend to determine the way in which evidence will be interpreted.

The first strand of evidence is based on the science of genetics. The evolution of different species can be understood by reference to the similarity or otherwise of the genetic material in their cells. It is understood how mutation of this material occurs, and thus how new variants within species come about. The principles of natural selection and the survival of the fittest are then thought to favor the better adapted species. If this general picture is seen to be true in the development of, say, butterflies, why should it not also account for the development of mammals from amphibians and reptiles?

The Secret Doctrine accepts that modifications within a species do indeed occur in this way, but as stated above, says that new species arise on the basis of new astral prototypes which are projected into the physical world at periodic intervals. This corresponds well with observed fact. It is recognized from the fossil record that evolution appears to develop in bursts. This theory is called *punctuated equilibria*. It is as if a new species arises all of a sudden, and then many variations arise, based on the new type. Science is at a loss to account for such sudden leaps in development. They postulate sudden catastrophic events, such as meteor strikes, to account for the demise of the reptiles and the rise of the mammals. But this does not explain why mammals in particular, in this instance, should be the beneficiaries.

The basic similarities in the genetic material in man and animal are also open to another interpretation. The occult view is that all animal forms extant today are ultimately derived from human prototypes, whether in this Round or in earlier Rounds. Thus the observed divergences between species need not be interpreted as man being the highest or most developed animal, but rather as animals being so many imperfect and partial expressions of human prototypes.

The second strand of evidence cited by biologists is the fossil record. If this is patchy overall, it is positively sparse as far as man is concerned. Remains of homo sapiens, which are tens or hundreds of thousands of years old, are not plentiful, but neither are they in dispute. Occultism would merely point to the wide variety of human stocks extant today in order to account for the remains thus far identified. However, the farther back in time we go, the fewer the fossil remains we find. *The Secret Doctrine* says that remnants of the giant Atlantean race were still in existence one million years ago and more, but were fast degenerating. It is they who were the parents of many of the more primitive tribes found alive today, and also as isolated fossilized remains. In other words, far from painting a picture of progressive linear development, these remains actually depict a cyclic process of degeneration and decay.

Another point in regard to the fossil record involves the ostensible progression from simple to complex. It is only natural for biologists to assume that there is a causal link between one stage and the next. But from the occult viewpoint this is an illusion in many cases. As stated above, new mammal stocks are derived from astral prototypes which develop into physical counterparts in chronological sequence. As it happens, mammals follow amphibians, but this does not necessary mean that they were derived from amphibians. Events which follow one another are not necessarily causally connected.

The third strand of evidence is derived, as already mentioned, from molecular biology. The most startling finding, as mentioned, is that man and gorilla are 99 percent identical in terms of their DNA. This is interpreted by biologists to mean that man and ape shared a common ancestor about four and a half million years ago. But molecular biology can say nothing about the characteristics of that common ancestor. It is assumed that homo sapiens is a further development from that ancestor. But the occult account fits the facts equally well. As already pointed out, *The Secret Doctrine* states that the gorilla and its close relatives were produced from an interbreeding between man and ape. Thus man and gorilla would indeed share a common ancestor, but it would be a wholly human ancestor. The human stock continues as human, while the hybrid tends to revert to type. In this case the type is that of its ape-like mother.

If the two theories, the scientific and the occult, were to be treated strictly on their merits, then both would be seen to be viable explanations of the available evidence. The fact that the account given in *The Secret Doctrine* has not been given a fair hearing is something I would now like to address.

The subtitle of this present work concerns Mme. Blavatsky's contribution to world thought. It would be legitimate to ask whether the ideas put forward in *The Secret Doctrine* on the question of evolution have had any impact on modern thought. If we were to compare the effect of Darwin's *Origin of Species* with that of *The Secret Doctrine* in this area, we would have to concede that the former has carried the day. It is Darwin's theories which are taught as fact in schools. But who has heard of theosophy and its ideas concerning evolution? Ostensibly then, the answer must be that, in this area at least, the occult doctrine has had little impact.

This leads us to ask other questions. For instance, was it ever envisaged that the scientific community would turn to *The Secret Doctrine* for information? Plainly not, for we are not comparing like with like. *The Secret Doctrine* addresses a far wider issue: that of the pernicious effects of scientific materialism. It may be that Mme. Blavatsky and her acknowledged coauthors were not concerned with any one issue, but rather with the whole scientific rationale.

It is, perhaps, difficult for us, who have been brought up with the fruits of scientific materialism, to conceive of a time when the major issues addressed by science encompassed another nonmaterial dimension. For example, it is not so very long ago that the science of astronomy was still interwoven with that of astrology. Scientists have tried to rewrite history in this respect. Newton is remembered for his *Principia*; we try to pretend that his interest in astrology was an aberration, a superstitious relic. We laugh at the alchemists for imagining that base metals could be transmuted by chemical means into gold. The same could be said concerning the principles of ancient Chinese medicine. Where is the Chi which flows along the meridians, and where are the meridians themselves? Some grudgingly concede that, despite the "obviously false theory," some therapeutic effects do result from its use. Mesmer was derided as a charlatan, but today hypnotism is reasonably respectable, although no one knows how it works.

It would not be difficult to make a case to the effect that the nonmaterial was recognized as an important factor in just about every culture except our own. It is only since the Age of Reason, the so-called Enlightenment, that Western thinkers have derided all such notions as superstitions. Reason and logic have become the only means by which nature can be studied. If a question is not susceptible to the scientific method, then the question is not worth asking. This stance leads to the absurd position wherein such areas as thought, feeling, intuition and consciousness, all of which are of manifest reality to everyone, are dismissed as mere epiphenomena of matter. Thought and consciousness are reduced to the electrical behavior of the brain.

The major contribution of *The Secret Doctrine* to modern thought is the establishment of a metaphysical framework on which can be built a viable alternative to the materialist's worldview. It demonstrates that metaphysics does not only deal with the origins and nature of both cosmos and man, but also with the manifest processes around us. Thus it is important to show that the application of the principles enunciated in Volume I of *The Secret Doctrine* lead, inter alia, to an alternative explanation of the origin of man's physical form, as has been reviewed in this paper.

It is hardly to be expected that those who defend the very

bastions of scientific materialism are themselves likely to be convinced by arguments such as these. But the scientists themselves are a result of a climate of thought whose origins can be traced back several centuries. *The Secret Doctrine* has, to use the words of a Mahatma, "laid the foundations of a new continent of thought."

16
H. P. Blavatsky and Contemporary Science

RALPH HANNON

> Since only a certain portion of the secret teachings can be given out in the present age, if they were published without any explanations or commentary, the doctrines would never be understood even by theosophists. Therefore, they must be contrasted with the speculations of modern science.
>
> *The Secret Doctrine*, I, 480

The study of theosophy implies not only ancient wisdom but also an ongoing, continually reemerging cycle of growth in knowledge and understanding—a cycle which includes all the modes of knowing. In today's world, this must preeminently include the domain of science.

Looking back to H.P.B. and the emergence of theosophy, we realize that it would be impossible to replicate that teaching exactly today. The science embodied in 19th century theosophical writings—which in many cases were grounded in a direct experience of the "sacred"—will inevitably appear antiquated and anachronistic to a contemporary scientist. But this fact itself offers an interesting paradox. It is true that science has changed enormously since the days when H.P.B. wrote, and that many of her comments about science are no longer valid, by reason of that change. On the other hand, modern science now accepts many of her concepts as correct. How are these two situations to be reconciled? Perhaps they emerge as a koan, and no further discussion is useful. Perhaps, however, it is the lack of discussion that has led to the paradox.

It should be noted that a very thorough effort at examining the relationship between science and theosophy was made in 1938, in honor of the semi-centenary of the publication of *The Secret Doctrine*. This was later revised and published in two volumes under the title *Where Theosophy and Science Meet: A Stimulus to Modern Thought*, edited by D.D. Kanga. Although much of the science in the book is out of date, the treatment of theosophical concepts is excellent.

I should like to begin this discussion by making a brief comment on the science of the 1880s and 90s, when *The Secret Doctrine* was written. It is my contention that H.P.B., with the help of the Masters, was able to see far into the future and realize that certain scientists, such as the chemist Sir William Crookes, would be helpful in introducing theosophy to the world by correlating it with science, which was much respected in those days. I will subsequently move quickly through the history of quantum physics, and consider some current theories and concepts that parallel *The Secret Doctrine's* premises.

The Science of HPB's Day

As the quotation which opens this article illustrates, H.P. Blavatsky relied a great deal on the science of her day when she wrote *The Secret Doctrine*. Each volume of that work contains a section called "Science and The Secret Doctrine Contrasted," which comprises almost 25 percent of the text. Since so much space as well as time and effort were given over to these discussions, it seems important to see why they were included, rather than dismissing them as outdated.

In these two sections, we note that H.P.B. agrees with some of the scientists of her day, while disagreeing with many of the scientific theories accepted at that time. One point that seems significant is that H.P.B. seemed to favor the positions taken by Sir William Crookes, especially when she attempted to point out correlations between theosophy and science. Crookes, in turn, evinced a reciprocal interest in theosophy. In 1883, when A.P. Sinnett returned with his wife to England, he developed a close friendship with Crookes, and was probably instrumental in Crookes's decision to join the Theosophical Society on November 20, 1883—the same day, incidentally, that Mrs. Crookes and C.W. Leadbeater joined. Col. Olcott and H.P.B. also visited Crookes's laboratory, as their friendship developed.

Crookes's particular area of scientific interest was spectroscopy, and his place in the history of scientific development was insured by his invention of the Crookes Tube—a prototype for the television tubes and fluorescent lighting in use today. His real fame as a scientist, however, came with his discovery of a new element, now called thallium, which led to his election to the Royal Society in 1863, long before he met H.P.B.

Crookes was also an ardent investigator of spiritualist phenomena. In fact it was his fearless investigation of psychic phenomena, under strict test conditions and in the face of scientific ridicule, that attracted the attention of the Masters who (it appears from their letters) helped him in certain occult ways. Several passages in the *Mahatma Letters* support this statement:

> . . . then he added that one of Master's Chums . . . a Syrian . . . had very seriously remarked that something ought to be done for Mr. Crookes, and Master had agreed with him. . . .[1]

> I never thought he [Crookes] was so learned till I heard Master's opinion about him and his aura. Master says, there is no one higher than him in chemistry in England, nor elsewhere. . . .[2]

> You speak of Massey and Crookes. . . . We advise and never order. But we do influence individuals. . . . To say and point to Edison and Crookes and Massey would sound much like boasting of that which can never be proven. And Crookes has he not brought science within our hail in his "radiant matter" discovery? What but occult research was it that led him first to that.[3]

> So the great Mr. Crookes has placed one foot across the threshold for the sake of reading the Society's papers? Well

> and wisely done, and really brave of him. Heretofore he was bold enough to take a similar step and loyal enough to truth to disappoint his colleagues by taking his facts public. . . . We have no favorites, break no rules. If Mr. Crookes would perpetrate Arcana beyond the corridors the tools of modern science have already excavated, let him Try.[4]

The "Society's papers" referred to in the last quotation were some of the chapters in *The Secret Doctrine* manuscript. More information about Sir William Crookes and his relationship to The Theosophical Society can be found in reference.[5]

The importance of the role of Sir William Crookes should not be underestimated. It was his work that led J.J. Thomson, in 1897, to identify and measure the charge to mass ratio of the electron. This was a major step in developing the 1913 Bohr model of the atom. Even though this model was based on the planets revolving around the sun ("as above, so below"), it had some strange implications. If the Bohr model was to be correct, then it appeared that scientists had to accept the idea that an electron moving in a particular orbit could suddenly dematerialize, and just as suddenly reappear somewhere else. It is reported that the German physicists Otto Stern and Max von Laue found Bohr's idea so shocking that they vowed to give up physics if by chance the theory turned out to be correct. One of the problems with the Bohr model was that it worked only for the hydrogen atom. In 1926 Erwin Schrodinger developed quantum mechanics, which corrected the difficulty, at least in part.

Quantum Theory

Max Planck introduced *the concept* of quantum mechanics as far back as 1900, when he said that light was emitted in little bundles of energy which he called "quanta." Prior to this development, it had been thought that light was propagated only in waves. (Today we refer to this situation as the wave/particle duality.) And here we should especially notice H.P.B.'s prophetic statement when she said that

Crookes's "discovery of radiant matter will have resulted in a further elucidation with regard to the true source of light, and revolutionized all the present speculation."[6]

A discussion of quantum mechanics would take us too far astray, but numerous references can be given.[7,8,9,10] However, there are certain salient points that should be made before going any further. In the quantum mechanical world, individual atoms do not behave like anything we encounter in the familiar macroscopic world. For example, it is impossible to determine accurately both the position and the momentum of a particle at the same time. This results from the Heisenberg Uncertainty Principle, which sets an inherent upper limit for measuring submicroscopic objects. In other words, it is impossible to pin down the exact nature of the electron.

Furthermore, the determination as to whether an electron should be thought of as a particle, or as a wave, or as a particle/wave, depends on how we take a measurement. The Schrödinger quantum mechanical equation incorporates both the particle properties, in terms of mass, and the wave properties, in terms of wave function—which has no real physical meaning! What is significant is the square of the wave function, for this gives the probability of finding the particle at a particular point in space. The implications of these discoveries were so great that Niels Bohr said, "Anyone who is not shocked by quantum theory has not understood it."

Hence we see that quantum mechanics, which seems so decisive, definitive and clearcut in its practical applications, is actually based on uncertainties, probabilities and bizarre ideas. Most scientists simply coexist with quantum mechanics and its strange philosophical implications.

Contemporary Science

Current science sometimes appears to have been invented by Lewis Carroll's White Queen, who often believed six impossible things before breakfast. Normally, theory and experiment must act in concert if the result is to be called "science." When theoretical speculation leaves experiment too far behind, the result is no longer physics; it has become metaphysics.

We are now going to walk along that gray area which lies between physics and metaphysics, always keeping in mind that a comparison between theosophy and science must be at best a labor of compromise. And what is more, the compromise must be constantly renewed, because science is evolving at such a rapid rate. This situation is epitomized in a well-known story about two scientists who were looking at some mathematical equations on a blackboard. One turns to the other and says, "What's most depressing is the realization that everything we believe will be disproved in a few years."

Dark Matter

One area of contemporary science that is of great interest both to the scientist and to the theosophist is what is called "dark matter." Simply stated, this means that there is more matter in the universe than can be seen. Indications of where some of this dark matter may be are given by the motions of stars and galaxies. But where is the rest of it, and what *is* it?

If the theory is correct, it would appear that most of the mass in the universe is "dark," that is, invisible to any existing telescope or other observational device. In fact, evidence now indicates that what is visible may account for only approximately 10 percent of the galaxies' actual mass. The "missing mass" can only be accounted for by the existence of a new kind (or kinds) of matter. Dark matter is probably the dominant form of mass in the universe.

H.P.B. seemed to speak directly to this fact when she wrote:

> There are millions and millions of worlds and firmaments visible to us; there are still greater numbers beyond those visible to the telescopes, and many of the latter kind do not belong to our objective sphere of existence.[11]

Theosophists in general accept the periodicity of the

cosmos. The current scientific theory which supports this ancient understanding is called the "Big Bang." Basically, this theory holds that the universe, as we understand it, started from an explosion which marked the beginning of time. The force of this was such that the universe will continue expanding until at some point the process stops, and then the universe will start to contract. Eventually it will condense back to its starting point, when the cycle will be repeated.

One of the current problems facing this theory is whether the expansion of the universe *will* stop. The answer to this question depends on two factors: (1) how fast the universe is expanding, and (2) how strongly the force of gravity (determined by the average density of mass within the universe) holds that mass together. At the moment, the average density of visible matter in the universe is less than 2 percent of that which is needed to halt the universe's expansion. The conclusion is that *if* the universe is cyclic, at least 80 percent of the total mass within it must be made up of something other than "visible" matter.

H.P.B. may have given us another hint with respect to the solution of this problem when she wrote:

> Hence, when 'other worlds' are mentioned . . . the occultist does not locate these spheres either outside or inside our Earth . . . for their location is nowhere in the space known to, and conceived by the profane. They are . . . blended with our world, interpenetrating it and interpenetrated by it.[12]

Virtual Particles

Another passage in *The Secret Doctrine* might be applicable not only to dark matter but also to the world of subatomic particles:

> . . . the Secret Doctrine, postulating that conditioned or limited space (location) has no real being except in this world of illusion, or, in other words, in our perceptive faculties, teaches that every one of the higher, as of the lower worlds, is interblended with our own objective world; that millions of things and beings are, in point of localization

> around and in us, as we are around, with, and in them; it is no metaphysical figure of speech, but a sober fact in Nature, however incomprehensible to our senses.[13]

This could be a reference to "virtual particles," which are very mysterious even in terms of today's boldest scientific speculations.

The standard theory of subatomic particles says that they are made up of quarks and leptons. For example, electrons belong to the lepton family, and protons and neutrons are made up of quarks. But now the mystery deepens. Scientists believe that surrounding every quark there is a cloud of particles *that are briefly materialized from the vacuum*. These are called "virtual particles" because they cannot be detected directly; they owe their ephemeral existence to Heisenberg's Uncertainty Principle. It will be remembered that according to this principle, the law of conservation of energy can seemingly be violated if that violation is so brief as to be "unnoticed." The energy needed to create virtual particles can be "borrowed" from the vacuum surrounding the quark because there is some uncertainty about the average energy level of the vacuum over any interval of time. The shorter the interval, the more uncertain the energy, and thus more energy becomes available for materializing virtual particles. The spontaneous creation and subsequent annihilation of virtual particles in the vacuum are called the "fluctuation of the quantum field."

With this in mind, let us consider the following passage:

> Nevertheless, such invisible worlds do exist. Inhabited as thickly as our own is, they are scattered throughout apparent space in immense number; some far more material than our own world, others gradually etherealizing until they become formless and are as "breaths."[14]

One interesting exercise is to reread the above paragraph on virtual particles while substituting the word "deva" for "virtual particles." On a macroscopic scale, this would provide an adequate explanation for devas. Yet most orthodox scientists would never accept this approach, for they would point out that the uncertainty principle works only on the subatomic level of reality, and is not applicable elsewhere. On the other hand, if our universe *is* a small part of a much larger living reality, as most theosophists hold it to be, virtual particles would provide an interesting explanation.

All of this, we realize, is speculation arising from current scientific theory. At the same time, it should be remembered that this is what H.P.B. recommended that we do.

Conclusion

Today, scientists are learning to speculate boldly. Theosophists have long been accustomed to do the same. However, there needs to be a serious effort to balance theosophical and scientific theories against each other. We might paraphrase Dr. Annie Besant's statement, as follows:

> Closely linked are true metaphysic and [scientific] practice. No practice is sound which is not based on true metaphysic. No metaphysic is true, that is, vital, which does not flower into sound practice. Both are necessary if we are to unfold into perfection our divine nature.[15]

Theosophists are firmly convinced that the future will confirm their intuition that the universe, far from being the dead mechanism conceived by orthodox science, is a living process evolving toward unity. To the esotericist who is also a scientist, this conviction is already a fact.

The world has great need for this inquiry into the fundamental unity of the universe, which transcends or includes all mechanical descriptions or laws. The next advance in human knowledge must bring about a realization of the *life* in which the whole universe participates—in which all things "live and move and have their being."

The Secret Doctrine approach to this great issue may be couched in a more antique phraseology than we are accustomed to, but it nevertheless points us very clearly in the right direction.

Notes

1. *The Letters of H.P.B. to A.P. Sinnett*, Letter 53, p. 226.
2. Ibid.
3. *The Mahatma Letters to A.P. Sinnett*, 3rd ed., Letter 47, pp. 267-8.
4. Ibid., Letter 59, pp. 335-6.
5. *Proceedings Symposium on S.D.*, Wizards Bookshelf, San Diego, 1984, pp. 24-27 (Reprinted in *The Theosophical Research Journal*, Vol. I (4), pp. 91-96).
6. Blavatsky, H.P., *The Secret Doctrine*, Vol. I, TPH, 1978, p. 621.
7. Gribbin, John, *In Search of the Big Bang*, New York: Bantam Books, 1986.
8. Gribbin, John, *In Search of Schrödinger's Cat*, New York: Bantam Books, 1984.
9. Pagels, Heinz, *The Cosmic Code*, New York: Bantam Books, 1983.
10. Capra, F., *The Tao of Physics*, Shambhala, 1975.
11. Blavatsky, H.P., *The Secret Doctrine*, Vol. I, TPH, 1978, p. 605.
12. Ibid.
13. Ibid., pp. 604-5.
14. Ibid., p. 606.
15. Besant, Annie, *An Introduction to the Science of Peace*, p. 53.

V

H. P. Blavatsky's Influence on Society and the Arts

17

Some Credentials of The Secret Doctrine

F. L. KUNZ

I

In the West the word "community" is likely to prompt an image of some peaceful urban settlement united by roads, telephones, and other facilities and served by schools, libraries, temples, churches, banks, and comparable institutions. Associated with these amenities is a somewhat heterogeneous aggregate of aspirational ideals and ideas. The whole of this psychophysical complex is usually called "civilization." Now that we have such means as rapid transportation and electronic communications, we humans hope to establish a settled, peaceful, planetary community. There are many obvious minor obstacles, such as language diversity, and others far more intractable: nationalism, international monetary and trade policies, and centuries of commitment to reckless competition, monstrous waste, and an excessive preoccupation with things physical and transient. There is something especially sinister and significant in the possibility that the next war may be fought fiercely, all-out, with what are politely called overkill weapons that can destroy civilization.

It is well that the people of the United States are discovering that physical facilities such as drains, supermarkets, and television do not insure true welfare. But it has been dismaying of late to realize that the secular school and college system affords no way to transcend civilization. We shall see that education could provide the solution, for a specific reason: Today's physics and chemistry have become a species of demonstrable metaphysics. In their special area of competence (matter and energy) they are providing secular, public, step-by-step evidence of the validity of the cosmology and the ontology that were prevalent in ancient cultures prior to the gory triumph of civilization.

That classical state of mind was summarized for the first time in English in a unique work, *The Secret Doctrine*, by H.P. Blavatsky. So it is quite possible for the layman to acquaint himself with the scheme. If one does so, it becomes clear that we of the West have for centuries not known enough about the nature of man and of the universe in which he has emerged to enable us to establish a genuine community at any level, and that the Far East is now rapidly abandoning that wisdom which once it employed.

Because of its uniqueness as a statement in a modern language of the classical scientific metaphysics required if we are to rise above civilization, I propose here to identify some of the credentials of *The Secret Doctrine*. We shall start the inquiry with an example of a community in that sense which is appropriate to Greece and Egypt at their peak. To make clear what is meant by the verb "to commune," we shall examine briefly the most mathematical of the arts. We shall refer to those of its principles which are established and employed in modern exact science.

II

Like all other true arts, music rests upon principles which no one can change and which are expressed not only in nature (wherein they constitute acoustics) and in man, in whom they are implicit and lead to music as a free and creative art. All over the world, and in all ages, the diatonic scale, the audible overtones, structural beat, and the like have been and are employed, though with varying degrees of conscious mastery, completeness, and sophistication. Children are endowed by nature with psychospiritual and physiological equipment which enables them to show at a very early age that they have joined the musical community, which is worldwide, because it arises from laws of nature no one can change. The *science* of acoustics, then, furnishes foundations for the principles of an *art* which, at its best, can bring immense benefit and additional unity to any and eventually to all people. Universality is thus insured at two levels: one, that of nature (acoustics), the other that of the human spirit.

Now when one studies modern field and particle physics, one discovers that they are in all fundamentals conformable to laws which are like those of music. The latter occurs in a physical continuum (the atmosphere), whereas the former reveal the existence of nonmaterial continua. Furthermore, the sequence of possible audible sounds is itself an infinitely graded continuum from the lowest audible tone to the highest, as can be demonstrated on a plunger pipe. Next comes the critical fact that at every point in the sound spectrum any and every tone creates its own natural quantized overtones in the major mode whence all music, as an art, takes off, the composer being free to create expressions of his own inspiration. Thus from any tone the whole system of music arises naturally. Fields and quanta are great new truths of physics. Music and the new physics are therefore two formulations—one in affective and the other in intellective terms—of the true law-abiding nature of the universe. When we observe a small child's first joyous entry into the musical community we would do well to recognize him as a citizen of the cosmos, and therefore fitted to be a citizen in a united world community: We commune with the Indians, the Russians, and any and all peoples through music, through science, through all forms of valid knowledge and wisdom based on knowledge. Hence a world-wide community can be achieved when the curriculum has been revised the world over.

We are implying—and it is true—that when a child sings he is expressing, at the human level, principles embodied in atoms and other self-organized natural systems. He is proclaiming his powers as a localization in and of the cosmos. For example, the boundaries (parameters) of all crystals provide small whole number ratios. It is possible to lay out the pattern of the crystal and to interpret the space intervals of the atoms as musical intervals, as Viktor Goldschmidt showed so long ago. Thus we can write and can hear the music of common table salt (sodium chloride) or the music of the diamond (pure carbon) or the music frozen in the snowflake. In Indian philosophy harmonious sound of language and of music are taken as representations of our senses of the characteristics of a field called the *akasha*. Something comparable has appeared in the West in physics, the quantized radiation field, where the photon is the basic particle. Can there be a true human community in which the education neglects or does violence to these relationships? Education should be mainly evocation.

A genuine human community may thus be defined as a society in which the laws of nature and the principles of the arts are sufficiently well understood so that what *is* good cannot only be to some extent determined and politically embodied in constitutional and case law, but can be agreed upon and made available in the schools and colleges, so that everyone will understand in some adequate sense the universe and the true nature and needs of a human individual as a localization in and of it. We are born with endowments which, if nourished, would enable us to know and to use our psychospiritual resources well and to obey intelligently and unitedly the sovereign realities.

III

There has never hitherto been a human society politically and economically organized as a nation, in which enough was known and lived out to serve children adequately. But there is ample evidence that in classical times enlightened individuals joined together in sacred pursuits in organizations which powerfully influenced nations. The true workings of these groups were secret for two obvious reasons:

1. Not everyone is willing to try hard to live out what he knows, as did the ancient brotherhoods; and not

everyone has the same capacity for enlightenment.

2. Tyranny, slavery, illiteracy, and other features were quite as antithetic to any opposite political and social expression of spirituality as are the stark ignorance and the dark physicalism of our own times, which is no less hostile to absolute altruism. That such enlightened groups existed, no one can doubt any more than he can deny the existence of the Masonic Order. But what they knew and taught is another question. It is answered in *The Secret Doctrine*.

IV

In the West (to which by and large we confine these remarks) Greece and Egypt are examples of societies in which the multitude was generally and emotionally (not intellectually) familiarized with and conditioned to live in accord with various forces of nature—through the prevalence of appropriate arts and religious customs which were contrived and sustained in and by such small altruistic communities of people who, by supreme efforts, achieved some mastery of themselves and won an accord with, and control over, various powerful psychospiritual forces of nature, of which modern scholars have lost all intelligible account.

Since about 1875, some of these forces have been studied by societies for psychical research, so far rather fruitlessly as to meanings. Unfortunately, the beginnings of such organizations came at a time (about 1875) when science was at its nadir in materialism. The arrogance of some of the early investigators insured the defeat of the very inquiries they aimed to make. In consequence of the attitude of the investigators, they were limited in their studies largely to mediums, clairvoyants, and telepathic sensitives who had little or no control over these gifts. Some students of these matters who were more truly cultivated than other men—such as Edward Bulwer, Lord Lytton, in England and G.H. Fechner in Germany—searched more deeply and felt obliged to go their own individual ways. The result of psychical research has been the accumulation of a vast body of diversified data, much of it recorded by skilled observers, but nearly all of it even today a mere collection, innocent of any theoretical systematization, and hence in disjunction with science generally. In classical societies there prevailed a sophisticated animism[1] in which the rare phenomena of poltergeists (telekinesis), mental communion (telepathy), transpatial perception (clairvoyance), veridical visions of future events (precognition) were natural parts of a comprehensive philosophy of nature which, in all its main features, was (as remarked above) the same in Greece as in Egypt. That such a philosophy *could* have existed can now readily be demonstrated, because the finest sciences of our times justify its fundamentals, as we shall see. To grasp its cosmology, ontology, and epistemology, the reader may have to make long-sustained efforts to purge his mind of physicalism, the heir to materialism, still prevalent even in science and pervasive in education. It is also necessary to bear in mind that the ancient true altruistic communities were founded and led by people who lived lives which accorded with the system. Therefore the metaphysics was tested in the laboratory of individuals whose psychospiritual activities and actual physical conduct proved the principles.

V

The best known example in Europe was the community recreated from an earlier and decadent form by Pythagoras after his visits to India, Egypt, and elsewhere. Subsequently, Plato himself, drawing upon Egypt, renewed that community which went on to serve not only Hellas, but Rome and Italy and pre-Christian Europe generally until the break-up of the system of the Empire.

We need no longer rely solely on scholars expert in Greek to tell us in English what Plato meant. For when we grasp the metaphysical significance of field and particle physics we discover to our delight that there is now new demonstrable evidence that Plato and the Pythagoreans knew what they were talking about when they discoursed on life and man. A reader who cares to look into this will do well to study *Plato in Sicily* by G.R. Levy, Faber & Faber, London, 1956, and to ponder *Great Thinkers on Plato*, edited by Barry Gross, G.P. Putnam, New York, 1968.

It is necessary always to bear in mind that in the true communities in the classical cultures, the guiding influence was not religion, by itself, but a metaphysics in which the religion and the science of the times were fused and which became a self-directed way of life for those who understood it best. The Pythagoreans were vegetarians because they knew that needless killing corrupts the killer. The history of the Levant and of Europe shows how, in due course, theologians created a system of beliefs independent of science. Even within this essentially irrational movement, the classical scientific metaphysics of Greece survived as a dying force in a line of descent from Ammonias Saccas of Alexandria (who contrived the term Theosophy in its Greek form), Plotinus in Rome, Origen, St. Augustine, and others.

In the Far East centers for perpetuation of that ancient, universal, value-laden natural system never died out. In Europe and the Mediterranean area, many sacred enclaves, such as Delphi, had to be forcibly closed, so vital were they. Whole groups, such as the Albigenses, were exterminated. Nevertheless, through the ages the doctrine lived on, more or less openly in India and in secret in Europe.

This is not the occasion to trace the break-up of the Christian dogmatic theological system. It was doomed to lose its power when science came back to life in Europe. Our concern is with the present state of science which, since Newton, has more and more justified the classical metaphysics. The reason why ancient secret communities could express their enlightenment in their mode of life is clear. The mode of life was in conscious accord with the good, the latter having been arrived at from the true and the beautiful. The residual question in this present essay therefore is this: What is the nature of an enlightenment in which the truths of science (the laws of nature) and the ultimates in spirituality are one and the same?

As of today, only a fair (but firm) beginning can be made

in the restoration of the classical state of mind. For the proofs available to us are drawn as yet only from the sciences of matter and energy. In contrast, the ancients sought their evidence in the phenomena of protoplasmic life and achieved their justification in personal and communal ways of truly spiritual life.

Modern field and particle physics is a deductive-exact science, derived from postulates, mathematically structured and empirically justified. It has one advantage: It can be employed to *demonstrate* the truth of its metaphysics; and I make bold to say that the method can and will before long be applied to biology and to man.

Instead of quoting from *The Secret Doctrine* I shall presently therefore turn to the contributions of recent leading geniuses in the scientific community and state briefly what they have achieved, in order to establish here the essential nature of the metaphysics of the classical community.

As noted above, these essentials were formulated in English for the first time and published in London in 1889 under the title *The Secret Doctrine*. Even at that date some of the modern proofs of the validity of the doctrine were available, from Isaac Newton, Auguste Bravais, and James Clerk Maxwell.

VI

H.P. Blavatsky was one of the small company of geniuses in whom the motivation is absolute altruism. Now and then such individuals appear. They know enough of the law to realize that there can be no compromise with worldliness, that only total self-discipline will ally them with the divine source, and that the truest philanthropy is complete commitment to living out and to teaching of the doctrine. They do, most naturally, react to false accusations, abuse, and villification addressed to them. They are human. But nothing deters them from their duty, which is mankind's welfare; and they harbor no ill feelings and certainly do not respond in kind to slanders. It is almost impossible to understand such people unless one has privileged opportunities to work with them.

In this matter a certain cynicism has permeated the learned world; and therefore I have little hope of stating the case here and now in these few words. Let me therefore instead merely recommend to the reader that he study an instance, the life of the real Francis Bacon, whose name was blackened for us in an infamous essay by Macaulay. If the appropriate members of a faculty of a university (historians in particular) were to pursue the issues raised and met in the undernoted books,[2] they might come out with the conviction that Shaksper, that illiterate village roisterer, ostler, and occasional small-part actor, could not possibly have written the plays which bear his name, spelled Shakespeare. No individual who wants to know need wait upon an academic inquiry. He may investigate for himself. He will be exhilarated and re-educated by the discovery that geniuses obedient to absolute altruism do occur. The circumstances of no one of them resemble exactly those of any other. For the arduous process of self-fulfilment is intended to produce not uniformity, but uniqueness. A Blavatsky is not a Bacon. And there are many levels of this utter commitment to truth and love. Can one deny that Joan of Arc went to her death in obedience to the guidance she had? There have been great revealers in all societies and in all ages, people who have found out that the greatest good which can be conferred upon their fellow men is to teach, especially to convey that which their lives embody. They are people who act on their wisdom. Plato risked his life three times in his visits to Sicily, where there was a faint hope that through Dion, the tyrants Dionysus I and his son, Dionysus II, could be guided toward democracy by the philosophical wisdom which Plato had achieved.

VII

H.P. Blavatsky was born in 1831 in an aristocratic Russian family, being on her mother's side a scion of a Dolgorouky. From her earliest years it was recognized that she was endowed with psychical powers. At first, these were not under her control. During that time she would have seemed to be a suitable subject for study by persons familiar with parapsychological phenomena: clairvoyance, poltergeist, and the like. But from those early years her visions also included rapport with an adept in occult arts, and he was the true lodestar of her life. She first wandered in Egypt, Greece, and Italy and the Levant in search of experiences with people gifted and seeking like herself. Later she sought in the New World, among American Indians. All along, her battle to control her powers was unremitting. At one stage she went through a fearful crisis in which finally she triumphed over her psychobiological nature, and in due time she found her way to India and to Tibet, where the training at this higher level perfected her mastery over her personal self.

What is involved in such a desperate engagement with nature's finer forces is not even now recognized in organized Western psychical research. It has, of course, long been known in the East and especially in India that there is a specific self-disciplinary method which can lead to self-mastery.

Well before 1875, then, Mme. Blavatsky was in complete conscious command of her clairvoyance and other supernormal resources; and she was therefore admirably endowed to achieve virtually limitless rapport with the records of the past and even to sketch the outlines of the future. Having not even a theory of the petty and occasional random precognitions and psychometric experiences which they record, organized psychical research groups have not even a glimmering of the workings of nature, as seen by persons who are within themselves *in command* of such faculties.

The Secret Doctrine, then, is a compilation in which one finds assembled the cosmology and ontology common to the classical cultures of India, Egypt, Greece and every other true ancient community. There is no other work like it in any modern language. What is more, it was written down by the putative author under the guidance of Personages who know the difference between deductive-exact science and hypothetical-approximate science. Although the employment of the former method is conspicuous in the work of Newton, Einstein, and others, yet to this day its true character and unique consequences are not made clear in education.

The literature associated with H.P. Blavatsky's life and work is considerable and fascinating. In it are a few volumes of written communications from her coadjutors, in particular *The Mahatma Letters to A.P. Sinnett* and *The Letters of the Masters of the Wisdom*. Therein we read (as early as the 1880's) that exact science will presently justify the classical scientific philosophy. As noted above, it has already done so amply in physics. I shall therefore now summarize some of the findings of field and particle physics as a ready way to remind students of *The Secret Doctrine* of its essential teaching, that the ultimate real is a nonmaterial continuum, Brahman, in the Indian nomenclature; and that man (as Atman) is rooted therein, and so on. In brief, the beauty of the new physics is that it shows how, from and in the nonmaterial boundless reality, the discrete "material" systems of nature—atoms, crystals, plants, animals, planets, solar systems—all arise. This is possible today because the new physics shows that matter is but energy localized in and in accord with the fields. The reader will please forgive me if the next few paragraphs, brief of necessity, are obscure.

VIII

More than any other individual since the days of Isaac Newton, Einstein has demonstrated scientifically the reality of nonmaterial continua and has shown how one proceeds in order to understand the *derivation* of the *discrete* material structures and processes which constitute the transient world, from and in accord with the real universe which latter, in contrast, is *continuous* in time and in impartible, boundless space.

Einstein's co-contributors, after Newton, were Bravais, J.C. Maxwell, Max Planck, and then a younger generation which concentrated immense talent upon the aforesaid *derivation* of the discrete from the continuous. Among them were Bohr, de Broglie, Dirac and, in particular,

Erwin Schrödinger, who wrote the equation which defines and employs those permissible discretenesses which, at the very root of physical nature, are mandatory if waves are to become particles, light specifically becoming photons.

It was under such leadership that a public doctrine was, by 1928, enunciated for physical science in perfect agreement with identical concepts in Blavatsky's great work *The Secret Doctrine.* There we read of Brahman (the ultimate real continuum) and Prakriti, the material basis of nature. Among the continua in that ultimate continuum is *akasha*, the harmonious quantized field.

Recently the failure of quantum theory in nuclear physics led some physicists to make a fresh start with Einstein's conviction that the space and space-time of nature alone are real. Their study, called geometrodynamics, has led to the view that there are ultimate vacua in great numbers involved with energy in an atom. Such vacua remind one of the *mulaprakriti* doctrine of the Vedanta. The new physicists' tentative calculations of the number of such vacua in an atom bring the theory into the range of the observations and laborious counts made by C.W. Leadbeater who, as early as 1884, was a trusted junior colleague of Mme. Blavatsky and became an important investigator on his own account.

IX

The main point in *The Secret Doctrine* and in field physics has been made, namely, that the real universe is nonmaterial, continuous, boundless, and presumably everlasting, whereas the world of galaxies, solar systems, atoms, and particles, is discrete and perishable. We need to add that the ancients held that man, as a consciousness, is rooted in the former. Hence the leaders of the classical communities understood spirituality and right conduct in a special sense. What is more, they understood the magnitude of the task of living out the truth.

The life of the compiler of *The Secret Doctrine*, as one such embodiment of ultimate good, repays study. As to the work itself, exact science and its philosophy will more and more fully validate it, as the decades pass. If, however, one desires to achieve in oneself the metamorphosis required if the ultimate reality is to be one's standard, then knowledge of the example of those who have gone before seems indispensable. We have sketched the credentials of the book. To grasp those of its scribe, something more even than the fusion of art and science is required. Plato saw this. To him the arts and beauty and the sciences and truth were the extremities of a line. By triangulation out of the one dimensional line one reaches the good. H.P. Blavatsky achieved that transcendence. An understanding of her personal victory is certainly not less important for us than our intellectual mastery of her monumental work on metaphysics. It is suggested that the reader familiarize himself with the book *Incidents in the Life of Madame Blavatsky* by A.P. Sinnett (L.W. Bouton, New York, 1886; Theosophical Publishing Society, London, 1913).

In addition to Mr. Sinnett's useful account, early volumes of *Old Diary Leaves*, H.S. Olcott's record of the early days of The Theosophical Society, are helpful reading as introductory to a study of *The Letters of H.P. Blavatsky to A.P. Sinnett.* Taken without any preparation, the *Letters* may prove to be misleading except for readers who have acquired elsewhere and somehow understanding of the strange regulations which govern the lives of genuine absolute altruists. In appearance they may seem to be merely human, but in fact they are celestial visitors, and their important acts can be rightly judged only if the criteria employed are appropriate to their other-worldly motives.

Notes

1. William MacDougall saw this modern lack and wrote of it in *Body and Mind, a Defence of Animism.*
2. By Alfred Dodd: *Francis Bacon's Personal Life-Story; The Secret History of Francis Bacon.* (The latter contains the Sonnets in correct chronological order. Both books are now out of print.) By Bertram G. Theobald: *Enter Francis Bacon.*

18
H.P.B.'s Attitude Toward Social Reform

KATHERINE A. BEECHEY

Madame H.P. Blavatsky's whole attitude to social reform may probably be summed up in a few words, for she identified herself almost completely with Theosophy and its teachings: "Let everyone become a Theosophist, a true brother to his fellowmen, and half the world's social problems would be solved." She saw in the society of her time two great evils: caste and religion in the East, and class in the West. To quote from an article which she wrote for *The North American Review*:[1]

> Everyone entering the Society is supposed to sympathize with the theory of essential brotherhood, a kinship which exists on the plane of the higher Self, not on that of racial, social and mental disabilities and antipathies. These elements pertain to the physical man and are the result of unequal development under the law of evolution. . . . It is the physical body only which has racial type, color, sex, hatreds, ambitions and loves. So then, when we postulate the idea of universal brotherhood we wish it understood that it is held in no Utopian sense, though we would not dream of realizing it at once on the ordinary plane of social or material relations.
>
> Most assuredly, if this view of the kinship of all mankind could gain universal acceptance, the improved sense of moral responsibility it would engender would cause most social evils and national asperities to disappear; for a true

altruism, instead of the present egotism, would be the rule the world over. So we have written down as the first of our declared Objects this altruistic asseveration, and have been working practically to bring about a beginning of the better law.

Continuing her article (which was published in *The Theosophist* for May 1957 in greatly condensed form, under the title "Fourteen Years of Theosophy,") she writes:

> Let us see what has actually been accomplished during the fourteen years of the Theosophical Society's existence.... First as regards Object number one, let it be noted that we have done things on the broadest possible scale, dealing with nations in the mass as well as individuals and small groups.
>
> Colonel Olcott and I removed from New York to Bombay at the beginning of the year 1879, at which time we had just established relations between Western students of Oriental mysteries and a few Hindus and Sinhalese. In the East we found division between sects, castes and races. . . . Now the traveller will be struck with the brotherliness which has begun to prevail. Soon after our arrival in Bombay our Society began to grow, branches rapidly sprang up and it became necessary to hold annual conventions of delegates representing the now widely-expanded Society.
>
> Responsive to the President's call, thirty odd branches sent as their representatives, Hindu, Parsi, Buddhist, Mohammedan, Hebrew and Christian fellows to the first convention in Bombay. . . . The platform was successively occupied by speakers of the above-named religions, who vied with each other in fervent declarations of mutual tolerance and goodwill. . . . Thus the clear note of universal brotherhood was struck . . . where previously there had been only sectarian hatred and selfish egotism. This was in 1882. Annually since then the convention has met as a parliamentary body to transact the Society's business and not the least sectarian or race discord has occurred. The whole of India became leavened with the benign influence . . . of the delegates in their respective states and nations. . . .

An interesting light is thrown on the meeting of the

various religions, nationalities, and castes in India in a letter which Madame Blavatsky wrote to her aunt, Mademoiselle Nadine Fadeew, on the 21st February 1880, from Bombay.[2] The following is an extract from her letter:

> ... I am writing in a hurry. Miss Hume the daughter of the Lt. Governor of Punjab is my guest since three days.... She came especially to be initiated into the signs and the secret word, as she joined the Theosophical Society 10 months ago. Yesterday night there was a very impressive ceremony, with all the staff and officials, presidents, secretaries, librarians and fellow-members. Only there were no neophytes.
>
> Miss Hume, Honorable Scott Ross, engineer, Parsi, worshipper of the fire, Dewan (Prime Minister) of the Maharajah of Holkar (idol worshipper), and a poor Hindu merchant from Bombay. Don't lose patience. This description has its purpose. You see 5 different diametrically opposed personalities. Different socially, religiously, nationally and in their social status. After the *initiation* Miss Hume a proud lady who lived for 10 years in India, and according to her own statement has never touched the hand of any native, was the first to shake hands with the poor Hindu merchant, touching his cup and calling him brother. The idol-worshipper, a real fanatic only three months ago, who regarded the very touch of a foreigner as polluting, calls brother a Parsi fire-worshipper and a merchant who lost the privileges of his caste because of his reformatory tendencies, *takes tea with them*, which is a great sin in the eyes of Brahmins.

Turning to the class situation in the West, H.P.B. continued, in the article in *The North American Review*:

> This is what we have done in India.... As to Europe, as we began to work in earnest here only three years ago, the effects begin to be hardly perceived as yet.
>
> Still, in London, in the very centre of the most luxurious materialism, we have founded in the East End the first Working Woman's Club, wholly free from theological creeds and conditions. Hitherto all such efforts have been sectarian and have imposed special religious beliefs; ours is based on

brotherhood alone, and recognizes no differences in creed as a barrier.

When the Club opens a few weeks hence the members will find themselves in a bright and pleasant home, with books, papers and music at hand, and a band of their better-educated sisters will take in rotation, night after night, the duty of helping and guiding—not controlling—the evening recreation. Only those who know the dreary lives of our poor East End girls . . . will understand the brotherly nature of the service thus rendered to them.

We (the cultured class) make outcasts of these less fortunate members of our family, set them in a special part of the town, amid squalid surroundings and coarsening influences, and we then complain that their roughness shocks our refinement, their brutality jars on our delicacy! Here, then, against class division, as in India against caste division, the Theosophical Society proclaims the Brotherhood of Man!

We learn more about the above-mentioned Working Woman's Club from Mrs. Annie Besant's *Autobiography*, first published in 1893. Dr. Besant writes:[3]

Early in the year 1890, H.P.B. had given her £1,000 to use in her discretion for human service, and if she thought well, in the service of women. After a good deal of discussion she fixed on the establishment of a club in East London for working girls, and with her approval Miss Laura Cooper and I hunted for a suitable place. Finally we fixed on a very large and old house, 193 Bow Road, and some months went in its complete renovation and the building of a hall attached to it. On August 15th it was opened by Madame Blavatsky, and dedicated by her to the brightening of the lot of hard-working and underpaid girls. It has nobly fulfilled its mission for the last three years.

Very tender was H.P.B.'s heart to human suffering, especially that of women and children. She was very poor towards the end of her earthly life, having spent all on her mission, and refusing to take time from her Theosophical work to write for the Russian papers which were ready to pay highly for her pen. But her slender purse was swiftly emptied when any human pain that money could relieve came in her way. One day I wrote a letter to a comrade that was shown to her, about some little children to whom I had carried a quantity of country flowers, and I had spoken of their faces pinched with want. The following characteristic note came to me:

"My Dearest Friend,—I have just read your letter to— and my heart is sick for the poor little ones! Look here; I have but 30s. *of my own money* of which I can dispose (for as you know I am a pauper, and proud of it), but I want you to take them and *not say a word.* This may buy thirty dinners for thirty poor little starving wretches, and I may feel happier for thirty minutes at the thought. Now don't say a word, and do it; take them to those unfortunate babies who loved your flowers and felt happy. Forgive your old uncouth friend, useless in this world!

ever yours,
H.P.B."

Perhaps one of H.P.B.'s reasons for deciding to spend her £1,000 on a Working Woman's Club may have been due to her own experience of such a club when she first arrived in New York on 7th July 1873. As is well known, when she was about to embark in France for New York she saw on the quay a poor woman with her children who had been swindled out of her passage money by some unscrupulous agent. H.P.B. promptly exchanged her first-class passage for steerage, in order that the poor woman might go on the boat. H.P.B. arrived in New York practically penniless, for she found that the money with which her father had regularly supplied her was not forthcoming. It was only later that she learned that her father had died and her relatives did not know her address or where she was living. After reaching New York, she somehow found her way to a co-operative house at 222 Madison Street which had been established by forty working women in a tenement area. She stayed there for some months.

It seems that at that period New York was extremely Victorian in its outlook, and no woman traveling alone would be received in any good hotel. She must be accompanied by a male relative. Thus a respectable woman who had to go out into the world to work found it difficult to find accommodation. The typewriter had not then been invented, and women who worked were mostly teachers, people who could sew, or those who could get work in some very poorly-paid trades. In her efforts to procure work, H.P.B. was helped by her friends at this co-operative house which, incidentally, lasted only a few months, as the promoters had neither capital nor business experience. These friends introduced her to a firm of shirt and collar makers, for whom she designed picture advertisement cards and sewed cravats. She tried her hand also at doing intricate fancy leather work, but found that it did not pay. After a short while, the French lady who visited the house and went with H.P.B. to the Eddy farmstead, invited H.P.B. to live with her until her money should arrive from Russia. When her legacy finally arrived, H.P.B. moved to a poorly furnished top-floor flat in Henry Street, with a saloon on the ground floor, but kept in touch with her former friends of Madison Street.

We are indebted for these particulars to Miss Elizabeth G.K. Holt, a member of The Theosophical Society in Newark, New Jersey, who lived in the same co-operative house with H.P.B. for some months. Her reminiscences of her contact with H.P.B. were published in *The Theosophist*,[4] the manuscript being still in the archives at Adyar. It is not possible to quote at length from this manuscript, but Miss Holt describes H.P.B. as living in a room on the second floor but spending most of her time in a common sitting room plus office, where mail was received and the members met.

> But she seldom sat alone; she was like a magnet, powerful enough to draw round her everyone who could possibly come. I saw her, day by day, sitting there rolling her cigarettes and smoking incessantly. . . . Madame continually described herself as being under the authority of unseen powers. . . .

She was therefore taken to be a Spiritualist. Miss Holt says she "never looked upon Madame as an ethical teacher. For one thing she was too excitable" but "in mental or physical dilemma, you would instinctively appeal to her, for you felt her fearlessness, her unconventionality, her great wisdom and wide experience and hearty goodwill—her sympathy with the underdog."

H.P.B. held strong views about the giving of charity, as may be seen by her answers to "Enquirer" in *The Key to Theosophy*, where again she identifies herself with Theosophy:

> The Theosophical ideas of charity mean *personal* exertion for others; *personal* mercy and kindness; *personal* interest in the welfare of those who suffer; *personal* sympathy, foresight and assistance in their troubles or needs. We Theosophists do not believe in giving money (N.B. if we had it) through other people's hands or organizations. We believe in giving to the money a thousand-fold greater power and effectiveness by our personal contact and sympathy with those who need it. We believe in relieving the starvation of the soul, as much as if not more, than the emptiness of the stomach, for gratitude does more good to the man who feels it than to him for whom it is felt.[5]

To the Enquirer who said that "millions and millions were spent annually on public or private charity" H.P.B. replied:

> Oh, yes, half of which sticks to the hands it passes through before getting to the needy; while a good proportion or remainder gets into the hands of professional beggars, those who are too lazy to work, thus doing no good whatever to those who are really in misery and suffering.[6]

Elsewhere in the same book,[7] replying to Enquirer's question: "Surely the T.S. does not stand altogether aloof from the social questions which are now so fast coming to the front?" H.P.B. replied:

> The very principles of the T.S. are a proof that it does not—or, rather, that most of its members do not so stand aloof. . . . All Theosophists are only too sadly aware that, in Occidental countries especially, the social condition of large masses of people renders it impossible for either their bodies or

> their spirits to be properly trained. . . . As this training and and development is one of the express objects of Theosophy, the T.S. is in thorough sympathy and harmony with all true efforts in this direction.

Asked what she meant by "true efforts," since each social reformer has his own panacea and each believes his to be the one and only thing which can improve and save humanity, H.P.B. replied:

> This is the real reason why so little satisfactory social work is accomplished. In most of these panaceas there is no really guiding principle, and there is certainly no one principle which connects them all. Valuable time and energy are thus wasted; for men, instead of co-operating, strive one against the other, often, it is to be feared for the sake of fame and reward rather than for the great cause which they profess to have at heart, and which should be supreme in their lives. . . . Every Theosophist, therefore, is bound to do his utmost to help on, by all means in his power, every wise and well-considered social effort which has for its object the amelioration of the conditions of the poor. Such efforts should be made with a view to their ultimate social emancipation, or the development of the sense of duty in those who now so often neglect it in nearly every relation of life . . . his duty will lie in the direction of forming public opinion. And this can be attained only by inculcating those higher and nobler conceptions of public and private duties which lie at the root of all spiritual and material improvement.

H.P.B. goes much more deeply into the subject of social reform in the section of *The Key to Theosophy* on "The Relations of the T.S. to Political Reforms,"[8] stating briefly the theosophical principles as: "universal Unity and Causation; Human Solidarity; the Law of Karma; Re-incarnation. These are the four links of the golden chain which should bind humanity into one family, one universal Brotherhood."

Although an altruist, Madame Blavatsky did not much approve of philanthropists generally. In an article entitled "Let Every Man Prove His Own Work" which appeared in *Lucifer* for November 1887,[9] she writes:

The religious philanthropist holds a position of his own.... He does not do good merely for the sake of doing good, but also as a means towards his own salvation . . . its devotees are little better than the idol-worshippers who ask their deity of clay to bring them luck in business and the payment of debts. . . .

The secular philanthropist is really at heart a socialist and nothing else; he hopes to make men happy and good by bettering their physical position. No serious student of human nature can believe in this theory for a moment. There is no doubt it is a very agreeable one, because if it is accepted, there is immediate, straightforward work to undertake. . . . Life-long philanthropists, who have started on the work with a joyous youthful conviction that it is possible to "do good" have, though never relaxing the habit of charity, confessed to the present writer that, as a matter of fact, misery cannot be relieved. It is a vital element in human nature, and is as necessary to some lives as pleasure to others. . . .

The social question as it is called, the great deep waters of misery, the deadly apathy of those who have power and possessions—these things are hardly to be faced by a generous soul who has not reached to the great idea of evolution and who has not guessed at the marvellous mystery of human development . . . a law inexorable, by which man lifts himself by degrees from the state of a beast to the glory of a God. The rapidity with which this is done is different with every living soul; and the wretches who hug the primitive task-master, misery, choose to go slowly through a treadmill course which may give them innumerable lives of physical sensation—whether pleasant or painful, well-beloved because tangible to the very lowest senses. . . .

It takes a very wise man to do good works without danger of doing incalculable harm. A highly developed adept in life may grasp the nettle and by his great intuitive powers, know whom to relieve from pain and whom to leave in the mire that is their best teacher. . . . Kindness and gentle treatment will sometimes bring out the worst qualities of a man or woman who has led a fairly presentable life when kept down by pain and despair. . . .

> Theosophists are obliged to work in the world unceasingly. . . . None know more keenly and definitely than they that good works are necessary; only these cannot be rightly accomplished without knowledge. . . . To the public and our critics we say, try to understand the value of good works before you demand them of others, or enter upon them rashly yourselves. Yet it is an absolute fact that without good works the spirit of brotherhood would die in the world; and this can never be. Therefore the double activity of learning and doing is most necessary. We have to do good, and we have to do it *rightly*, with knowledge.

In *Lucifer*, for December 1887,[10] H.P.B. replies to some of the criticisms aroused by her article of the previous month:

> We maintain that more mischief has been done by emotional charity than sentimentalists care to face. The practical results of his labours have to be examined . . . whether he does not sow the seeds of a greater—while relieving a lesser—evil. Mere physical philanthropy . . . is worthless. The gradual assimilation by mankind of great spiritual truths will alone revolutionize the face of civilization and ultimately result in a far more effective panacea for evil than the mere tinkering with superficial misery. Prevention is better than cure. Society created its own outcasts . . . and then condemns and punishes.
>
> Theosophy teaches that *perfect absolute justice* reigns in Nature, though short-sighted man fails to see it in its details on the material and even psychic plane, and that every man determines his own future. . . .

In the *Collected Writings of H.P. Blavatsky*, vol. 8, p. 85, H.P.B. writes, under the title, "Misconceptions R" regarding progress on the physical plane:[11]

> Are three-quarters of humanity happier due to the progress of science and its alliance with industry? . . . Theosophical missionaries aim also at a social revolution. But it is a wholly ethical revolution. It will come about when the disinherited masses understand that happiness is in their own hands, that wealth brings nothing but worries, that he is happy who works for others, for those others work for him, and when the rich realize that their felicity depends upon

> that of their brothers—whatever their race or religion—then only will the world see the dawn of happiness.

The above extracts, although they may seem somewhat long, could be added to at much greater length if one had time to search more thoroughly the published writings and letters of Madame H.P. Blavatsky, but they will serve to show the trend of H.P.B.'s views on charity, philanthropy, and social reform generally, and her attitude to them as an ardent member, as well as one of the Founders, of The Theosophical Society.

Notes

1. No. ccccv, August 1890, pp. 173-186.
2. *H.P.B. Speaks*, Theosophical Publishing House, Adyar, vol. 1, p. 226.
3. Adyar edition, 1937, pp. 461-462.
4. December 1931, pp. 257-266, under the title, "A Reminiscence of H.P. Blavatsky in 1873."
5. *The Key to Theosophy*, 1889, p. 244.
6. Ibid., p. 243.
7. Ibid., p. 232.
8. Ibid., pp. 231-237.
9. Vol. 1, pp. 161-169, H.P.B. *Collected Writings*, vol. 7, p. 166.
10. See H.P.B. *Collected Writings*, vol. 7, p. 295, "Answers to Queries."
11. Written in reply to an article on "Revolution" by "Aleph" in the *Revue du Mouvement Social* (issued May 1887) and published in the French magazine *Le Lotus* (Paris, vol. 1, no. 6) translated into English by B. de Zirkoff. See H.P.B. *Collected Writings*, vol. 8, p. 86.

19
H. P. Blavatsky and Ireland's Literary Renaissance

W. EMMETT SMALL

Compressed into a period of twenty or thirty years toward the end of the 19th and beginning of the 20th centuries, we see a unique example of impregnation, birth, and flowering—for however briefly—of a Seed of Thought in a matrix made fertile by devotion to a stirring idea. That Seed was Theosophy. The matrix was Ireland and Irish minds dedicated to the idea of resuscitation of her ancient greatness. The birth was the Celtic Literary Revival.

> Towards the end of the Eighties there came into being what might certainly be termed a literary "movement" in Ireland, the presence in Dublin of a number of writers working together, imbued with the same ideals and in constant relation to one another. All were alive with the same enthusiasm for a national tradition in literature, and had found in O'Grady the necessary revelation. They concentrated and condensed, as it were, the hitherto scattered elements of revival, and gave a very desirable homogeneity to the rather isolated or unrelated efforts of individual writers in England and Ireland.[1]

Students of world literature know of this extraordinary literary renaissance, but perhaps only historians realize "the germinative power of Theosophy and its doctrines which were potent factors" in its flowering,[2] and some may be surprised at the extent of John Eglinton's endorsement when he writes that

> a branch of the Theosophical Society was founded, which if all were told, was as truly the nucleus from which the Irish Literary Renaissance originated as were the contemporary Gaelic and literary societies: indeed, Yeats once declared that in a few years it had done more for Irish literature than Trinity College in its three centuries.[3]

That "branch" was the Dublin Lodge of The Theosophical Society founded in 1886. Ernest A. Boyd in his authentic history of this period says that its members included "the younger writers, W.B. Yeats, Charles Johnston, John Eglinton, Charles Weekes and George W. Russell (AE), to mention only some of the names which have since come into prominence in Irish literature;" and that "the study of mysticism was the common factor" which brought them together.

> They created a literary life in Ireland just at a time when some fusion of intellectual activities was most essential to the future of the Revival, and, by living and working in and for their own country, strengthened the roots of Irish authorship.[4]

This was the group that would proclaim universal brotherhood and understanding and the esoteric tradition of the inner divinity of man and the oneness of all mankind as practical objectives all can follow and attain. This was the group that would seize the Promethean fire of Theosophy, who would recognize as their inspirer one trained and disciplined who came with that Ancient Wisdom to shock and shake to its foundations the materialistic props and stanchions of the last quarter of the 19th century. Ireland, these Irish hearts and minds, rejoiced, accepted the challenge, responded, and became knights errant in speech and song and deed, making sure the world knew that the old truths were alive again to transform the clay of man to kingly gold.

So in this Celtic Literary Movement we witness a

phenomenon of most interesting theosophic significance. Before us, as audience, is drama enacted on a stage of world history where critically we can today view the actors and judge the acting and its results. There is no doubt or question of the record. It is not too far in the past for impress and picture to have faded from memory, nor too close to our present to blur scholarly perspective. It is a phenomenon that stirs reflection and invites deduction to the end that from its study some measure of its unique import may be gained.

Professor Charles J. Ryan of Theosophical University (Point Loma, California) presses the same point.

> The facts of the important literary work initiated by this Lodge should be known to all . . . as an example of the real standing of the Theosophical Movement as shown by its power to inspire new achievements in the thought-life of the world.[5]

The power of the Theosophical Movement—a global force or energy alive in all ages but not always visibly traceable in world events—is seen in its effect on this other minor yet important movement of national and literary significance, and we come to recognize through investigation that the Celtic Renaissance has the distinction of being the clearest example in our historical day of a definite measurable "wave" or "awakening" or "Movement," an impulse from the great ideas of the Perennial Philosophy, the religion-philosophy-science today known as Theosophy. Conditions for this efflorescence were more than likely somewhat more ideal than those surrounding earlier similar attempts. Ireland was a small enough stage on which to enact the drama, not too large in area or too populated to diffuse a focused energy. The Irish mind was ready, conditioned by a background of closeness to the gods and a natural pantheism which saw all things in nature infilled with divinity, which set up no physical barrier between unseen and seen but saw Man as Hero, the Cuchulainn of the Spirit, shouting with the Sons of God, marching ever toward Lugh the Sunbright in war against Matter and the joyous conviction of eventual victory of Spirit.

Movements, as such, must devolve around a personality or personalities who focus the light of the sun through their own human glass. As we review the history of this Celtic Revival one single individuality looms above all others, George W. Russell, known by his pen-name AE (for the diphthong in Aeon). His whole life was an active meditation for the welfare of Ireland: first as mystic, poet, dreamer-philosopher, and in later years as economist, editor of *The Irish Statesman*, and encourager and inspirer of the younger generation of Irish literary personalities.

Of AE and his place in history we have generous recognition: "a visionary and a mystic . . . the most vivid personality in Ireland today";[6] "AE and W.B. Yeats, the two pillars of the Irish Literary Renaissance";[7] "the greatest of Irish poets";[8] "undoubtedly towered over the contemporary scene";[9] W.B. Yeats and AE "were to dominate the entire literary revival and affect the whole intellectual life of Ireland in their time";[10] "one of the noblest figures in the Irish intellectual movement."[11]

Ella Young, who, among others, felt the touch of AE's mysticism, leaves this impression of her first meeting with him in her charming autobiography of "things remembered accurately and inaccurately":

> His eyes were of a strange blue, very luminous. In the dusky room he made a semblance of light about himself. Gods and Heroes, Days and Nights of Brahma, Mountains, Fire-Fountains, Lakes, and Forests loomed and faced and scintillated through his talk.[12]

And George Moore, "irrepressible and acidic," wrote of AE:

> When he left me, a certain mental sweetness seemed to have gone out of the air.[13]

Highest place as a poet in the Celtic Movement is by acclaim given to William Butler Yeats, but the personage with the widest influence on his own and succeeding generations is accorded AE. He is the mystic, the Celt with deepest vision; the Theosophist, the seer with a universal outlook.[14]

How did this theosophy that "pervaded his whole life"[15] come to him? It came from inner growth, contemplation, brooding and meditation. But in a positive, thunderous way it came with the establishment of the Dublin Lodge of The Theosophical Society and with the study of *The Secret Doctrine* by H.P. Blavatsky, from association with friends saturated with the same enthusiasms. AE "drew his cosmogony from *The Secret Doctrine* and his psychology from kindred sources. . . ."[16]

> To the end of his days he treasured H.P. Blavatsky's magnum opus, *The Secret Doctrine*, the very cornerstone upon which the Theosophical Society was built. . . . Upon his very deathbed AE discoursed on some of the central doctrines of theosophy—karma, reincarnation, Patanjali and the Oversoul.[17]

AE himself wrote in his later years:

> I had no private doctrine: nothing but H.P.B., eked out, for beginners, by W.Q.J.;[18] the Bhagavad Gita; Upanishads; Patanjali; and one or two other classics. I did what I could to keep always in line with the Message of H.P.B.
>
> My own writing is trivial, and whatever merit is to be found in it is due to its having been written in a spiritual atmosphere generated by study of H.P.B. and the sacred books of the East.[19]

And in a letter written in the same year as his death, 1935, to the Irish writer Sean O'Faolain, AE gently chides:

> You dismiss H.P. Blavatsky rather too easily as "hocus pocus." Nobody ever affected the thought of so many able men and women by "hocus pocus." The real source of her influence is to be found in *The Secret Doctrine*, a book on the religions of the world, suggesting or disclosing an underlying unity between all great religions. It was a book which Maeterlinck said contained the most grandiose cosmogony in the world . . . it is one of the most exciting and stimulating

> books written for the last hundred years. It is paying a poor compliment to men like Yeats, Maeterlinck, and others, to men like Sir William Crookes, the greatest chemist of modern times, who was a member of her society, to Carter Blake, F.R.S., the anthropologist, and the scholars and scientists in many countries who read H.P.Blavatsky's books, to assume that they were attracted by "hocus pocus."[20]

AE had first been a founding member of the Hermetic Society, its recognized leader and guide; but now that name was dropped and he and his friends formed, as we have seen, the Dublin Lodge of the Theosophical Society. This Lodge became as vital a factor in the evolution of Anglo-Irish literature as the publication of Standish O'Grady's *History of Ireland*, the two events being complementary to any complete understanding of the literature of the Revival. The Theosophical Movement provided a literary, artistic and intellectual center from which radiated influences whose effect was felt even by those who did not belong to it.

Further, it formed a rallying-ground for all the keenest of the older and younger intellects, from John O'Leary and George Sigerson, to W.B. Yeats and AE. It brought into contact the most diverse personalities, and definitely widened the scope of the new literature, emphasizing its marked advance on all previous national movements.[21]

To those earlier movements (the Pan-Celtic Society, London Society, Dublin Society, etc.) the theosophical influence lent needed spiritual dynamism, free from politics or even a narrow nationalism, but encouraging all that was essentially Irish yet also universal.

The story of the formation of the Dublin Lodge is interesting. Edward Dowden, well-known English literary critic, may in a special way be said to be held responsible—ironically, for he was not one of the circle interested in Theosophy or the writings of Madame Blavatsky, but rather antagonistic to them. A discussion of A.P. Sinnett's *Esoteric Buddhism* and *The Occult World* was being held at Professor Dowden's house. W.B. Yeats was present. The review of the books induced Yeats to read these pioneer theosophical volumes and to recommend them to a school friend, Charles

Johnston. Johnston took fire immediately, interested others in the philosophy, and in 1885 the "Hermetic Society" was formed. T.W. Rolleston, editor of the *Dublin University Review*, published a long article by Johnston on "Esoteric Buddhism." Then Johnston sought out Mr. Sinnett and other Theosophists in London, became a Fellow of the Theosophical Society, obtained other recruits, and these in 1886 became the charter members of the famed Dublin Lodge of the Theosophical Society.[22]

Of the writers who were part of this literary and theosophical movement Yeats was the first to become widely known. Indeed he had already published several books. But mysticism *per se* was not a major part of his inspiration. The only volume of his which carried impress of distinct theosophic thought and speculation was *The Celtic Twilight*, published in 1893 but written before that date. He had no part in the collaboration of those who were the contributors to the pages of *The Irish Theosophist*, a monthly magazine "devoted to Universal Brotherhood, the Study of Eastern literature and occult science," the first number of which appeared in the fall of 1892. It was a journal destined to become a veritable organ of the Literary Revival. In nearly every issue were stories, poetry, essays by AE, John Eglinton, Charles Weekes, Charles Johnston, Fred J. Dick.

> As writers, editors and publishers they are directly and indirectly responsible for a considerable part of the best work in Anglo-Irish literature.[23]

The volume of AE's verse and prose was not great, but it was one-pointed, deep, and continuously consistent in its theosophic and mystic belief. He was ever loyal to the inspiration given him by H.P.B. In the main his cosmogony, psychology, and ethics were derived from her teachings as given in her great works *The Secret Doctrine, Isis Unveiled, The Voice of the Silence,* as well as W.Q. Judge's many articles in *The Path* magazine and his posthumous work *Letters That Have Helped Me.*[24] The great ideas of the Theosophy of all ages ring clear and resonant. AE declares:

> I account it the highest wisdom to know this of the living universe that there is no destiny in it other than we make for ourselves. . . .
>
> I believe that for myself and for all of us there has been an eternity of being.[25]

Man, he asserts,

> is the originator of his own fate, that countless aeons ago the immortal element in each one deliberately decided to embark upon the hazardous journey which would involve numberless incarnations, a multitude of painful experiences, forgetfulness of the very goal for which the sacrifice had been made. Ultimately, however, the destiny of every man would be accomplished, that is, to become the ruler of a star; the "foreseeing spirit would shine at last like the stars of morning triumphant among the Sons of God."[26]

Merchant in his comprehensive thesis on AE paraphrases his "Irish Promethean's" theosophic philosophy.

> The material universe is an emanation of the divine will and all things are sustained by it. Dead matter does not exist, for all things vibrate with the life which is imparted by the unfaltering will. The earth, for example, is a living entity. It is the outer garment of a being that is also evolving. Ordinarily we perceive but the outer form, and say that matter is inert and lifeless; but for the seer, the person who becomes aware of a higher dimension of being, the sustaining life, without which matter would be inconceivable, is evident.
>
> Law rules all things—from the birth of a star or the creation of a solar system, to the ordered pattern of a snowflake. The motions of the planets in their courses, the evolution of a solar system through the long passage of time—naught is haphazard or meaningless. This belief in the essential orderliness of the universe is summed up in one word—karma. Never for a moment did AE relinquish or doubt this hypothesis that eternal justice governs the universe. Every cause has its appropriate effect—and the world as we see it is the effect of a mighty will that created it.[27]

AE believed religion and science complement each other,

that they are not, as orthodox education teaches today, irreconcilable.

> The more the scientist knows about religion the subtler is his exploration of Nature likely to be. The more the religions know about science the more likely are they to make their doctrine appear a true interpretation of the Universe.[28]

Indeed it was AE's belief that a new religion would eventually emerge, a blending of the philosophy of East and West, a truly universal religion. To George Moore he said:

> The fault I find with Christianity is that it is no more than a code of morals, whereas three things are required for a religion—a cosmogony, a psychology, and a moral code.[29]

AE found these three in the Theosophy of H.P. Blavatsky. "Cosmogony," he writes,

> describes the background of man's life on earth. It concerns the creation of the universe, and the purpose of life. Psychology deals more specifically with the mind of man—how he can use it to shape the course of his destiny, and attain liberation. Ethics emphasizes those rules of conduct which one should observe—the actual way of life which would follow from a careful consideration of cosmogony and psychology. In other words, cosmogony indicates why the world was created; psychology investigates the limitations and powers of the human mind; ethics points out how men should act in such a world.[30]

Above all, perhaps, AE believed in meditation. He practiced it all his life, not—we are inclined to believe—a meditation consisting of repetition of mantras at set times, of traditional postures, of controlled breathings, but a brooding on the great ideas, the sustaining inner life of all religions and philosophies; the creation and abiding self-generated "atmosphere" or thought-direction which would surround the poet throughout all his daily routine and from day to night and night to day and day to year throughout his lifetime. A meditation which AE especially recommended

> was first mentioned by the Buddha several thousands of years ago. It was an attempt to develop an attitude of good will towards all human beings. Friend and foe are both included, inasmuch as such distinctions are spiritually invalid. As AE writes, the Buddha told his disciples "to let our minds pervade the whole wide world with heart of love." The result of this meditation is to break down the wall which separates our ego from that of others. Our separation from them is then seen to be an illusion. . . . An unbreakable bond unites us with all other human beings and the greater our love, the more our lives interpenetrate that of others.[31]

With the death of AE and most of his confrères in Theosophy, the spear-point of the Irish Renaissance lost its force. A younger generation of writers had indeed been inspired by him, such as Padraic Colum, James Stephens, Seumas O'Sullivan, Susan Mitchell, Alice Milligan, Ella Young, and others, but their writings do not carry the same theosophic message. Much less did Joyce's. In fact Joyce did not consider himself "a product of the Irish Renaissance."[32] He had met AE and AE appreciated his brilliance, but felt "a little sadly" about his burying himself "in a jungle of words."[33] He readily acknowledged that Joyce had created a new style and influenced many, but he questioned the worthwhileness and soundness of the content of his writing.

And so the Celtic wave of enlightenment passed. As we look back and review that drama and how hearts were moved and minds illuminated, we ask: What teaching brought by H.P. Blavatsky stirred most deeply those Irish disciples? It wasn't so much the scientific aspect of *The Secret Doctrine*, though they did not deny its inherent science. It was the grand cosmogony that fascinated them, the idea of active intelligences behind all manifestation, star and atom; the illusive nature of matter that appealed to the natural magic they saw in the universe; the divinity at the heart of stone and flower and beast and man and galaxy; the assurance that man, already in his essence a god, would someday live and act and *be* that god; the whirling appearance and disappearance of universes, their rebirth on a higher evolutionary plane. They quickly grasped and were enthralled with the idea that the Neo-platonists, as the ancient Egyptians, the Chaldeans, the old Hindus, and their own ancient bards, drank at the same Source of Ancient Wisdom as did H.P.B., and that therefore what she brought and so bountifully and explicitly explained in the pages of *Isis Unveiled* and *The Secret Doctrine* were universal truths, not narrowed down to a single country or community.

All this they were able to draw in inspiration from the Source and make immediate application of to Ireland. It is the immediacy of this recognition of ancient teaching and its application on a national scale that lends such stunning drama and visual excitement to the whole period known as the Celtic Literary Revival. What Ireland experienced will ever be unique because of two vital factors that then played their mutually necessary roles. H.P.B. was alive and teaching; and Ireland as a nation was ready. H.P.B. and her colleague of the T.S., W.Q. Judge, and the ancient Theosophy of the ages, were there amongst them, vibrant, challenging, inspiring. What an opportunity! Ireland seized it.

My literature professor of many years ago, Kenneth Morris, himself not Irish but proudly Welsh, who as a young man knew and appreciated AE, declared with characteristic Celtic flourish that "the whole Celtic Renaissance was born in the rooms of the Dublin Theosophical Society." He ended his series of lectures, "The Crest-Wave of Evolution," given at Theosophical University, Point Loma, California, in 1918-19, with the declaration:

> The Celtic Renaissance is only a promise. Theosophy only bides its time until the storm of the world has subsided. It will take hold upon marvelous Ireland yet. . . . When she had but a feeble candle of Truth, in those ancient times, she stood up a light-giver to the nations; how will it be when she has the bright sun shining in her heart?[34]

Who can say Morris's prophetic tongue nay? This much we know: the inner light that the Celtic Movement radiated it owed in strictest sense to H.P.Blavatsky, or rather to the persuasive power of the Eternal Truths she enunciated; and whatever new movement, born of an outburst of similar creative activity, may flash across the historical stage in some better aeon to come—in Ireland again or in another land—we may know it also will owe its power and effulgence to that same solar Energy H.P.B. drew on and partook of and was representative of.

> ...we may find scores of societies, groups, cults, periodicals, all influenced, consciously, by the heritage of idea—the agelong wisdom—that H.P.B. restored to the West. . . . The Intelligences that despatched H.P.B. as Messenger to her Age did not err. Her Mission has been accomplished. She changed the current of European thought, directing it toward the sun.[35]

The Celtic heart knew. See how it knew and took command!

Addendum

H.P.B.'s close interest in the welfare of the Dublin Lodge of the Theosophical Society is attested by the 1891 New Year card designed and drawn by her and sent the Lodge with greetings in English, Gaelic, and Russian. One side of the card in her handwriting reads "To the 'Dublin Lodge' of the TS Happy New Year 1891 & CEAD MILLE FAILTHA (A Hundred Thousand Welcomes) S Novim Godom, S Novim Schastyem (Wishing you a New Year with New Happiness) from your servant H.P.B." In the left-hand top corner written diagonally are the words: "This is the back of the card; the front is behind!"

The other side, with a border of Egyptian hieroglyphics, the rim of a rising sun, the Winged Disc, a snake or serpent representing the *S* superimposed over the *T* [TS] and a lotus design of three symbols, has the words in capital letters: "NEW YEAR'S GREETINGS"; and boxed on the right-hand side: "Can there be bliss when all that lives must suffer? Shalt thou be saved and hear the whole world cry?" —*Voice of the Silence.*

A facsimile of this is published in C.J. Ryan's *H.P. Blavatsky and the Theosophical Movement*, facing p. 276.

Notes

1. Boyd, Ernest A.: *Ireland's Literary Renaissance*, p. 213.
2. Bragdon, Claude: *Merely Players*, p. 44.
3. Quoted by Bragdon, *loc. cit.*
4. Boyd, Ernest A.: *Ireland's Literary Renaissance*, pp. 212-13 *et seq*.
5. Ryan, Charles J., *H.P. Blavatsky and the Theosophical Movements*, p. 275.
6. Morris, Lloyd, *Celtic Dawn*, p. 25.
7. Merchant, Francis, *AE: An Irish Promethean*, p. 215.
8. Dunsany: quoted in a letter to Merchant, op. cit. Appendix A.
9. Ibid.
10. Gwynn, Stephen: *Irish Literature and Drama in the English Language*, quoted by Merchant, ibid.
11. Legouis and Cazamian: *A History of English Literature*, quoted by Merchant, op. cit.
12. Young, Ella: *Flowering Dusk*, p. 31.
13. Moore, George: *Salve*, p. 21.
14. Boyd, E.A.: op. cit., Ch. X "The Dublin Mystics."
15. Bax, Clifford: *Rosemary for Remembrance*, Letter by AE, p. 56.
16. Norman, F.H.: *The Theosophical Forum*, Feb. 1936.
17. Merchant, F.: op. cit., p. 17.
18. W.Q. Judge.
19. *The Canadian Theosophist*, XVI, pp. 193-94, Aug. 1935.
20. Eglinton, John: *A Memoir of AE*, pp. 164-65; also quoted in *Reincarnation in World Thought* by J. Head and C.L. Cranston, p. 152.
21. Boyd, E.A.: op. cit., pp. 214-15.
22. Boyd, E.A.: op. cit.; Merchant, op. cit.
23. Boyd, E.A.: op. cit.
24. Norman, H.F.: *The Theosophical Forum*, Feb. 1936.
25. AE: *The Candle of Vision*.
26. AE: *Imaginations and Reveries*, 'The Hero in Man,' p. 145.
27. Merchant, F.: op. cit., pp. 25-26.
28. Gibbon, Monk: *The Living Torch*, p. 210.
29. Moore, George: op. cit., p. 50.
30. Merchant, F.: op. cit., pp. 21-22.
31. Merchant: op. cit., p. 32.
32. Lady Gregory: *Journals*, p. 119.
33. AE: *The Living Torch*, p. 139; also quoted in Merchant: op. cit., p. 220.

34. Morris, Kenneth: *The Theosophical Path*, XXI, July 1921, "The Irish Illumination."
35. Neuberg, Victor B.: *The Aryan Path*, V, 277-78, 1934.

20
The Influence of H. P. Blavatsky on Modern Art

GERRIT MUNNIK

History will eventually tell us to what extent Theosophy and the work of H.P. Blavatsky have influenced a number of art movements and schools, especially in the first quarter of this century. Even now, half a century later, the biographies and writings of the artists of these groups reveal their contacts with theosophical literature or with The Theosophical Society itself. Among them are such great names as Piet Mondrian, Wassily Kandinsky, Paul Klee, and Malevich, all artists of world fame who have contributed to the founding of a new philosophy in the "World of Art."

It is now very clear that a definite change took place in the "World of Art" practically simultaneously with the revealing of the inner truths in *The Secret Doctrine* by H.P. Blavatsky. André Malraux, France's Minister of Cultural Affairs and eminent writer in the field of art, begins the introduction of his book, *The Metamorphosis of the Gods*, with this statement: "It is now common knowledge that a new age dawned and its painting came to birth somewhere round 1860."[1]

As H.P. Blavatsky in her day traced back to their inner source the truths of religions and philosophies, of symbols and allegories, so the artists of that period began searching for means to express inner values rather than outward appearances. The change was gradual at first, but it was accelerated as inner values were discovered and new methods explored.

Not to conform with the visual had at one time seemed unintelligent; now the symbolic art of Egypt, Mexico, Asia, and even Africa were being displayed in the museums of the world, emancipated from their reputation as barbaric artifacts and recognized as great works of art with deep spiritual values.

Art was no more solely a means of communicating emotions, as Tolstoy defined it, but "The feelings we experience when gazing at pieces of great art . . . can hardly be conveyed by words associated with pleasure, even the delight of the eye, or with the traditional idea of beauty . . . the emotions which they inspire in us are of a quite different kind."[2]

The Impressionists were the first to explore that inner light at the end of the last century. They achieved certain effects by the use of pure color, while the lines began to adopt a different function. Forms were not so much to be copied from nature, but were purposely distorted in order to emphasize inner characteristics. Later, these distortions would even evolve into symbols and, still later, disappear altogether from the world of appearances and become pure abstractions. An attempt was made to come in touch with primordial creative forces described in the ancient oriental literature which H.P. Blavatsky expounded in *The Secret Doctrine*. It was the teachings of the parent doctrine that inspired the above mentioned artists to preserve them in their work.

"The public must be made acquainted with the efforts of many world-adepts, of initiated poets and writers in the classics of every age, to preserve in the records of humanity the knowledge at least of the existence of such a philosophy, if not actually of its tenets."[3]

Among artist groups who incorporated these tenets in their philosophy and their work, those of the avant-garde review *De-Stijl* in Holland come foremost. This periodical was founded in 1917 by Piet Mondrian. Besides Mondrian, the architect De Bazel was an active member of The Theosophical Society in Holland. Many outstanding buildings were designed by him, and he contributed greatly to the development of the so-called "Nieuwe Zakelijkheid," the modern trend in architecture, furniture design, and weaving. De Bazel may not be as world famous as Mondrian but this may be because the reputation of architects is usually limited to the areas where their work can be observed.

Piet Mondrian joined The Theosophical Society in 1909. Like many artists, he had a sensitive and mystical nature, and he learned to evaluate his experiences through theosophical teachings. He was an ardent reader of the works of H.P. Blavatsky, Annie Besant, and Rudolph Steiner. Eduard Schure's *Les Grands Initiés* made a lasting impression on him.

Martin James wrote: "Mondrian's theosophy was more than a personal quirk. Several artists around 1910 sought through it deeper and more universal values, meaning behind meaning, new dimensions to understanding. The thought that the ancient seers perceived and imparted a veiled wisdom, that behind the many guises of truth there is *one* truth, is partly based on Oriental and Neo-Platonic ideas. It easily links with the romantic and symbolist theory of illumination, which gives the artist extraordinary, even occult power of insight into the nature of the world, the reality behind appearances—a new content for art."[4]

H.P. Blavatsky certainly regarded great artists of the world as belonging to those who have insight when she wrote: ". . . in the beginning of times, the Rulers of Mankind, when incarnated as Kings of the 'Divine Dynasties,' they gave the first impulse to civilization, and directed the mind with which they had endued men, to the inventions and perfection of all the Arts and Sciences. . . . To these . . . is ascribed the invention of letters (the Deva-nagari, or alphabet and language of the Gods), of law and legislature, of architecture. . . ."[5]

In his search for truth and liberation we see clearly in Mondrian's work how he gradually discarded the unessentials in form and color, emphasizing only that which speaks of the real and the eternal. He drove his principles to the ultimate, sacrificing all that did not belong to the basic creative power, leaving only the vertical and the horizontal lines and the three primary colors, yellow, red, and blue for the mode of his song. With these bare basics he made the attempt to channel on our human level the cosmic creative forces which the great god Shiva exercises in his several transformations, after first having acted as the Great Destroyer.

". . . Shiva, as Shvetalohita, the Root-Kumara, from moon colored *white*; in his next transformation, he is *red* . . .; in the third *yellow*; in the fourth *black*."[6] Blue and black are often identical in meaning: darkness made visible.

One wonders whether Mondrian was conscious of the four stages of the alchemical process, namely, *black*, the latent force in primordial matter; *white*, the first transmutation, mercury; *red*, the passion, sulphur; and *yellow*, the final gold.

In the first issues of *De Stijl*, Mondrian wrote down the basics of his principles which obviously were inspired by theosophical teachings. The most important were: the creation of a collective style; the integration of arts and techniques, especially in architecture. Forms should derive from inner life rather than from exterior vision and be limited to the horizontal-vertical order only; colors to the three primary and the three non-colors—white, black, and grey.

These were the new rules for aesthetics, based on pure relationship of lines and pure color, the only means capable of a pure manifestation of the universal force which is to be found in all things.

These rules appear to us now quite rigid, and in time other artists of the group became less dogmatic. Mondrian, however, remained faithful till the end. The fundamentals of Theosophy and the teachings of *The Secret Doctrine* were his strongest inspiration in establishing his abstract art. It is said that after his death only three books were among his possessions—all theosophical works.[7]

Two other famous artists whose work and thinking were strongly influenced by the theosophical philosophy were

Wassily Kandinsky and Paul Klee, both connected for a time as teachers in the Bauhaus in Weimar and later in Dessau, Germany. Kandinsky himself wrote: "[Spiritual] methods are still alive and in use among nations whom we, from the height of our knowledge, have been accustomed to regard with pity and scorn. To such nations belong the people of India, who from time to time confront our scholars with problems which we have either passed without notice or brushed aside. Madame Blavatsky was the first person, after a life of many years in India, to see a connection between these "savages" and our "civilization." In that moment rose one of the most important spiritual movements, one which numbers a great many people today, and has even assumed a material form in the Theosophical Society. This Society consists of groups who seek to approach the problem of the spirit by way of *inner* knowledge. Their methods, in opposition to positivism, derive from an ancient wisdom, which has been formulated with relative precision. . . ."[8]

Not only in his thinking was Kandinsky inclined to the East. He actually had Oriental blood in his veins, and his work emanates these qualities in both color and form. He was not interested in the visual arts alone; his ideal was to incorporate all the arts in one universal symphony in which sound can be seen and color and rhythm heard in a spiritual state of consciousness. There are two kinds of art forms, he said, those of today and those of the past. The first is external and has no future. The second is internal and contains the seed of the future.

Jean Gasson describes the idealism of Kandinsky: "The idealism of young Kandinsky was influenced to some extent by the theory of Rudolf Steiner, a fascinating man whose lectures he attended, as well as by the doctrines of Annie Besant and Madame Blavatsky. He was also for a time inspired by Edward Schuré's *Grands Initiés*.[9]

As Rudolf Steiner experimented with color in healing, so did Kandinsky try to coordinate a system of analogies between form-giving and color and tone. The horizontal line expresses cold and its color is black, while the vertical is the opposite—warmth. The intermediaries between the two call for color. The right angle is red, the circle blue. The curved line expresses tension and its repetition indicates rhythm. As a theosophist he was keenly conscious of the occult meaning and influences of the different colors, and also in his linear designs he succeeded in expressing meaningful powers. His interplay of lines is often like a personal calligraphy, mostly abstract, but vibrant with the clarity of Chinese ideograms and symbols—with inner meaning.

Kandinsky shared his new philosophy of the "World of Art" with Paul Klee, his friend and associate in the Bauhaus school. Of the two, Klee was perhaps the more mystical, as he was always aware of an inner power which urged him on in his creative search for truth and liberation. For he wrote in his diary in 1918: "My hand is entirely the tool of a distant will."[10] His emphasis was placed on origins, on the return to basic forces in cosmos and microcosmos. His work relates in that respect to spontaneous children's drawings, or to the caveman's designs and symbols. For "the end is already latent in the beginning."[11]

Klee was also a musician, and in his lectures he often touched upon the intimate relationship of all the arts.[12] His colors relate clearly to the sounds in nature, and in his linear structure he often expresses a rhythm related to the musical counterpoint. In this repetition of lines and themes he combines, in a subtle way, dance, music, and design. Even musical notes and bars and keys often suggest this universality in his work, as he combines calligraphy and pictorial forms in a manner similar to that of the masters of the Sung dynasty in China.

Was Klee perhaps aware of the existence of a mystic language used in the inner worlds as a means of communication? A language of color and sound to which one of the Masters refers: "How could you make yourself understood by, command in fact, those semi-intelligent Forces, whose means of communication with us are not through spoken words, but through sounds and colors in correlation between the vibration of the two? It is this "correlation" that is unknown to Modern Science, although it has been many times explained by the Alchemists."[13]

Klee was very much interested in the new dodecaphonic music of Arnold Schönberg and he applied this system to his own theory of color, so definitely linking the two arts together in a limitless variety of possibilities. He talked about chromatic color scales in major and minor keys. He considered rhythm as a spatial and temporal value, relating it to the abstraction of numbers.

In this relation, H.P. Blavatsky speaks as follows: "Esoteric Science teaches that every sound in the visible world awakens its corresponding sound in the invisible realms, and arouses to action some force or other on the Occult side of Nature. Moreover, every sound corresponds to a color and a number (a potency spiritual, psychic or physical) and to a sensation on some plane."[14]

It is still premature to evaluate the full impact of Theosophy on the pioneers of the modern art movement mentioned here. Many of the writings of the artists have not yet been published; many of the notes of their pupils have not yet been worked out—pupils who are continuing in their footsteps.

Neither Klee nor Kandinsky claimed that he had founded or explored in all directions a new art which was fully matured. But it is clear that these artists planted the seed for new expressions on levels of human consciousness that had not previously been touched—levels that will eventually lead to a new future. They had this in common with H.P. Blavatsky's teaching, a teaching which has only partially lifted the veil but which has promised even greater revealings of the truth in the future.

Notes

1. Malraux, André, *The Metamorphosis of the Gods*, p. 1.
2. Ibid., p. 1.
3. Blavatsky, H.P., *The Secret Doctrine*, Adyar ed., vol. 1, p. 66.
4. *Art News*, 1957.
5. Blavatsky, H.P., op. cit., vol. 3, p. 363.

6. Ibid., vol. 2, p. 251.
7. Seuphor, Michel, *Piet Mondrian: Life and Work*, p. 309.
8. Kandinsky, Wassily, *Concerning the Spiritual in Art*, p. 32.
9. Gasson, Jean, *Wassily Kandinsky—the Man and His Work*, p. 18.
10. Grohmann, Will, *Paul Klee*, p. 214.
11. Ibid., p. 214.
12. In this connection, it may be of interest that another musician, Alexander Scriabin (1872-1915) was deeply interested in Theosophy, and this interest is said to have greatly influenced his later works, especially Symphony No. 3 *The Divine Poem*, (1905), *The Poem of Ecstasy* (1908), and *Prometheus: A Poem of Fire* (1913).
13. Blavatsky, H.P., op. cit., vol. 2, p. 239 (footnote quoted from *The Occult World*, by A.P. Sinnett)
14. Ibid., vol. 5, p. 431.

21
Kandinsky and Theosophy

JOHN ALGEO

Wassily Kandinsky is universally acknowledged to be one of the most important artists of the twentieth century. Because his nonobjective paintings were early and well-known examples of the genre and because his writings about art attracted many readers including other artists, he has even been called the originator of abstract art. He was certainly one of the first and most influential of modern painters in the abstract or nonrepresentational style.

Kandinsky's work, both his practice and his theory, can also be viewed as an artistic expression of theosophical ideas. The extent to which Kandinsky was influenced by Theosophy and sought deliberately to find an artistic correlate for theosophical teachings is a matter of dispute. Some art critics believe that the influence of theosophical thinking on Kandinsky's work is clear; others minimize such influence and look instead for other sources of his ideas and techniques.[1] It has been shown, however, that Kandinsky had contact with Theosophy through books and lectures, and it can be shown that his writing and painting are in accord with theosophical principles.

That Kandinsky knew of and had a high regard for the theosophical worldview is demonstrated by this remark in *Concerning the Spiritual in Art*:

> Mme. Blavatsky was the first person, after a life of many years in India, to see a connection between these "savages" and our "civilization." From that moment there began a tremendous spiritual movement which today includes a large number of people and has even assumed a material form in the *Theosophical Society*. This society consists of groups who seek to approach the problem of the spirit by way of *inner* knowledge. The theory of Theosophy which serves as the basis to this movement was set out by Blavatsky in the form of a catechism in which the pupil receives definite answers to his questions from the theosophical point of view [*The Key to Theosophy*, 1889]. Theosophy, according to Blavatsky, is synonymous with *eternal truth*. (13)

The present essay is a small contribution to the recognition of Wassily Kandinsky's sympathy with theosophical ideas by noting their presence in his book on the theory of art: *Concerning the Spiritual in Art (über das Geistige in der Kunst).* The theory Kandinsky puts forth in it is harmonious with Theosophy and incorporates concepts that are central to theosophical thought. Kandinsky wrote this work in 1910; it was first published in late 1911 or early 1912 and was translated into English in 1914. There are several versions of the work in German and Russian, as well as several English translations.[2] In it Kandinsky demonstrates a considerable knowledge of Theosophy and expresses various ideas that have theosophical analogues. Kandinsky's ideas may well have other, nontheosophical analogues as well—but the similarities with theosophical teachings are too numerous and too extensive not to suggest that Kandinsky derived some of his ideas from Theosophy or, at the very least, found in Theosophy a welcome confirmation and explanation of his own view of the world.

Spirit versus Matter

The very title of the book *Concerning the Spiritual in Art* and its dominant theme are centrally relevant to Theosophy. The book is about Kandinsky's belief in the importance to art of the "spiritual." By *spiritual* Kandinsky means 'conscious, aware, purposeful, meaningful'; the word does not denote a vague religious ideal, but a quite precise concept that stresses the presence of consciousness and purpose in otherwise supposedly dead, unconscious matter.

Kandinsky wrote this book, as he painted his pictures, to combat the "nightmare of materialism," which he associated with despair born of "lack of purpose and aim," thus turning life into "a senseless game." In a passage omitted from the Russian version of his essay, Kandinsky associated materialism with atheism, often disguised as orthodox religion; with conformity in political ideas; with socialism in economics; with positivism in science; and with naturalism or realism in art (10-11). For Kandinsky, naturalistic, representational art depicts only the surface appearance of things and thus loses the inner meaning that he sought to express in his abstractions.

Materialist art is preoccupied with the "how" of art, with technique and with art for art's sake. Spiritual, that is, conscious, purposeful art, is concerned instead with "what," the meaning of things (8). This way of looking at representational versus abstract art is a reversal of that fostered by traditional art criticism, which sees representation as "what" and abstraction as "how." However, Kandinsky was no fin de siecle esthete. He regarded art without content as trivial, unworthy of serious consideration:

> If we . . . devote ourselves purely to combination of pure colour and abstract form, we shall produce works which are mere decorations, which are suited to neckties or carpets. (47)

Kandinsky classified his own paintings into three groups, partly reflecting their kind of meaning (57):

1. Impressions: "a direct impression of outward nature, expressed in purely artistic form." In these paintings, objects are still recognizable, although not in a narrowly realistic form; they represent the impressions the artist has of objects.

2. Improvisations: "a largely unconscious, spontaneous expression of inner character, the non-material nature." These paintings contain no recognizable objects, but

colored shapes by which the artist expresses his own feelings; they are "improvised," that is, done without conscious planning and preparation.

3. Compositions: "an expression of a slowly formed inner feeling, tested and worked over repeatedly and almost pedantically" (Motherwell 77). These paintings include recognizable objects, but ones that have been "stripped" and "veiled." A stripped object is one whose representation has been simplified to an outline of the essential features of the object, without detail. A veiled object is one placed in a context where it is unexpected or amid colors that hide it. These paintings are carefully constructed, and Kandinsky often made a series of studies leading up to a canvas. The results may look casual, but are the result of detailed planning. Of these paintings, Kandinsky said, "Reason, consciousness, purpose play an overwhelming part."

Kandinsky's "compositions" are his most important paintings, and they are the ones that express most fully "reason, consciousness, purpose." They are the most meaningful of his works. Nevertheless, Kandinsky cautions that meaning is to be found in everything:

> It is never literally true that any form is meaningless and "says nothing." Every form in the world says something. But its message often fails to reach us, and even if it does, full understanding is often withheld from us. (29n)

Kandinsky's insistence on the presence of consciousness and meaning in art and his rejection of materialism, which includes artistic realism, echoes H.P. Blavatsky's rejection of materialism in *The Secret Doctrine*. In the preface to that work, she described its aim as fourfold, of which the first was "to show that Nature is not 'a fortuitous concurrence of atoms,' and to assign to man his rightful place in the scheme of the Universe" (p. viii).

For Blavatsky, as for Kandinsky, the flaw of materialism is its view of ultimate reality as consisting of dead matter, without consciousness or purpose. "Spirit" is synonymous with the latter. Kandinsky concluded his theoretical statement of the aim of art with a vision of its future:

> I should like to remark finally that, in my opinion, we are fast approaching a time of reasoned and conscious composition, in which the painter will be proud to declare his work constructional—this in contrast to the claim of the impressionists that they could explain nothing, that their art came by inspiration. We have before us an age of conscious creation, and this new spirit in painting is going hand in hand with thought towards an *epoch of the great spiritual.* (Motherwell 77)

Art is to become increasingly a conscious expression; art and thought together are becoming more self-aware and will serve to increase self-awareness in others. A time of significantly increased self-awareness is what Kandinsky means by the "epoch of the great spiritual." In *The Secret Doctrine, maha-buddhi* (literally, "the great spiritual") is another name for what is also called *mahat*, the cosmic equivalent of self-consciousness in the human being, the divine mind (1: 334, 451). Kandinsky anticipated a time when maha-buddhi, the great enlightenment or awareness, would be the normal state of consciousness; and he thought that art would play a role in bringing that time into existence.

The Inner Life and the One Life

Kandinsky found all things, even supposedly dead matter, vital and alive. Thus he praised Cézanne for his perception of the inner life of things:

> Cézanne made a living thing out of a teacup, or rather in a teacup he realized the existence of something alive. He raised still life to such a point that it ceased to be inanimate.
>
> He painted these things as he painted human beings, because he was endowed with the gift of divining the inner life in everything. (17)

The casual reader might mistake these words for metaphor. But they are intended literally. Cézanne did not simply paint a teacup with such skill that it seemed to be alive—that is not what Kandinsky is saying. Rather he says that Cézanne "realized the existence of something alive." Cézanne captured on canvas something real—the life of the "inanimate" because "he was endowed with the gift of divining" it. Teacups, like all objects, have a life in them. Only the diviner, the seer, can perceive it.

For Kandinsky, the perception through art of the inner life of things was akin to a mystical experience. In his autobiography he tells of that perception:

> Everything "dead" trembled. Not only the stars, moon, woods, flowers of which the poets sing, but also a cigarette butt lying in the ashtray, a patient white trouser button looking up from a puddle in the street, a submissive bit of bark that an ant drags through the high grass in its strong jaws to uncertain but important destinations, a page of a calendar toward which the conscious hand reaches to tear it forcibly from the warm companionship of the remaining block of pages—everything shows me its face, its innermost being, its secret soul, which is more often silent than heard. Thus every still and every moving point (= line) became equally alive and revealed its soul to me.[3]

As Kandinsky put it in an essay "On the Question of Form": "Even dead matter is living spirit."[4]

In her "Summing Up," half way through the first volume of *The Secret Doctrine* (1:274), Blavatsky writes:

> Everything in the Universe, throughout all its kingdoms, is *conscious*: *i.e.,* endowed with a consciousness of its own kind and on its own plane of perception. We men must remember that because *we* do not perceive any signs—which we can recognize—of consciousness, say, in stones, we have no right to say that *no consciousness exists there.* There is no such thing as either "dead" or "blind" matter, as there is no "Blind" or "Unconscious" Law.

The omnipresence of life in matter is both a theosophical doctrine and a principle of art in Kandinsky's theory and practice.

Self-Knowledge, Maya, and Synesthesia

Realistic art is stuck in the surface appearance of things. It is only as artists strive "towards the abstract, the non-material" that they approach true knowledge of the world and of themselves. By such striving, "consciously or unconsciously they are obeying Socrates' command—Know thyself" (19). In the work of art, "the more obvious is the separation from nature, the more likely is the inner meaning to be pure and unhampered" (50).

The theory of abstract art—that the realism of surface appearances is misleading—is the artistic correlate of the theosophical doctrine of maya—that the world of perception is an impermanent illusion in comparison with the underlying noumenon:

> The Universe is called, with everything in it, *Maya*, because all is temporary therein, from the ephemeral life of a fire-fly to that of the Sun. Compared to the eternal immutability of the *One*, and the changelessness of that Principle, the Universe, with its evanescent ever-changing forms, must be necessarily, in the mind of a philosopher, no better than a will-o'-the-wisp. (*SD* 1:274)

When the arts are limited to the manifold variety of surface phenomena, they are strikingly different from one another. However, as each of the arts rises out of the limits of representational materiality, it approaches all of the others. Music is already one of the least material, least representational of arts; therefore, it is an art to which others, such as painting, must assimilate. However, in some ways, painting is in advance of even music, for the latter is restricted to presentation in time, whereas a picture can be grasped atemporally, its whole meaning conveyed at a moment.

Synesthesia, the unification of sensory impressions, by which colors are heard and sounds are seen, is what one would expect to find as consciousness is raised from the multiplicity of the phenomenal world to the unity of the noumenal world. And unity is the cardinal theosophical principle, reiterated in many ways by Blavatsky:

> The radical unity of the ultimate essence of each constituent part of compounds in Nature—from Star to mineral atom, from the highest Dhyan Chohan to the

> smallest infusoria, in the fullest acceptation of the term, and whether applied to the spiritual, intellectual, or physical worlds—this is the one fundamental law in Occult Science. (*SD* 1:120)
>
> The fundamental Law in that system [of the Secret Doctrine], the central point from which all emerged, around and toward which all gravitates, and upon which is hung the philosophy of the rest, is the One homogeneous divine *Substance-Principle*, the one radical cause. (*SD* 1:273)

In harmony with the concept of an ultimate unity, Kandinsky sees art as rising toward that unity. As the arts approach one another, not by superficial imitation, but rather by a fundamental growing together, they become increasingly strong in spiritual values, that is, they become more revelatory of the inner nature of things, of the artist, and of the observer:

> And so the arts are encroaching one upon another, and from a proper use of this encroachment will rise the art that is truly monumental. Every man who steeps himself in the spiritual possibilities of his art is a valuable helper in the building of the spiritual pyramid which will some day reach to heaven. (20)

The monumental art, rich in spiritual possibilities, is also a unified art in which sensory impressions are unified by synesthesia. The experience of sensory conflation may be an ordinary one; Kandinsky mentions the case of one man who could not eat a certain kind of sauce without tasting "blue"—that is, seeing a blue color (24). But it may also be an extraordinary experience. In his autobiography, Kandinsky tells of "two experiences which stamped my entire life and which shook me to the marrow." One was seeing a painting by Monet in which he could recognize no object. The other was hearing a performance of Wagner's *Lohengrin* during which he "saw" the sounds:

> The violins, the deep bass tones, and, most especially, the wind instruments embodied for me then the whole impact of the hour of dusk. I saw all my colors in my mind's eye.

> Wild, almost insane lines drew themselves before me. I did not dare use the expression that Wagner had painted "my hour" musically. But it became entirely clear to me that art in general is much more powerful than I had realized. (26)

Later Kandinsky was himself to write a stage composition, *The Yellow Sound*, integrating sound and sight.

Periods and Cycles

Kandinsky's mention of the epoch of the great spiritual at the end of *Concerning the Spiritual in Art* balances the opening of that book, in which he states that "every work of art is the child of its age. . . . It follows that each period of culture produces an art of its own which can never be repeated" (1). Kandinsky views history as a succession of periods of culture, each with its own unique style of art and its own unique characteristics.

The theosophical view of history, the primary subject of the second volume of *The Secret Doctrine*, is fully in accord with Kandinsky's view. To be sure, Theosophy emphasizes the cyclical pattern of life:

> This second assertion of the Secret Doctrine is the absolute universality of that law of periodicity, of flux and reflux, ebb and flow, which physical science has observed and recorded in all departments of nature. (*SD* 1:17)

However, theosophical cyclicity is not a strict repetition of earlier experiences, but rather a repetition with cumulating variation. The world changes, grows, evolves through its cycles. In each cycle, a new faculty or "principle" develops, so each cycle is unique, as Kandinsky maintained.

The cycles include vast periods of planetary evolution called "rounds" and shorter, but still extremely long periods of human evolution called "races." According to the evolutionary scheme of *The Secret Doctrine*, our planet is now in a period of its evolution in which passion and desire are dominant, and our species is in a period in which intellect is dominant. The whole evolutionary pattern has cycles within cycles, each emphasizing its own characteristic. And thus at any given time there is a unique combination of characteristics, "which can never be repeated."

The Ancients and Primitivism

Past cycles represent not lesser forms of culture and intelligence than ours, but different forms. In some ways the perceptions of reality and the styles of art of the past may have much to teach us. And in some ways we may resonate inwardly with the worldviews of earlier eras. Kandinsky says that when such inner resonance exists,

> the logical result will be a revival of the external forms which served to express those inner feelings in an earlier age. An example of this today is our sympathy, our spiritual relationship, with the Primitives. Like ourselves, these artists sought to express in their work only internal truths, renouncing in consequence all consideration of external form. (1)

Primitivism, a renewed respect for the value of simpler cultures, was a characteristic of early modern art exemplified, for example, in Gauguin's South Sea paintings.

Kandinsky himself saw an analogy between art turning to primitivism and modern investigators who had lost faith in the positivist methods of science turning to the ancients:

> Just as art is looking for help from the primitives, so these men are turning to half-forgotten times in order to get help from their half-forgotten methods. However, these very methods are still alive and in use among nations whom we, from the height of our knowledge, have been accustomed to regard with pity and scorn. To such nations belong the Indians, who from time to time confront those learned in our civilization with problems we have either passed by unnoticed or brushed aside with superficial words and explanations.

Kandinsky saw the new interest in and respect for Indic philosophy and literature, which were being fostered by Theosophy and the writings of H.P. Blavatsky, as a parallel to the attention artists were paying to primitivism.

Blavatsky herself repeatedly emphasized that modern Theosophy is no new idea or innovation, but merely a restatement of an ancient teaching that can be seen in the writings of earlier cultures, especially the Indic:

> The Secret Doctrine is the accumulated Wisdom of the Ages, and its cosmogony alone is the most stupendous and elaborate system: *e.g.*, even in the exotericism of the Puranas.

Blavatsky's book is ultimately a commentary on fragmentary passages from an "Archaic Manuscript" (1:1) and throughout her works she stresses the value of ancient wisdom and "primitive" skills. The respect for antiquity and apparently primitive cultures is a unifying attitude in Theosophy and Kandinsky's theory of art.

The Teachers

In ancient times and modern alike, humanity is blessed with certain persons having "a deep and powerful prophetic strength" and "a secret power of vision" (4), persons who see and point the way to others. In a famous metaphor, Kandinsky likened humanity to an acute-angled triangle, whose base consists of the mass of humanity. At the apex of the triangle are a few beings, and ultimately often a single one:

> His joyful vision cloaks a vast sorrow. Even those who are nearest to him in sympathy do not understand him. Angrily they abuse him as charlatan or madman. (6)

Despite the abuse and rejection, the teacher at the apex, by personal effort, succeeds in inspiring and motivating those below, so that eventually they rise toward his position. In turn they inspire those still lower in the triangle to follow, so that eventually the entire triangle moves upwards—all as the effect of the labor of the few or the one with vision at the top.

Kandinsky's triangle of humanity is theosophical in two ways. First, it envisions humanity as consisting of persons at different stages of progress, at different stages of intellectual evolution. And second, it envisions each level of humanity as aiding and assisting those less advanced to progress, with the self-sacrificing individual of sorrows, the bodhisattva, at the top, living only to raise the rest of humanity to greater spirituality—that is, to greater self-awareness. Kandinsky's triangle is a hierarchical structure, consisting of orders within orders. Elsewhere he speaks of the composition of a painting in terms that could also be applied to the composition of humanity in the triangle:

> The general composition will naturally include many little compositions which may be antagonistic to each other, though helping—perhaps by their very antagonism—the harmony of the whole. These little compositions have themselves subdivisions of varied inner meanings. (30n)

Order within order, this view of Kandinsky's closely echoes well-known theosophical teachings about the hierarchies of Dhyan Chohans and of the teachers of humanity and their students, who have forgone efforts at individual progress in order to devote themselves to the betterment of the human condition and the improvement of the state of the world.

Meliorism and Messianism

The consequence of the upward movement of the triangle and the labors of the bodhisattvas at its apex is the gradual improvement of the human condition. Kandinsky quoted with approval Blavatsky's vision of the future betterment of humankind at the end of *The Key to Theosophy*:

> The new torchbearer of truth will find the minds of men prepared for his message, a language ready for him in which to clothe the new truths he brings, an organization awaiting his arrival, which will remove the merely mechanical, material obstacles and difficulties from his path.

And then Blavatsky continues: "The earth will be a heaven in the twenty-first century in comparison with what it is now," and with these words ends her book. (13-14, quoting *Key* 307)

For Kandinsky, the improvement of the world and the human condition is the purpose of art. That improvement can result only from an increase in self-awareness, that is, an increase in spirituality. Like Blavatsky, Kandinsky saw universal and human history as governed by an evolutionary impulse that responds to purpose as well as causes.

Subtle Worlds

Although he did not develop the concept in detail, Kandinsky posited the existences of subtle worlds of matter, in which feeling and thoughts have form and existence as material entities:

> Thought which, although a product of the spirit, can be defined with positive science, is matter, but of fine and not coarse substance. (9)

Similarly, he wrote of " 'non-matter,' or matter which is not accessible to our minds" (13). In his view, and that of Theosophy, thoughts and feelings are part of the atmosphere around us. They constitute a realm of subtle matter in which we live, just as we live in the realm of gross matter that we call the physical world. We are affected by the thoughts and feelings that make up that subtle world, just as we are affected by the air and water of this physical world. We are all surrounded by an aura of that subtle emotional-mental matter:

> Frequent attempts have shown that such a spiritual atmosphere can belong not only to heroes but to any human being. Sensitives cannot, for example, remain in a room in which a person has been who is spiritually antagonistic to them, even though they know nothing of his existence. (16n)

In speaking of the atmosphere of feelings and thoughts within which we move, just as we do within the physical atmosphere, Kandinsky observes:

> For this atmosphere is like air, which can be either pure or filled with various alien elements. Not only visible actions, thoughts and feelings, with outward expression, make up this atmosphere, but secret happenings of which no one knows, unspoken thoughts, hidden feelings are also elements in it. Suicide, murder, violence, low and unworthy thoughts, hate, hostility, egotism, envy, narrow "patriotism,"

> partisanship, are elements in the spiritual atmosphere.
>
> And conversely, self-sacrifice, mutual help, lofty thoughts, love, unselfishness, joy in the success of others, humanity, justness, are the elements which slay those already enumerated as the sun slays the microbes, and restore the atmosphere to purity. (42)

The existence and nature of worlds subtler than the physical is one of the most characteristic Theosophical doctrines. Kandinsky held that the ability of art to modify the nature of those subtle environments, either directly or through the response of human beings to the physical art work, was the means by which it could further evolution, "restore the atmosphere to purity," and hasten the epoch of the Great Spiritual.

Inner Harmony and Vibration

Referring to the artistic theory and practice of Maeterlinck (another artist of the time who was heavily influenced by Theosophy), Kandinsky says:

> The word may express an inner harmony. This inner harmony springs partly, perhaps principally, from the object which it names. But if the object is not itself seen, but only its name heard, the *mind* of the hearer receives an abstract impression only, that is to say as of the object dematerialized, and a corresponding vibration is immediately set up in the *heart*. (15)

Kandinsky finds a parallel phenomenon in the leitmotifs of Wagner and the musical impressions of Debussy. The idea that the hearer resonates, vibrates in sympathy, with the content of words and music provides a model for Kandinsky's theory of the operation of visual art. In a similar way, seeing objects or pictures will cause the viewer to resonate with their meaning—to respond, by means of the vibration of matter in the subtle worlds, to the vibrations that the objects or pictures involve.

Kandinsky repeatedly talks of "vibration" as the method by which we respond to our surroundings. So in his autobiography he remembered events in his early university life that "made the strings of the soul sensitive, receptive, especially susceptible to vibration" (24). In *Concerning the Spiritual in Art*, he talks about color, form, and the object itself as involving a "corresponding vibration in the human soul" (26, 29, 32). It is easy to take such talk as metaphor of a kind prevalent in turn-of-the-century discourse. However, vibration is the theosophical explanation of how feelings and thoughts are influential on living beings, and Kandinsky could not escape being aware of that.

The theosophical view of all matter, dense and subtle, as vibrations at different frequencies within an ultimate substance provided Kandinsky with an explanation of how art could affect humanity and the world. The vibrations within our psyches and minds respond to the vibrations around us, and in turn influence those outer vibrations. Our feelings and thoughts respond to those of others, and help to shape the atmosphere of feelings and thoughts in which we all live.

This vibrational theory of perception bridges the gap between matter and spirit (consciousness). It also explains degrees of perception. Everyone perceives the physical impression of colors, and responds variously to them according to their associations.

> But to a more sensitive soul the effect of colors is deeper and intensely moving. And so we come to the second main result of looking at colors: *their psychic effect*. They produce a corresponding spiritual vibration, and it is only as a step towards this spiritual vibration that the elementary physical impression is of importance. (24)

As we learn to respond to subtler perceptions, that is, to subtler vibrations, the differences between the senses become less acute and synesthesia more pronounced. Kandinsky concludes his theoretical consideration of the psychological working of color with these words:

> *It is evident therefore that color harmony must rest only on a corresponding vibration in the human soul; and this is one of the guiding principles of the inner need.* (26)

That statement is to be taken, not metaphorically, but literally.

The Colors and the Gunas

As part of an extended discussion of the value of colors, Kandinsky takes the three primary colors as expressing three fundamental characteristics of things (37-40). In that way they are like the Hindu gunas, "strands" or qualities of matter, of which the whole universe is built in the Indic tradition.

Yellow is "the human energy which assails every obstacle blindly, and bursts forth aimlessly in every direction." It has "an insistent, aggressive character." It is parallel in abnormal human nature with "violent raving lunacy." These qualities suggest that for Kandinsky yellow is the color of the guna called *rajas* 'violent activity' by the Hindu tradition.

Blue, as the dark color, is the opposite of yellow. "The ultimate feeling it creates is one of rest. When it sinks almost to black, it echoes a grief that is hardly human." Its correspondence among the gunas is *tamas* 'inertia.'

Red is a mediating color. "The unbounded warmth of *red* has not the irresponsible appeal of yellow, but rings inwardly with a determined and powerful intensity. It glows in itself, maturely, and does not distribute its vigor aimlessly." In these qualities, Kandinsky's red parallels the guna of *sattva* 'harmony.'

Kandinsky develops the value of other colors as well, and ends with a circular color chart containing the six main chromatic variations. Of this chart he says:

> As in a great circle, a serpent biting its own tail (the symbol of eternity, of something without end) the six colors appear that make up the three main antitheses. (41)

In this comment, Kandinsky uses the serpent swallowing its own tail, which forms part of the seal of the Theosophical Society, with the same basic symbolism it has in theosophical use. It is a small matter, but shows how extensive are the parallels between Kandinsky and theosophical thought and symbolism.

The Inner Necessity and Swadharma

As Kandinsky's comment about color harmony and vibration in the human soul suggests in its final words, he believed that in each person is an inner *Notwendigkeit*—need, necessity, inevitability, essential—which ultimately determines all outward forms and actions. That inner essential is what the Hindu tradition refers to as the *swadharma* of a being—its self-nature or inner foundation. In *The Secret Doctrine*, Blavatsky speaks of it in these words:

> The Universe is worked and *guided* from *within outwards*. . . . and man—the microcosm and miniature copy of the macrocosm—is the living witness to this Universal Law and to the mode of its action. We see that every *external* motion, act, gesture, whether voluntary or mechanical, organic or mental, is produced and preceded by *internal* feeling or emotion, will or volition, and thought or mind. (1:274)

We are not merely automata reacting automatically to external pressures in sophisticated versions of the Pavlovian response. Behavioral psychology cannot explain human behavior. Our actions cannot be reduced to conditioned reflexes. An irreducible core of it is the result of an "inner necessity"; we are "guided from within outwards." The goal of evolution, of the changing spirits of the ages, is to realize the inner necessity in outer form:

> In short, the working of the inner need and the development of art is an ever-advancing expression of the eternal and objective in the terms of the periodic and subjective. (34)

William Butler Yeats, another student of H.P. Blavatsky's, put the same idea in these words: "Eternity is in love with the productions of time." In evolution, we move toward a goal; but the goal is set from within.

Inner/Outer, Esoteric/Exoteric

Kandinsky's distinction between inner and outer realities is drawn in several ways in *Concerning the Spiritual in Art*. Speaking of form, he observes that it serves as a way of separating one colored surface from another:

> That is its outer meaning. But it has also an inner meaning, of varying intensity, and, properly speaking, *form is the outward expression of this inner meaning*. (29)

Kandinsky's pervasive recognition of inner and outer realities echoes the theosophical distinction between the esoteric and the exoteric. The very title of Blavatsky's *The Secret Doctrine* shows how essential is the concept of esoteric, hidden, or inner reality to theosophical thought.

As with Blavatsky, Kandinsky's inner meaning is not something deliberately hidden to keep it from the vulgar crowd, but rather a truth whose perception requires a form of knowing that has to be developed. This secrecy is a challenge to discovery, and its discovery is what brings us to the Epoch of the Great Spiritual.

Art and Yoga

For Kandinsky, art was more than a pastime, more than a livelihood, more than a profession, more than a form of expression. For Kandinsky, art was the means by which the artist comes to know the world and himself, and the means by which he serves his fellows, helping them also to such knowledge. For Kandinsky, art was a form of yoga. The artist is not

> king of the castle but rather a servant of a nobler purpose. He must search deeply into his own soul, develop and tend it, so that his art has something to clothe, and does not remain a glove without a hand. (54)

Every artist has a threefold responsibility, which is (1) to exercise the talent he has—to express the inner necessity within him, (2) like every person, by actions, feelings, and thoughts to create a spiritual atmosphere, and (3) to use his artistic ability specifically to shape that spiritual atmosphere:

> Painting is an art, and art is not vague production, transitory and isolated, but a power which must be directed to the improvement and refinement of the human soul—to, in fact, the raising of the spiritual triangle. (54)

Kandinsky was a theosophical artist not only because his practice was influenced by theosophical models, not only because his theory reflects theosophical concepts, but especially because his motive for the practice of his art was to improve the human state. For Kandinsky that was the purpose of art. That is also the essence of Theosophy.

Notes

1. Among the studies presenting evidence for a theosophical basis of Kandinsky's art are Sixten Ringbom, "Art in 'The Epoch of the Great Spiritual': Occult Elements in the Early Theory of Abstract Painting," *Journal of the Warburg and Courtauld Institutes* 29 (1966): 386-418, and *The Sounding Cosmos*, Acta Academiae Aboensis, ser. A, 38 (Abo, Finland: Abo Academy, 1970); and Rose-Carol Washton Long, *Kandinsky: The Development of an Abstract Style* (Oxford: Clarendon, 1980).
2. M.T.H. Sadler, trans., *Concerning the Spiritual in Art* (New York: Dover, 1977), a reprint of the first English translation of 1914; unless otherwise noted, citations to the work are to this edition. Robert Motherwell, ed., *Concerning the Spiritual in Art* (New York: Wittenborn, Schultz, 1947), a revision of the first English translation with changes supplied by Nina Kandinsky. John E. Bowlt and Rose-Carol Washton Long, eds., *The Life of Vasilii Kandinsky in Russian Art: A Study of "On the Spiritual in Art"* (Newtonville, Mass.: Oriental Research Partners, 1980, 2d ed. 1984), a translation of the Russian edition of 1914, which omits the explicit theosophical references.
3. Wassily Kandinsky, "Reminiscences" (*Rückblicke*) in *Modern Artists on Art*, ed. Robert L. Herbert (Englewood Cliffs, N.J.: Prentice-Hall, 1964), 23-24.
4. *The Blaue Reiter Almanac*, ed. Klaus Lankheit (New York: Viking, 1974), 173.

Recommended Books

On Blavatsky and her Work

A list of books and pamphlets dealing with H.P. Blavatsky, her life and work. Articles published in theosophical journals are not included:

Arundale, Francesca. *My Guest—H.P. Blavatsky*. Adyar: Theosophical Publishing House, 1932.

Barborka, Geoffrey A. *H.P.B., Tibet and Tulku*. Adyar: Theosophical Publishing House, 1974.

Besant, Annie. *H.P. Blavatsky and the Masters of the Wisdom*. London: Theosophical Publishing House, 1907; Krotona, 1918.

Blavatsky, H.P. *Collected Writings*. Volumes I through XIV, index in progress. Issued by the Theosophical Publishing House, Wheaton. Every volume contains chronological surveys. Volume I contains detailed data concerning H.P. Blavatsky's family background and early life.

Bragdon, C. *Episodes from an Unwritten History*. Rochester, NY: The Manas Press, 1910.

Butt, G. Baseden. *Madame Blavatsky*. London: Rider & Co., 1925.

Carrithers, Walter A., Jr. *The Truth About Madame Blavatsky*. An Open Letter to the Author of *Priestess of the Occult*. Covina, CA: Theosophical University Press, 1947.

Cleather, Alice Leighton. *H.P. Blavatsky: A Great Betrayal*. Calcutta: Thacker Spink & Co., 1922.

———. *H.P. Blavatsky: Her Life and Work for Humanity*. Calcutta: Thacker Spink & Co., 1922.

———. *H.P.Blavatsky as I Knew Her.* Calcutta and London: Thacker Spink & Co., 1923.

de Zirkoff, Boris. *The Dream that Never Dies.* W.E., Small, ed. San Diego: Point Loma Publications, 1983.

———. *Rebirth of the Occult Tradition: How the Secret Doctrine of H.P. Blavatsky Was Written* (pamphlet). Adyar: Theosophical Publishing House, 1977. Also used as the introduction to the 1978 two-volume edition of *The Secret Doctrine.*

Endersby, Victor. *The Hall of Magic Mirrors: A Portrait of Madame Blavatsky.* A Hearthstone Book, New York: Carlton Press, 1969.

Hall, Manly Palmer. *The Phoenix.* Contains a study of H.P.B. as "The Russian Sphinx." Los Angeles: Philosophical Research Society, Inc., 1931-32 and 1968.

Humphreys, Christmas. *The Field of Theosophy: The Teacher, The Teaching and The Way,* (small booklet). London: Theosophical Publishing House, 1966.

H.P.B.—In Memory of Helena Petrovna Blavatsky by Some of her Pupils. A large number of articles by people who knew H.P.B. personally. London: Theosophical Publishing House, 1891. Second ed., London: 1931.

Keightley, Bertram. *Reminiscences of H.P. Blavatsky* (small booklet). Adyar: Theosophical Publishing House, 1931.

Kingsland, William. *The Influence of H.P. Blavatsky's Teachings upon Western Thought* (pamphlet). London: The Blavatsky Association, 1926.

———. *The Real H.P. Blavatsky: A study in Theosophy and a Memoir of a Great Soul.* Includes the author's analysis of the S.P.R. Report. London: John M. Watkins, 1928.

Mead, George R.S. *Concerning H.P.B.* Originally of 1904. Reprinted as Adyar Pamphlet No. 111.

Neff, Mary K. *The "Brothers" of Madame Blavatsky.* Adyar: Theosophical Publishing House, 1932.

———. *Personal Memoirs of H.P. Blavatsky.* New York: E.P. Dutton & Co., 1937.

Olcott, Henry Steel. *Old Diary Leaves. The True Story of the Theosophical Society,* Volume I. New York & London:

G.P. Putnam's Sons, 1895. Five other volumes appeared in the series, published by the Theosophical Publishing House in subsequent years.

Ransom, Josephine. *Madame Blavatsky as an Occultist.* London: Theosophical Publishing House, 1931.

Redfern, Thomas H. *The Work and Worth of Mme. Blavatsky* (pamphlet). London: Theosophical Publishing House, 1960.

Ryan, Charles J. *H.P. Blavatsky and the Theosophical Movement.* Point Loma, CA: Theosophical University Press, 1937.

Sinnett, A.P. *Incidents in the Life of H.P. Blavatsky.* London: Geo. Redway, 1886. A second ed. published in London in 1913, incomplete.

Wachtmeister, Countess Constance. *Reminiscences of H.P. Blavatsky and The Secret Doctrine.* London: Theosophical Publishing Society, 1893; Quest Book, 1976.

Warcup, Adam. *Cyclic Evolution: A Theosophical View.* London: Theosophical Publishing House, 1986.

Waterman, Adlai E. *Obituary: The "Hodgson Report" on Madame Blavatsky—1885-1960.* Adyar: Theosophical Publishing House, 1963.

Whyte, G. Herbert. *H.P. Blavatsky: An Outline of her Life.* Adyar: Theosophical Publishing House, 1920.

On Science

A list of books on contemporary science that tend to corroborate H.P. Blavatsky's world view:

Bohm, D. *Wholeness and the Implicate Order.* Boston: Routledge & Kegan Paul Ltd., 1980.

Capra, F. *The Tao of Physics.* Berkeley: Shambhala Publications, 1975.

Ditfurth, H.V. *The Origins of Life.* San Francisco: Harper & Row, 1982.

Futuyama, D.J. *Science on Trial.* New York: Pantheon Books, 1983.

Gribbon, John and Jeremy Cherfas. *The Monkey Puzzle.* London: Bodley Head, Ltd., 1982.

Herbert, N. *Quantum Reality*. New York: Anchor Press/Doubleday & Co., 1985.

Hey, T. and P. Walters. *The Quantum Universe*. Cambridge: Cambridge University Press, 1987.

Jantsch, E. *The Self-Organizing Universe*. New York: Pergamon Press, 1983.

Jastrow, R. *Until the Sun Dies*. New York: Warner Books, 1977.

Kaku, M. and J. Trainer. *Beyond Einstein*. New York: Bantam Books, 1987.

Luria, S., S. Gould, and S. Singer. *A View of Life*. Menlo Park, CA: The Benjamin/Cummings Publishing Company, 1981.

Prigogine, I. *From Being to Becoming: Time and Complexity in the Physical Sciences*. San Francisco: W.H. Freeman and Co., 1980.

Segre, E. *From Falling Bodies to Radio Waves*. New York: W.H. Freeman & Co., 1984.

———. *From X-Ray to Quarks*. New York: W.H. Freeman & Co., 1980.

Sheldrake, R. *A New Science of Life*. Los Angeles: J.P. Tarcher, 1981.

Taylor, G. *The Great Evolution Mystery*. New York: Harper and Row, 1983.

On Art

These books document the influence of Theosophy on some well-known modern artists:

Kandinsky, Wassily. *Concerning the Spiritual in Art*. New York: Dover, 1977.

Regier, Kathleen J. *The Spiritual Image in Modern Art*. Wheaton, IL: Theosophical Publishing House, 1987.

Weisberger, Edward, ed. *The Spiritual in Art: Abstract Painting (1890-1958)* (catalogue for an exhibition). Co-published. Los Angeles: Los Angeles Museum of Art and New York: Abbeville Press, 1987.

QUEST BOOKS
are published by
The Theosophical Society in America,
Wheaton, Illinois 60189-0270,
a branch of a world organization
dedicated to the promotion of brotherhood and
the encouragement of the study of religion,
philosophy, and science, to the end that man may
better understand himself and his place in
the universe. The Society stands for complete
freedom of individual search and belief.
In the Classics Series well-known
theosophical works are made
available in popular editions.